Life in the Beautiful Game

To the next generation
— Louis and Georgie; Max and Tom; Big Max and Maya

Life in the
Beautiful Game

Bob Wilson

ICON BOOKS

Published in the UK in 2008 by
Icon Books Ltd, The Old Dairy,
Brook Road, Thriplow,
Cambridge SG8 7RG
email: info@iconbooks.co.uk
www.iconbooks.co.uk

Sold in the UK, Europe, South Africa and Asia
by Faber & Faber Ltd, 3 Queen Square,
London WC1N 3AU or their agents

Distributed in the UK, Europe, South Africa and Asia
by TBS Ltd, TBS Distribution Centre, Colchester Road
Frating Green, Colchester CO7 7DW

This edition published in Australia in 2008
by Allen & Unwin Pty Ltd,
PO Box 8500, 83 Alexander Street,
Crows Nest, NSW 2065

Distributed in Canada by
Penguin Books Canada,
90 Eglinton Avenue East, Suite 700,
Toronto, Ontario M4P 2YE

ISBN: 978-184831-018-6

Foreword

Through football I have been privileged to meet many characters, some famous, some infamous. They have all contributed in some way to the beautiful game's ever-changing face, to its greatness and occasional failings, and they epitomise the wide range of talent and methods that football is able to produce.

Their profiles tell much of my life story, as it criss-crosses early hopes and ambitions and then moves to the period in which I won acceptance with my peers as a professional keeper. Second careers in television and goalkeeping coaching allowed me the luxury of keeping in touch with the sport that I love and with those whose lives have been shaped by it.

Without football and Arsenal in particular, there would be no Bob Wilson, footballing addict, and I have to apologise that the book contains a lot of red and white within it. Hopefully you'll be surprised that those colours don't signify just the Gunners, but Manchester United's Red Devils and the Reds of Liverpool, as well as many others. Above all, the tales told and history of the game reflected are there to be enjoyed, and ultimately help raise more funding for the Willow Foundation, a charity that my wife Megs and I set up in memory of our daughter Anna and which provides 'Special days for seriously ill young adults aged 16–40'.

Since her death – six days before her 32nd birthday – the world of football has been a major force in helping us grow from a small local charity in Hertfordshire to a national organisation providing 1,400 special days in the year 2008 alone. We are in football's debt and I will always be thankful for what it has given me – amazing memories, wonderful friendships and a lifelong love of its ability to entertain more people around the world than any other game. Therein indeed lies its true beauty.

Bob Wilson

Contents

Acknowledgements

This is the third book in three years in which Oliver Pugh has entrusted his faith to me and so my thanks go to him for that and his invaluable input and support throughout that time.

I'd also like to thank Brian Rendell for his meticulous help on the many statistics which are included throughout the text, and my son Robert for taking the portrait photograph of me.

The greatest thanks go to Megs. My wife has always had the unenviable task of converting my longhand writings into a readable print. Apart from her typing skills, she happily guided me towards rewrites when it was, in her opinion, necessary, plus provided the one essential I have always needed as an author – encouragement. I will never be a literary genius but you can be assured that my writing comes from the heart.

The best game in the world

I fell in love with football long before a Christmas present of a shiny blue goalkeeping jersey determined the position I would play to professional level. The appeal for me lies in the basic simplicity of the game. One ball, one pitch, two goals, twenty outfield players, two goalkeepers. Forty-five minutes each way, win, lose or draw.

It's a game which has brought me fame and ultimately popular and professional recognition but at some cost. Physically it has led to two artificial hips, an impending new knee and arthritic joints which are a direct result of overuse and serious injury. A punctured lung, several broken ribs, a broken ankle, broken wrist, broken arm, dislocated elbow, various breaks of fingers and numerous stitches over a wide area of my anatomy!

Has it been worthwhile? You bet.

For all the tears and heartaches there have also been smiles and joy. As a kid, an amateur player and as a professional, the game of football has always fascinated me, filled me with excitement and never ceased to amaze. Without football, and without Arsenal Football Club, there would be no Bob Wilson as the public know him.

To be given the platform to present sport on television or develop the specialisation of goalkeeping coaching would not have happened without the success I achieved as an Arsenal player. Making the public aware that there should be a UK charity which was dedicated to helping seriously ill young adults from the ages of 16 to 40 and securing the fundraising that has taken it to national status, would not have been accomplished without such success either.

The irony within my love for football lies in the position I chose – that of goalkeeper – the true purpose of which is to negate the very objective and attraction of the game to the public, which is the scoring of goals. However, if the truth be told, the art of goalkeeping runs the art of goalscoring very close in the popularity stakes with fans. In no other positions can your star rise quicker and shine brighter than if you score a pile of goals or make sensational saves. The difference is that missing a goalscoring opportunity pales into insignificance rapidly, whereas a silly error between the sticks is ridiculed forever and a day. Believe me I should know.

Since the laws were drawn up back in 1863, the game has produced great matches and equally unforgettable characters. Different generations have their own heroes. During my life the game has changed dramatically; sport science, training and dietary methods have all led to a faster game. Changes in the makeup of the ball itself are intended to produce more goals but in turn they have brought greater difficulties for goalkeepers. The biggest difference, however, is in players' wages. Not one footballer of yesteryear, including my own era, could retire at the end of a playing career. Not even George Best, the first to be given superstar status.

Now players' salaries are huge and in some people's eyes obscene. If there is fault it does not lie at the player's door. It is directly linked to television, to the selling of the game domestically and around the globe. Sponsorship and commercial activities have added to the wealth at the top level. Dangers and difficulties are ever-present for the elite clubs, as well as for those who find everyday a struggle to survive.

Thankfully, at this moment, the fans, who have always been the lifeblood of the game, are still prepared to make sacrifices in order to support their team. They are drawn by great talent on the pitch and a feeling that they belong to a club and its history. Each generation recalls the games, the characters, the stories.

As a fan, professional player, coach and TV presenter I have had the added fortune of meeting many of the game's great names face to face, both on the field and off it. My biggest reward has never been the honours and medals won, but the acceptance, in what I consider to be a golden era in the game's history, among my fellow pros that I was on a par with them, that I could play. It has enabled me to gain an insight into their fame and greatness that would not have otherwise been possible. It has reminded me also of how good football has been to me, how lucky I have been. I hope you enjoy these memories of the game and its players. They reflect all that is best about the game of football.

Players' club appearances

Statistics shown are complete career records including all cup and league games.

Those shown with an * are for league appearances only.

During the years of the Second World War, 1939–45, all British domestic football matches were suspended.

Stanley Matthews

'Stan used to put the ball on my centre parting. They don't do that anymore.'

Tommy Lawton, 1985, England centre forward

'Stan was unique. He never went for 50-50 balls, didn't score many goals and was not good in the air. But on his days he was unplayable. He beat fellows so easily, with such pace and balance, often taking on four or five at a time.'

Joe Mercer, 1970, former England colleague

⚽ ⚽ ⚽

I cannot claim to have known Stan Matthews well, but on the occasions that I spent time in his company I learned about what drove him on to play until his 51st year and how much he regretted that his talent and entertainment value was never rewarded in similar fashion to the players of the 90s and beyond.

To the majority of football-crazy kids of the 50s, Stan's name was synonymous with not only football in England, but around the world. I was barely twelve years old when I sat glued to a black and white television screen and watched what has since been referred to as 'the Matthews Final' – Stan's Blackpool team versus Bolton Wanderers at Wembley in the 1953 FA Cup Final. It was a 'Roy of the Rovers' story, with Blackpool trailing 3–1 and only half an hour left on the clock. Stan Matthews seemed to be heading for a hat-trick of FA Cup Final defeats after losing in 1948 and 1951. He was

1

38 years old with time seemingly running out on his career. How wrong we all were on both counts. Matthews played on in top class football until 6 February 1965, just five days after his 50th birthday. In the dramatic last quarter of that Cup Final in '53, he lived up to his nickname of 'The Wizard of the Dribble'.

His speciality of running at opponents, selling them a little dummy and then accelerating away from them at devastating pace over five to ten yards, turned the game in breathtaking fashion. He seemed to have a telepathic understanding with Blackpool's burly centre forward, Stan Mortensen, whose hat-trick would normally have won him the Man of the Match award. Instead all of those who witnessed Blackpool's victory know that the inspiration came from Matthews, not Morty, with the old boy setting up Bill Perry to clinch the 4–3 triumph. Amazingly for such an iconic player, the FA Cup winners' medal of 1953 remained the only reward he gained at the very top level of the game, although his genius was recognised when he was awarded the inaugural Football Writers' Footballer of the Year in 1948. He won this again in 1953, as well as a CBE in 1957 and in 1965 Stan became the first footballer to be knighted for services to sport.

He was looked on as a true gentleman, a fitting description for someone who was never booked in almost 700 league games. Stan did however hold strong opinions and attracted attentive audiences wherever he appeared in Britain or in the many countries he lived in or visited for the rest of his life.

One of these was Canada in the 80s where I was to meet Stan for the last time. He was coaching and spreading the word about the game when he was told that I was in Toronto conducting a goalkeeping course for players and coaches. He asked to meet up, which we did in a downtown Toronto hotel where we spent a couple of hours in pretty serious discussion about the state of football at that time and the ever-increasing spiral in players' wages. I would say Stan was at best disappointed that his talent had, for the majority of his career, earned him £20 a week and at worst, envious of where the game seemed to be heading. He talked about the amounts that players and agents took from transfer deals – at least 5 per cent then – and compared this to the miserly amounts he received back in 1947 when he was transferred from Stoke to Blackpool for £11,500.

I remember trying to convince Stan that although his generation of players and my own could never afford to just retire at the end of our careers, we still earned more than the man in the street and the national average. He forcibly put an argument that he was a great 'entertainer' and should be judged alongside singers and comedians like Sinatra and Bob Hope.

It didn't really come as a total surprise to me that Stan had an obsession about money because on the previous time that we had been together, at a sportsman's evening in England, he had waxed lyrical on the increase in wages for players that he felt did not match up to most of those of his time.

Basically Stan knew his own worth and it was hard to argue against him when he spoke with pride about the longevity of his career, including his 54 appearances for England that began on 29 September 1934 and ended on 15 May 1957, a span of 23 years.

Another subject on which he held powerful views was fitness and, in that respect, he was way ahead of his time and would certainly appreciate the modern thinking about diet and drink. Stan claimed that throughout his life he had been a teetotaller and vegetarian, and was proud of the lean, athletic figure that had been the basis of his longevity.

There are those who claim he was not very generous when speaking about his great rival, Preston North End's Tom Finney. That wasn't the case when I shared the stage with Stan. He was fulsome in his praise of Tom and actually acknowledged that they were equals in ability, and that Tom could do things he couldn't and vice versa. On the game in the 90s he was critical, but thrilled that Manchester United's Ryan Giggs in particular had reintroduced the art of dribbling into the game. No one was left in any doubt of his love of football.

A statue of Stan Matthews stands outside Stoke City's impressive new Britannia Stadium. The words carved into the plinth express perfectly the respect in which Stanley Matthews is held by the Potteries town and all who follow the game of football. It reads: 'His name is symbolic of the beauty of the game, his fame timeless and international, his sportsmanship and modesty universally acclaimed. A magical player, of the people, for the people.'

⚽ ⚽ ⚽

Sir Stanley Matthews

Born:
1 February 1915, Hanley
Died:
23 February 2000, Stoke-on-Trent

Position:
Right wing

Clubs as player:
1932–47 Stoke City, 259 games (51 goals)
1947–61 Blackpool, 379 games (17 goals)
1961–65 Stoke City, 59 games (3 goals)

Internationals:
1934–57 England, 54 caps (11 goals)

Clubs as manager:
1965–68 Port Vale

Honours as player with Blackpool:
1953 FA Cup

Honours as player with Stoke City:
1962 Promotion to First Division (aged 47)

Awards:
1948 FWA Footballer of the Year (first player to win this award)
1953 FWA Footballer of the Year
1956 European Footballer of the Year (first player to win this award)
1957 CBE
1965 Knighthood

– Billy 'Fatty' Foulke –

The heaviest keeper to appear in the Football League, his top weight was 26 stones (165 kg). Billy was born at Dawley in Shropshire in 1874, played for Sheffield United, Chelsea and Bradford City, and won international caps with England. He was 6' 3" tall (1.90 m) and in his early career weighed 22 stones 3 pounds. He wore size 12 boots and 24-inch collars. He once broke the crossbar when swinging on it and could fist a ball further than many players could kick it. After his career was over he set up a penalty-kick business on Blackpool Sands – a penny a shot and three pence back for each goal scored against him.

Matt Busby

His greatest achievement was to create the illusion of beauty in a craft wretchedly deformed from the beginning.

Eamonn Dunphy, 1991, *Strange Kind of Glory*

I said, 'What's happened?' She still said nothing. So I began to go through names. She didn't speak at all. She didn't even look at me. If they were gone she just shook her head. Dead … dead … dead … dead … dead … dead … dead … dead.

Matt Busby describing how his wife Jean told him about
the fate of eight of his team after
the Munich air crash, 1958

⚽ ⚽ ⚽

Certain moments in your life remain indelibly etched in the memory regardless of age. My meetings with Sir Matt Busby fall into that category.

Imagine an impressionable fifteen-year-old who desperately wanted to be a professional footballer learning that the greatest team of that time wanted to sign you, and that the creator of the brilliant and brash young champions of England considered you a possibility for his next generation of Busby Babes.

That is what faced me in 1957 as a result of my performances in goal for England at under-15 schoolboy level. The initial contact did not come from Matt Busby himself but his chief scout Joe Armstrong. The dapper little Armstrong acted as the United manager's eyes and ears when it came to assessing and recruiting emerging talent. United tried to sign two of that England schoolboy squad: a scraggy midfield lad from Manchester called Norbert Stiles, better known as Nobby, and a Chesterfield Grammar School goalkeeper named Bob Wilson.

United did their wooing with the style you would expect from a club who had just retained the First Division title, inviting my parents and me to Old Trafford to watch games and meet the United family, all expenses paid. Similarly they would ensure I wanted for nothing when travelling across the Pennines from Chesterfield to play in the junior United sides. Joe Armstrong was ever-present and when possible, first team coach Bert Whalley would sell the club to me. He didn't have to really. The Busby Babes were irresistible, living proof that kids could take on and defeat teams of greater experience.

Of all the visits I undertook to Manchester one stood out. It was a Charity Shield game between United and Aston Villa. Together with dad and mum, I was shown around Old Trafford and introduced for the first time to Matt Busby. Bert Whalley took me separately to meet the team. Captain Roger Byrne, Duncan Edwards, Harry Gregg, Tommy Taylor; they were all there – friendly, smiling, confident.

As for first impressions of Matt Busby, they were, as you would expect, very inspiring – a manager in his prime, proud of his achievements, of the club and team he had created. Behind the easy manner and smile there seemed to be a genuine interest in a boy whose background was very different to the majority of kids who fancied their chances as a footballer. There was no rush to get rid of us, possibly because my mum engaged him enthusiastically in comparing their separate childhoods around Glasgow. Sir Matt Busby actually hailed from Orbiston in Lanarkshire, while my dad was born in Ayrshire – three proud Scots recalling their roots.

United's manager had clearly been briefed on the better aspects of my game. He homed in on my ability to dive head-on at forwards' feet in identical fashion to his Manchester rivals' goalkeeper and my hero, Bert Trautmann of City, a player he greatly admired.

After the game, which United won, Bert Whalley asked me what I thought of Villa keeper Nigel Sims' faultless display. I expressed my admiration only to be told by the United chief coach that I could be even better if I signed for them. It was flattering, but all part of the Busby philosophy when taking on new players.

My dad was less impressionable than me. Invited to discuss my future privately with Busby, he eventually emerged from the manager's office with no sign of a smile and little indication of what had transpired. I left Old Trafford with Bert Whalley continuing his sell. 'Never forget how good you can be son' were his parting words.

Only on the way home did dad tell me that he had turned down the offer made by Busby and United for me to sign as an apprentice. He strongly believed that football was not a 'proper job', too risky by far as a profession for life. He insisted that it would be better for me to continue my education, get a qualification and, if I was still as keen to play, then weigh up the possibilities of playing football for a living. I'm glad he never saw how many tears I shed sitting on the back seat of the family car as we made our way back home. The dream seemed to be over.

After that initial meeting with Matt Busby, much happened before I was to meet the genial Scot again. Only six months later his life had hung in the balance and the last rites were delivered twice before he became a miraculous survivor of the Munich air crash. The inspirational Bert Whalley was not so fortunate and neither were eight of Busby's wonderful team. One of my schoolboy goalkeeping heroes, Frank Swift, died as well. The final toll was 23 dead. When I faced Busby again, I had left school, qualified as a physical education teacher and established myself as Arsenal's number one. Eleven years had elapsed when, prior to Arsenal's home game with Manchester United, my old teammate Norbert Stiles (by now a 1966 World Cup-winning hero) and I were chatting by the Highbury dressing rooms.

As the newly knighted Sir Matt appeared, Nobby said, 'Boss, you remember Bob Wilson don't you?' Not surprisingly Busby didn't, until Nobby and I between us reminded him of 1957. 'Pity you didn't sign for us son' was the United manager's response. There was good reason for the remark at that moment because the fickle finger of fate had seen Arsenal and Bob Wilson's star in the ascendancy, heading for European and domestic glory during the following two seasons. The great Manchester United, on the other hand, were in freefall. Sir Matt Busby's reign as manager had only months to run.

Sir Alexander Matthew 'Matt' Busby

Born:
26 May 1909, Orbiston, Glasgow
Died:
20 January 1994

Position:
Inside forward

Clubs as player:
1928–36 Manchester City, 227 games (14 goals)
1936–40 Liverpool, 125 games (3 goals)

Clubs as manager:
1945–69 Manchester United
1970–71 Manchester United

International teams as manager:
1958 Scotland

Honours as player with Manchester City:
1934 FA Cup

Honours as manager at Manchester United:
1948 FA Cup
1952 First Division and FA Charity Shield
1956 First Division and FA Charity Shield
1957 First Division and FA Charity Shield
1963 FA Cup
1965 First Division and FA Charity Shield
1967 First Division and FA Charity Shield
1968 European Cup

Awards:
1958 CBE
1968 Knighthood

– *British record score* –

The record scoreline for any British first-class match remains: Arbroath 36–Bon Accord 0. The game took place on 5 September 1885 and was a Scottish FA Cup 1st round tie.

There seem to have been extenuating circumstances for the remarkable score, notably an illness which had struck down the Bon Accord keeper and led to an outfield player standing between the sticks, something he had never done previously. Neither did it help that the visitors didn't possess any boots or playing kit, so turned out in ordinary shoes and working clothes. John Petrie was the Arbroath hero, scoring thirteen goals which also remains a record for any individual player. Not quite so surprising is the fact that the Arbroath goalkeeper did not touch the ball once during the game.

On the same afternoon Dundee Harp beat Aberdeen Rovers 35–0.

Frank Swift

Football is in his debt, both for the distinction of his goalkeeping and the rich vitality of his nature.

Geoffrey Green, *Soccer in the Fifties*

⚽ ⚽ ⚽

Bert Trautmann and Pat Jennings are the two goalkeepers from whom I gained most inspiration. However it was Bert's predecessor at Manchester City who first captured my imagination and set me on the undulating rocky road that is life for any keeper.

Frank Swift was a giant of a man, almost 6' 4" in height and with a hand span of 12" from little finger to tip of thumb. In the same way that Pat Jennings' hands have been called 'shovels', 'Big Swifty's' were referred to as Frank's 'frying pans'. I was eight when he was coming to the end of his career and began to read the stories of his greatness for club and country. Most of the tales included mention of his strength of character – like challenging his first City manager Wilf Wild about the miserly terms offered to him as a part-time pro – ten shillings a week. Frank evidently asked if he would get more if he played in the first team, at which a clause was agreed stating 'In the event of an appearance in the senior side, F Swift will receive twenty shillings a week'. Fourteen years later, in September 1946 and at the top of his trade Swift was still getting only £10 a week.

I met him only once. That was following an England schoolboys' trial held at Manchester United's Old Trafford ground. I hadn't played well, even before an injury left me out of the second half. After the game this wonderful man was introduced to me. By then he had become a respected journalist. He asked me if I was OK and wished me well. I told him I thought my nerves had got the better of me and that it was a regular problem. Frank just laughed and said it was natural to be nervous, often a good sign as long as it could be kept under control. He then proceeded to tell me that, as a young keeper for City, the days leading up to a game could be torture and on one occasion his fear and tension built to such an extent that he fainted at the final whistle. 'Don't worry,' he told me, 'most good footballers have to learn to conquer their nerves.' I thanked him, shook his hand and never saw him again. The date was 2 March 1957. Less than one year later on 6 February 1958 he was killed, aged just 43, one of 23 people to lose their lives in the Munich crash which devastated the Busby Babes.

What Frank failed to tell me during our brief time together was that his fainting episode came at the conclusion of a very public game, the 1934 FA Cup Final, in which, as a nineteen-year-old, he had helped Manchester City beat Portsmouth. Only later did I uncover the truth when I read his book *Football in the Goalmouth*.

It emphasises what still exists today – a player's ability to convince himself that he won't let his teammates down, that he can reproduce on match day what seems simple in training. In the week leading up to the final, Frank was wracked with fear. 'As the days passed I still couldn't believe I was going to keep goal in a Cup Final. One moment I'd be on top of the world, then I'd get terrible fits of despondency and tell myself I was far too young to think about playing in a Wembley side. I never confided in anyone, but I was plenty worried. When on the Tuesday the team was chosen, I remember the terrible sinking feeling I had in my stomach when I saw my name heading the list.'

Instead of calming Frank Swift, the announcement of the side only heightened his pre-match nerves. At the stadium it got worse as kick-off time loomed, especially when he saw a senior member of the team struggle to tie his boots with shaking hands. Another teammate spotted the goalkeeper's fright, grabbed him, led him to the bath area, slapped his face and then gave him a tot of whisky shouting at Frank 'Get back in there you big lug, nobody's going to eat you!'

Letting in a poor goal hardly helped his cause during the first half but gradually Frank's confidence increased. In the second 45 minutes Fred Tilson scored two goals for City, the second just four minutes from time, creating four minutes of excruciating tension and panic in the young keeper's mind. This is how Frank described it:

On either side of the posts, two or three photographers were still perched, presumably in the hope of snapping Portsmouth's equaliser should it come. One of them, probably seeing how tense I was, began to tick off the minutes for me. 'Three minutes to go!' The photographer's excited voice heightened the terrific tension. My heart was pounding away and I had difficulty in focusing my full attention on the field of play. 'Only two minutes left, Frank.' The play seemed a long way off, or was it because things were becoming a little hazy. 'One minute to go!' Mr Rous is looking at his watch. I wish he'd blow the whistle. 'Only 50 seconds, you're nearly there lad!' I thought how pleased mother would be and brother Fred at the glory which had come to their youngest member. I wonder if the Cup takes much cleaning … 'Forty seconds! You've done 'em now!' I try to remember the drill we've been given. Winning team goes up first. I expect I'll drop my gloves or my cap or both … I hope the King says something to me. I won't know what to say … 'Thirty seconds, it's your cup son!' Matt Busby smashes the ball into touch. I notice a flurry of movement near the entrance to the tunnel, leading to the Royal Box. The Guards have come out, ready to line up on the grass. Racing through my brain is the thought, 'I must shake skipper Sam Cowan's hand …' There's the whistle, it's all over! I stoop into the net for my cap and gloves, take a couple of steps out to meet Sam … and then everything went blank.

Frank's account of the day is so descriptive and it could have been written by numerous professional footballers, giving an insight into the pressures that can build inside the mind. He passed off his embarrassment thus: 'Fancy a strapping fellow like me fainting in front of all those people and the King.'

Ahead of Frank Swift lay another fifteen years of conquering his emotions. He learned to use humour as a mask for his true feelings. Frank was a one club man, his career at Manchester City spanning eighteen years. He was an inspirational force when City won the League title for the first time in 1937 and an inspiration to a young boy from Chesterfield. Frank Swift, my first mentor.

⚽ ⚽ ⚽

Frank Victor Swift

Born:
26 December 1913, Blackpool
Died:
6 February 1958, Munich

Position:
Goalkeeper

Clubs as player:
1933–49 Manchester City, 372 games

Internationals:
1946–49 England, 19 caps

Honours as player:
1934 FA Cup
1937 First Division

– *Football League history* –

1885	Professionals accepted
1888	Football League founded
1898	Promotion and relegation begins
1939	Numbers on shirts introduced
1951	White football introduced
1956	First major floodlit match between Portsmouth and Newcastle
1960	League Cup launched
1961	Maximum wage removed
1965	First substitutes introduced for injured players only
1966	Tactical substitutes achieved as well
1981	Three points for a win begins
1982	League Cup sponsored for first time (called Milk Cup)
1983	League Championship sponsored by Canon
1987	Play-offs introduced to settle promotions and relegation
1992	First Division break away and Premier League formed

Nobby Stiles

Eusebio is capable of giving us a lot of problems Nobby, so I want you to take him out of the game.

Sir Alf Ramsey's orders to Stiles,
World Cup semi-final vs. Portugal, 1966

What do you mean Alf; for this game, or for life?

Stiles' reply

If Nobby Stiles doesn't play, then England don't play.

Sir Alf Ramsey, 1966

Nobby never got the credit for his footballing ability because of his reputation as a hard man. He also looked a bit of a moody so-and-so when he wore those Mr Magoo glasses off the field, but in the United dressing room he was known as Mr Happy because he was such a bubbly character.

George Best

⚽ ⚽ ⚽

Ask me to name the individuals who had the perfect physique to play the game of football and I would instantly give you Johan Cruyff and Thierry Henry. Lean, athletic, quick, intelligent, technically gifted, they were both supreme mesomorphs, with bodies that seemed to be carved out of stone.

Amazing then that England included in their World Cup-winning XI of 1966 a small, extremely short-sighted, toothless little man called Nobby Stiles. On the field he needed the strongest of contact lenses; off the pitch he wore thick spectacles to assist his eyesight.

The lovely thing about football is that it caters for all sorts, as long as a player retains huge enthusiasm and a fierce competitive nature alongside a degree of skill. Nobby possessed all of these attributes.

Who will ever forget the spontaneous post match jig which Stiles performed at Wembley while holding the Jules Rimet trophy in one hand and, it is rumoured, his dentures in the other?

Throughout those World Cup finals, the lad from Collyhurst, Manchester, had effectively man-marked some of the greatest players in the universe, including one of the tournament's star performers, Portugal's Eusebio. He subdued them with biting tackles and menacing shadowing. I watched that semi-final against Portugal from the Wembley terraces. My career at Arsenal had hardly taken off in the three years I had been at the club. In my mind I doubted I would ever play consistently at the top level, let alone enter the international arena. What a different road it had been for Nobby Stiles, a lad I first met in 1957.

The venue was the Recreation Ground, Saltergate, and home of Chesterfield FC, the Spireites. The event was the first round proper of the English School's Shield, between Chesterfield Boys and Manchester Boys.

The lads from Lancashire ran us ragged, winning 3–1 and putting us out of the competition. In the dressing room after the game, I studied the programme in an attempt to find the name of their skinny inside forward who had scored a gem of a third goal to finish us off.

The programme read, 'Norbert Stiles, St Patrick's School'. 'What a player!' I thought. 'Now he's got a real chance of making it as a pro.' Forty-five days after our first meeting, Norbert Stiles and I shared the same dressing room, representing the North versus the South in an England under-15 schoolboys trial game at Cadbury's Bournville Ground in Birmingham. We won 3–0 and both Stiles and Wilson could be proud of themselves and their performances. Both of us made the 1957 England team against Northern Ireland, Scotland and Germany – three big games, all won with some style.

Before the season came to an end, Manchester United were knocking on the doors at the Stiles household in Manchester and the Wilson home in Chesterfield. We were the two players chosen by Matt Busby and United as those who could continue a production line labelled 'The Busby Babes'. Initially we would meet up and play for the United junior sides, but while Norbert Stiles became Nobby and gained early recognition, for Robert Wilson, who became Bob, there was the strong restraining hand of a dad who knew the pitfalls of being a professional footballer and who decided that a 'proper' career in the police force or teaching profession would preclude any gamble between the sticks, albeit at the home of the champions of the time, Manchester United.

It took some ten years or so before Nobby and I again shared the same pitch, but not the same team. European Cup glory had been added to his playing CV, a newly acquired position as Arsenal goalkeeper was all I had gained in return. However the pendulum had begun to swing away from United's success and veered towards Arsenal and a first European trophy for the Gunners in 1970, followed immediately by the second League Championship and FA Cup Double of the last century in the 1970–71 season.

Throughout those early days of being a teammate of Nobby's I would describe him as quite shy, but full of fun, nothing like the guy who was eventually to struggle with depression during the managerial days that followed his playing career.

The working-class boy from the heavily Irish Catholic community of north Manchester was an unlikely star and although ultimately he was the least-capped member of the 1966 World Cup XI with 28 England appearances, there are many, including me, who believe Nobby Stiles was the key man in Alf Ramsey's jigsaw and that without him World Cup glory may not have come England's way.

⚽ ⚽ ⚽

Norbert Peter 'Nobby' Stiles

Born:
18 May 1942, Collyhurst

Position:
Midfield

Clubs as player:
1960–71 Manchester United, 393 games (19 goals)
1971–73 Middlesbrough, 69 games (2 goals)
1973–75 Preston North End, 46 games* (1 goal)

Internationals:
1965–70 England, 28 caps (1 goal)

Clubs as manager:
1977–81 Preston North End
1981–84 Vancouver White Caps
1985–86 West Bromwich Albion

Honours as player with Manchester United:
1963 FA Cup
1965 First Division and FA Charity Shield
1967 First Division and FA Charity Shield
1968 European Cup

Honours as player with England:
1966 World Cup

Awards:
2000 MBE

– *Derek Dooley* –

The former Sheffield Wednesday centre forward had an exceptionally cheerful disposition. Always smiling, and interested in all things to do with football, his attitude to life and to the people he met was made that bit more special by the fact that the game of football had robbed him of his livelihood and the possibility of a great career. Derek was just 23 years old when he broke his right leg following a collision with the opposing Preston keeper. There was nothing malicious about the challenge for a 50-50 ball. Two days later, shortly before Dooley was to be discharged from Preston Royal Infirmary and embark on the road to recovery, gangrene was found to have infested the leg. Very quickly it was realised that to save his life the leg would have to be amputated.

At the time of the injury, 14 February 1953, Derek had scored 16 goals in 29 First Division games, which followed on from his debut season in which his 46 goals in 30 games took Wednesday to promotion. There was nothing subtle about his play. In fact he looked bulky and unrefined but he just had a wonderful knack of finding the net from impossible looking situations. His friendliness and lack of pity for himself made him a special person and he remained in Sheffield following his dreadful injury as a great servant to both the city's clubs, Wednesday and United.

Bert Trautmann

There have only been two world-class goalkeepers. One was Lev Yashin, the other the German boy who played in Manchester – Trautmann.

Lev Yashin

Bert for me was a very great goalkeeper because he made things look so easy. He was the first goalkeeper I ever saw start an attack by throwing a ball deep. I'd seen others, but he always looked for someone nearer the half-way line and by-passed the others. The big thing also for me was he was such a sportsman and played as if he owed us something because he was a German and had been a prisoner-of-war. If anything, we should give him a debt of gratitude for staying here and showing us what a great goalkeeper he was. I certainly learned a lot from him.

Gordon Banks

❀ ❀ ❀

Ask any top footballer from the late 40s and 50s about the best goalkeepers during that era and you would be guaranteed to hear a German name included, that of Bernhard Carl Trautmann. Similarly, if at that time you had asked the aspiring young teenage keeper that was me, who my hero was, the instant response would have been Bert Trautmann, one and the same person

Bert always was and always will be my greatest hero. I imitated his style of play simply because it was so natural in my own game. The death-defying plunge headlong at onrushing forwards' feet resulted in a broken neck for Trautmann during the 1956 FA Cup Final between Manchester City and Birmingham City. It not only led to legendary status but, by staying on the field, he helped the cup go to Maine Road Manchester.

The young Bob Wilson idolised this former prisoner-of-war, despite my father's reticence to me having a hero who was German. Dad's problem was understandable bearing in mind that he had lost friends and family fighting with the Highland Light Infantry in France during the Great War, and then lost his two eldest sons, Jock and Billy, two of my four brothers, in the RAF during the Second World War.

Only once did my father make it absolutely clear that he would always mistrust a German. As I stood on the platform at Chesterfield station in 1957 awaiting a train that would start my journey to play for England under-15 schoolboys against Germany in the Neckar Stadium, Stuttgart, my mum gave me a kiss and best wishes while dad simply gripped my two arms tightly and whispered with feeling, one word – 'Win!'

It's a moment I will never forget, nor the emotional turmoil it put me in as I weighed up my dad's feelings with the knowledge that my German hero was then the current Footballer of the Year in his adopted country, England. At fifteen years of age it was difficult for me to comprehend the rights and wrongs of war and its effect on relationships between countries. Only now can I appreciate that Bert Trautmann's humanity and goalkeeping heroics did more to bring together two warring countries than any politician could ever achieve.

I was almost 41 years old when I finally came face to face with my hero. On a television gantry high above Wembley Stadium just prior to the 1981 FA Cup Final between Trautmann's old club Manchester City and Tottenham

Hotspur. My excitement at the knowledge that I was about to have an ambition come true left me nervous in the extreme. I need not have worried. On spotting me, Bert made the first move, hand outstretched, beaming smile on the handsome famous face, 'Hello Bob. I know, I was your idol. Thank you. I'm glad.'

I have always wished that my dad had been with me at that moment, or on the other occasions when I have been able to spend time with Bert Trautmann. The last time was during the BBC's *This Is Your Life* programme of which I was the subject.

Twice during the recording of the show presenter Michael Aspel had made reference to Bert and I had instantly waxed lyrical. Both times I was left disappointed that he had not then appeared from behind the screens. Those in the know, however, knew how important Bert Trautmann had been in my life. To my delight Bert was the last guest that appeared. Such was my appreciation that I, unwittingly, clapped my hand behind his neck, that famous neck which had once been broken. With typical generosity Bert paid his tribute to me by complimenting 'Bob Wilson the footballer, Bob Wilson the television presenter and Bob Wilson the man'.

At the party that followed he charmed everyone and made me again wish that my dad had lived long enough to meet this hero of mine, who journalist Frank McGhee aptly described as: 'A man who insisted on keeping his German nationality because he felt that what a man is, is more important than where he is born.'

❀ ❀ ❀

Bernhard Carl 'Bert' Trautmann

Born:
22 October 1923, Bremen, Germany

Position:
Goalkeeper

Clubs as player:
1948–49 St Helens Town, 43 games*
1949–64 Manchester City, 545 games

Clubs as manager:
1967–68 Preussen Munster
1968–69 Opel Russelsheim

International teams as manager:
1972–74 Burma
1978–80 Liberia
1980–83 Pakistan

Honours as player with Manchester City:
1956 FA Cup

Awards:
1956 FWA Footballer of the Year
2004 OBE

– *Numbered shirts* –

Although shirts with numbers on them appeared in two games on 25 August 1928 – Arsenal players away at Sheffield Wednesday and the Chelsea team who met Swansea – they were then banned. Numbered shirts were worn for the first time in the 1933 FA Cup Final but went from 1–22. The eventual winners, Everton, started with their keeper wearing 1 and their opponents, Manchester City, were numbered from 12 to 22, the latter being City's goalkeeper.

Stan Cullis

Stan Cullis famously put a heavy emphasis on fitness and strength and the overall impression of Wolves was of muscularity and raw power. Yet there was also a thread of artistry running through the side, and they provided a procession of players for the England team. The Cullis theory was a simple one. He argued that one long ball, accurately placed, could do the work of three or four short passes and in half the time. The modern name for it would be 'route one'. Not pretty, but extremely potent.

Norman Giller, *Billy Wright: The Official Biography*

⚽ ⚽ ⚽

Stan Cullis was the greatest manager in Wolverhampton Wanderers' history. In his first season in charge at Molineux he became the youngest manager to win the FA Cup as Wolves beat Leicester City to win the 1949 final and lift their first trophy since 1908. He was just 31 years of age. Five years later Stan's team took their first league title. Two more First Division titles followed in 1958 and 1959, with a hat-trick of championships missed narrowly in 1960. Lifting the FA Cup that season hardly compensated a man like Cullis.

That was the year I first met him, shortly after a Wolves XI had beaten our Loughborough College team 5–2 in a friendly at Molineux. I must have had a half-decent game because Stan immediately asked me if I would like to spend some time during vacations from studies, college commitments permitting, with Wolves. That's exactly what I did, often hitching a lift to go and play in a reserve or third team game. At holiday times I would spend a few days in Wolverhampton substituting educational learning for football knowledge. Strangely it was education that created a bond between Stan and me. Whenever I visited he would call me into his Molineux office for a private chat and cross-examine me about the importance of education and the best schools available. He was keen that his son received what he hadn't: a sound grounding that would be a springboard to a successful career. I believe his lad went to Repton School and Cullis was proud that he was an achiever there. Stan had served as a physical training instructor in both Britain and Italy during the Second World War conflict so he showed a special interest in my Loughborough training from the footballing side of things.

Without doubt he was one of the most intense men I have met, almost hypnotic in discussion and as I remember it, with a slight lisp and a strong Black Country accent. The success he achieved at Wolves around this time made him as famous as Manchester United's Matt Busby. Like Busby, Cullis ensured that I came into contact with his star players, such as keeper Malcolm Finlayson, Ron Flowers and Peter Broadbent, and Bill Slater who was especially engaging for me as he too was an educationalist and later worked at Birmingham University.

Cullis also sorted out the 'digs' during my flying visits, a house no more than 150 yards from Molineux where the mother of another famous Wolves player, Bill Shorthouse, looked after me. One of my roommates was the instinctively talented Peter Knowles who could have enjoyed footballing greatness but settled for life as a Jehovah's Witness.

I loved my time in the company of Stan Cullis and Wolves but when it came to making a choice of where to teach prior to turning professional a bitter conflict materialised.

The Wolves board summoned me to explain why I was hesitating to sign a contract that would give me £30 a week once I had fulfilled my probationary year of teaching. It was a nerve-wracking experience for a college boy and although Stan Cullis and the chairman, Stanley Baker, were very understanding of my dilemma, another member of the board, John Ireland, accused me of wanting money to sign and courting other clubs' offers. That was not the case. Initially I put any immediate decision on hold and just carried on doing my best for Wolves.

On 23 March 1962 I was en route to play for Wolves reserves at Burnley when I learned of a tragedy involving my family. An experimental Handley Page Victor bomber had crashed on top of my sister Jean's house at Stubton in Lincolnshire. Two airmen and two of my sister's home helps died. Jean and her husband both escaped death miraculously but were seriously injured. My nephew and two nieces were lucky to have left for school. Once I had established that there was nothing I could do to help, my dad told me to continue my journey and, if possible play for Wolves.

The Wolves staff were brilliant, leaving a decision on whether I should play until the next day. Stan Cullis thought it would be a real test of character but ultimately worthwhile. I did play at Burnley the following afternoon where ironically all players wore a black armband in a show of respect to miners who had recently lost their lives in a pit disaster.

Contact with Stan Cullis was lost once I had pinned my colours to the Arsenal mast, but I was to meet him during the second week of March 1968 when, at last, my chance to make the Arsenal goalkeeping position my own arrived in an FA Cup replay at St Andrews, home of Birmingham City whose manager was Stan Cullis.

He was friendly and encouraging after the game, but by then his City side had knocked Arsenal out of the cup with two Barry Bridges goals. Stan never was able to reproduce the success he'd enjoyed at Wolves but he became a very useful contact for me, especially when I too left the game and turned to a television career. Periodically I would receive a missive from him, sometimes praising but usually warning me about overstepping the mark when it came to critical comments about managers. Stan didn't mind what I said about players because I'd been one, but he distinctly disliked people who had never coached or managed a team telling them that they should or shouldn't do this or that.

No doubt he'll be looking down with great disdain on many of the pundits who today air their views so confidently and controversially.

My last meeting with Stan Cullis was at a footballing dinner in London which he attended with his son. He was looking frail and the ravages of stomach cancer were taking a toll on him. He told me that despite all the trophies and England caps won, he had never displayed any mementos of his vast achievements. To Stan it could be interpreted as showing off, an unnecessary boastfulness and one that his character and personality would simply not allow.

⚽ ⚽ ⚽

Stanley 'Stan' Cullis

Born:
25 October 1916, Ellesmere Port
Died:
28 February 2001, Malvern

Position:
Defender

Clubs as player:
1934–47 Wolverhampton Wanderers, 171 games

Internationals:
1937–39 England, 12 caps

Clubs as manager:
1948–64 Wolverhampton Wanderers
1965–70 Birmingham City

Honours as manager at Wolverhampton Wanderers:
1949 FA Cup
1954 First Division
1958 First Division
1959 First Division
1960 FA Cup

– *The Baggies* –

West Brom settled at their current home, the Hawthorns, in 1900. They soon became known as the Throstles, the Black Country name for the thrush, a bird seen in large numbers in the surrounding expanse of hawthorn bushes that gave their ground its name.

In its early days, the ground only had two entrances – one behind each goal. On match days, the stewards at each gate would collect the payment from fans entering the ground and place the coins in large cloth bags. When all the fans were in the ground, the stewards would then close the gates and carry the bags of money along the touchline – escorted by police – to a small office under the stand on the halfway line. Before long it became tradition for the fans to chant 'Here come the Baggies!' as the stewards passed the main stand. Over time, the team acquired it as their nickname as well.

During my time at Arsenal, we rarely came away from the home of the Baggies with a win and the humorous taunts from their fans live on in my memory.

John Osborne

John Osborne was West Bromwich Albion's goalkeeper as the Baggies beat Everton to lift the FA Cup in 1968. He hailed from my neck of the woods, Chesterfield, most famous for its crooked spire on St Mary's and All Saints church in the middle of the town. Running the twisted and warped spire a close second is the Derbyshire town's proven ability over many years to produce, nurture and groom some very good goalkeepers: Sam Hardy, Ray Middleton, Gordon Banks, John Lukic, Steve Ogrizovic, Alan Stevenson, Steve Hardwick have all made a name for themselves in the game along with John Osborne and Bob Wilson.

John was born on the outskirts of Chesterfield, at Barlborough. We were teammates in the Chesterfield Boys under-15 side in 1956. John was our captain and left half. I was the goalkeeper. No signs or talk then that the lanky midfielder would become a goalie in the professional ranks and make 250 league appearances for WBA. The transition took place in his late teens and Chesterfield FC were quick to recognise his ability between the sticks.

Soon 'Ossie' was on his way to the Hawthorns where he became a popular player with the Baggies fans. We often referred to and laughed about our period as teammates whenever we met. I was thrilled for him when he played a notable part in Albion beating Everton in an uninspiring '68 Cup final. He started the game nervously and was struggling initially with every high cross into the Albion box. Two solid saves during the first half changed his mood and confidence oozed from him throughout the second 45 minutes. There was no way through for Everton's Kendall, Harvey, Ball and Joe Royle.

Later in his career he required plastic knuckles in order to prolong his playing days. Like most keepers he suffered breaks, dislocations and sprains of both his hands. He called me to see whether our manager Bertie Mee, who was acknowledged as a leading physiotherapist, could give him advice over a hideously broken and distorted finger. Bertie saw John and after careful examination of X-rays and the finger itself, which seemed to point at right angles to the rest of his fingers, gave advice that made the Albion keeper turn pale: 'Bearing in mind you are a goalie and need to close your fist to punch the ball, there is only one way to proceed. I advise amputation for the offending finger.'

The room went very silent before John recovered his composure and, in thanking Bertie for seeing him, insisted he might just seek an alternative route other than losing a finger. For a time he continued to play by taping the broken finger as tight as he could to the next finger. Ultimately medical science produced plastic knuckles and a less traumatic solution to that offered by Bertie Mee. John Osborne went on to play for Shamrock Rovers in late 1978, playing in UEFA Cup Winners' Cup ties, in which he kept a clean sheet on two of his three appearances.

⚽ ⚽ ⚽

John Osborne

Born:
1 December 1940, Barlborough
Died:
7 November 1998, Worcester

Position:
Goalkeeper

Clubs as player:
1960–66 Chesterfield, 110 games as a junior – no senior appearances
1967–72 West Bromwich Albion, 312 games*
1978 Shamrock Rovers, 4 games

Honours as player with West Bromwich Albion:
1968 FA Cup

– *The Spireites* –

Chesterfield FC is the fourth-oldest football club in England and takes its nickname from the bizarre spire of the town's fourteenth-century Parish Church of St Mary's and All Saints. It rises to a height of 228 feet above the ground and leans perilously almost 10 feet to the southwest. What's more, from base to pinnacle it twists anticlockwise through more than 45°, and is still moving. The spire also just sits on top of the stone tower, balancing with no apparent fixing. How it remains standing I'm not quite sure.

Built in 1362, it remained straight for several centuries before it began to twist. There are several theories for the movements that have emerged over time. Some think that unseasoned or green timber was used; this was fairly common practice in the Middle Ages as it was less wearing on the tools of the time. Having said that, if green timber was used it was usually for less ambitious or permanent constructions than a 228-foot-high church spire! It's also thought that there may have been a shortage of skilled craftsmen at the time, after the Black Death had taken its toll on the area. Folklore also talks of two imps that were sent by Satan to do his evil work. Their first act was to twist the spire of Chesterfield Parish Church before heading off to wreak more havoc across the region.

I have huge affection for the crooked spire. It was at this church in my hometown that I began a relationship with a girl called Margaret Miles which continues to this day, albeit as Mrs or Megs Wilson!

Herbert Chapman

The Club, in Chapman's view, always needed to be greater than the individual. He would not tolerate anyone who, in his judgement, sullied its name.

Bob Wall, Arsenal Secretary, *From the Heart*

There was an aura of greatness about him. He possessed a cheery self-confidence. His power of inspiration and gift of foresight were his greatest attributes. I think his qualities were worthy of an even better reward. He should have been Prime Minister and might have been but for the lack of opportunities entailed by his position in the social scale.

Cliff Bastin, former Arsenal player

There are two kinds of visionary: those that dream of a whole new world and those who dream of just one thing. Chapman's vision was of the greatest football club in the world. His genius was in creating something close to that.

Bernard Joy, former Arsenal player

⚽ ⚽ ⚽

The first face I saw when I stepped into the marble halls of Arsenal's Highbury stadium in 1963 was Herbert Chapman. The fact that it was a bronze head sculpted by Jacob Epstein did not diminish the impact it had on me. I had already read and heard of this man's greatness, humility and reputation as one of the biggest innovators the game of football had ever seen.

Arsenal, without the Chapman years, would never have achieved its special place in the history of the game. When he accepted the offer made to him by chairman Henry Norris of £2,000 a year, the club had won nothing. It was easily the highest salary in English football paid out to a man, who late in 1920, had joined Huddersfield Town as assistant to secretary-manager Ambrose Langley. Within one month Langley put Chapman in charge and within five years Huddersfield had become the first English club to win a hat-trick of league titles. From his earliest days Chapman had shown himself to be exceptionally bright.

Born eight years before Arsenal FC, on 19 January 1878, he was the son of an illiterate miner and, against all the odds, completed a course in Mining Engineering which led to a variety of jobs in industry. Only after Huddersfield had become champions for the first time did Chapman desert his engineering career, at the age of 46. As an amateur he had played without distinction for a number of clubs, the longest spell ironically being two years with Spurs. As a manager he was inspired, both at Huddersfield and Arsenal, but not always tactically. When the offside law was changed in 1925 from three defenders to two (for explanation of this rule, see entry on the WM formation, below), he took advice from Charles Buchan, one of his players, as to how he could take advantage of the new law. Chapman's genius lay in picking great talent to fit particular roles: players like Cliff Bastin, Joe Hulme, David Jack and Alex James. His acute brain saw him turn part of his desk into a football field layout, with small models as players.

Tactics and any new ideas were encouraged by Chapman who, at that time, was referred to as secretary-manager, with a brief to run the whole club. He did that and more, with a series of boldly brazen ideas on improvements, not just to Arsenal Football Club, but the game as a whole. It comes as little surprise that many of Chapman's ideas were opposed vehemently by the Football Association. Innovation, even today, is regarded with caution by the game's governing body. In and around 1928, Chapman introduced numbers on his team's shirts for a match against Sheffield Wednesday. The FA promptly told him to revert to numberless kits and reluctantly he complied, although Arsenal reserves continued to play in them.

Next came a 45-minute clock at Highbury but that was banned as well by the powers that be, so Chapman made it into a 60-minute clock, which stood above the south end of the ground until 2006 when the last game at Highbury was played.

Because midweek fixtures were badly attended with kick-off at an unreasonable hour of 3.00 pm, he advocated floodlights. Guess what? He was not allowed to proceed with the idea. His initiative of a ten-yard penalty semi-circle did get the go ahead, but only ten years after he had proposed it and long after his death.

Herbert Chapman died very suddenly on 6 January 1934, as Arsenal were heading for a repeat of Huddersfield's hat-trick of League titles. Had he lived today he would still not have seen two other ideas of his come to fruition. One was to have goal judges to decide whether a ball was over the line or not, something he felt strongly about. Secondly his belief that to get correct decisions on the field of play, two referees were needed, not just one. At least Chapman's hopes that promotion and relegation would involve far more clubs were fulfilled to a degree in the 1973–74 season with an increase from two to three.

Undersoil heating; advocating for a single England manager rather than a committee of selectors; a coloured ball and the insistence on his players having part of their wages put into savings by the club ... all came from the Arsenal manager's brain.

Thankfully his employers were quicker to adopt his ideas than the FA. The Gillespie Road underground station, a few hundred yards from Highbury was renamed Arsenal thanks to his persistence. The marble halls and its underfloor heating of dressing rooms all helped create a special football club, but one of the best ideas, as far as I'm concerned, centred on the respect for the other team. On match days at Highbury flowers were placed in a variety of areas, including the boardroom, in the colours of Arsenal's opponents. Manchester United, Liverpool etc meant red flowers; Villa and West Ham claret and blue flowers; Newcastle, black and white, albeit dyed flowers. Respect for the opposition. Now there's a thought for the game of football as we know it today.

❀ ❀ ❀

Herbert Chapman

Born:
19 January 1878, Rotherham
Died:
6 January 1934, Hendon

Position:
Inside forward

Clubs as player:
1898–99 Grimsby Town, 10 games* (4 goals)
1899 Swindon Town, 3 games* (2 goals)
1901–02 Northampton Town, 22 games* (14 goals)
1902–03 Sheffield United, 22 games* (2 goals)
1903–05 Notts County, 7 games* (1 goal)
1905–07 Tottenham Hotspur, 42 games* (16 goals)

Clubs as manager:
1907–12 Northampton Town
1912–19 Leeds City
1921–25 Huddersfield Town
1925–34 Arsenal

Honours with Huddersfield Town as manager:
1923 FA Cup
1924 First Division
1925 First Division

Honours with Arsenal as manager:
1930 FA Cup
1931 First Division
1933 First Division

– *The WM* –

In 1925 the offside rule was amended so that an attacking player needed only two opponents in front of him and not three as was the case before. This obviously made the offside trap much more difficult to execute and saw the number of goals in the English First Division rise 43 per cent from 1,192 to 1,703 the following year.

In response, the great Herbert Chapman and his Arsenal captain Charles Buchan devised a system whereby the centre half was pulled back into a centre-back role in order to deal with the now more dangerous and prolific centre forward. To fill up the gap created in midfield, the two inside forwards were pulled back to create a four-man midfield, or magic square as it would later become known. When all was said and done, the general shape of the defensive players made up a W and the attacking players an M – a formation that became known as the WM.

Billy Wright

Billy was a wonderful teammate, who had time and a smile for everybody. As a player he was a manager's dream. He won the ball and dispatched it with minimum of fuss but with great efficiency. He was only five foot eight but played like a giant in the centre of the defence.

Tom Finney, England colleague

When Billy took off his England shirt with the three lions I fully expected to see three lions tattooed on his heart. Who knows, if it had not been for the Munich air crash (and the loss of the Man Utd players) Billy might easily have been the first player to lift the World Cup as England captain.

Bobby Robson, England colleague

I knew Billy wouldn't make it as a manager. He was far too nice. You need a ruthless streak and the skin of a rhinoceros. Billy liked to be liked, but you just cannot be a football manager and also popular with everybody. The players will eat you alive if you are too nice.

Stan Cullis, Wolverhampton Wanderers manager

⚽ ⚽ ⚽

I owe Billy Wright so much and yet my gratitude to him is tinged with less gracious memories. On one hand he is the man who brought me to Arsenal FC, initially gambled on my potential but then lost faith in me, never regained it and came so very close to ending my dream.

He was a footballing legend, his brilliant playing career encapsulating so many highs and containing several attributes

45

that the players of today would do well to study. For instance in the entire 1950s, when his club Wolves won three First Division titles to add to the FA Cup triumph of 1949, Billy Wright missed only 31 games. He didn't retire as a player until August 1959. Alongside his total of 541 appearances for Wolves he added 105 caps for England. He was never cautioned or sent off in his entire career.

The first England player to win a century of caps, he remains third behind Peter Shilton and Bobby Moore in international appearances for his country, captaining England throughout their campaigns in the 1950, 1954 and 1958 World Cup finals tournaments.

He enjoyed his status, was generous with his time and his smile but should have settled for the playing celebrity he had so deservedly earned. I think he should have turned away the offer of management which took him to Highbury in banner headlines in 1962 and ended in similar fashion with his sacking four years later, ironically as England became champions of the world.

My first meeting with Billy Wright in 1963 is as clear in my mind now as if it was yesterday. I was a college boy, into my last year of studies at Loughborough College, fulfilling my dad's order that I should qualify for a 'proper' job before pursuing a career as a professional footballer.

Throughout my amateur days at Loughborough I had been tapped up by several big clubs. My first club, Manchester United, had even come back during a goalkeeping crisis to sound out my availability. My presence in the British Universities team and the England Amateur and Olympic squads continued to confirm potential.

I had signed 'amateur' forms for Wolverhampton Wanderers, persuaded by manager Stan Cullis, the man Billy

Wright had succeeded as captain just after the end of the Second World War. Suddenly Arsenal were also expressing interest, initially through their physio Bertie Mee, who held a similar role with British Universities.

With the end of college days looming I needed to find a teaching position in order to fulfil my probationary year that would seal my teaching certificate. I also had to think hard about where my fiancée Megs and I would be best placed, especially for her to go on the stage as an actor following her own probationary period as a teacher.

The choice was simple. At that time, drama, which was her specialisation, was a subject established in and around the southeast of England. But in truth, it was not Megs' work that was the defining factor. It was the selling of Arsenal and Highbury by Billy Wright that re-kindled the ambition within me that had been subdued on that fateful day when my dad had turned down Manchester United six years earlier.

It was February 1963. I was 21 years old and my finals at Loughborough were looming. I had intended to travel to London in my old Ford Prefect, my first car, bought and sold for £50. Its reliability was questionable so a pal loaned me his sparkling Triumph Herald and after a few wrong turns around Islington, I suddenly spotted the historic art deco exterior of Arsenal's East Stand which somehow distinguished the club's unique style when set alongside any other English club.

On entering the marble halls, I was confronted by a bust of the man who had won three League titles at Huddersfield before creating the base at Highbury that saw his Arsenal repeat the feat in the early 30s. Chapman's face reminded me a bit of my dad, who this time would play no part in my choice of club or career. Then suddenly I was facing a real life legend, Billy Wright, blonde curly hair, small, smiling and persuasive. Cleverly he led me on a tour which left the two most important details until last; dressing room and pitch were preceded by directors' lounge, boardroom and trophy cabinets.

Famous faces and moments in the club's history lined the walls, while in the guest lounge claret and blue flowers remained from the previous home game, the colours of Aston Villa and just one of the little touches of respect for the opposition that always made Arsenal different.

Then he led me to the underfloor-heated dressing room, the massive bath and showering facilities and the boot room which had housed the footwear of immortals from Alex James to Joe Mercer. Finally Billy took me on the short walk that I got to know so well over the next twelve years as an Arsenal player and another 28 years as the club's goalkeeping coach. The narrow corridor passing the opponents' dressing room; the dark, cramped tunnel that also contained the players' guest room just off it; and then the emergence into daylight as we walked on the pitch. It sent shivers down my spine, the stands so majestic and high. Rather dramatically I have always likened this first sighting of Highbury to a stately cathedral. Certainly no ground I had ever been inside contained the aura of that created by Herbert Chapman.

Billy sensed what I was thinking and knew he had tempted me away from his old club Wolves. Little did he or I realise then that Wolves would challenge my registration, that a legal dispute would drag on for months until Arsenal, in typical style, paid a sum of £6,500 to the Wanderers, the first and only transfer fee paid for an amateur footballer.

My dealings with Billy over the next three years were rarely as happy as on that initial meeting. There was gratitude at being picked for the first team two months after joining the club – eight games played at the top level as an amateur schoolteacher, the last time that happened at Arsenal. For the majority of time though he held little belief that I could play at the highest level. Just once in three years did he pick me on merit, only for me to sustain a dislocated elbow at Fulham and, once repaired, disappear back into the 'stiffs', which was the affectionate name for the Arsenal reserves.

I also sustained another serious injury – from Billy himself. Playing outfield in a fun game on the Highbury pitch I used my pace to try and go past him. He was always a competitor though, caught me late and broke my ankle. The lowest point of our relationship came when he dropped me from the second team after a humiliating defeat at Highbury in a London Challenge Cup game against Hendon. 2–0 up after ten minutes, we contrived to lose 3–2. No other player in that team was punished although we had all played poorly.

It wasn't unusual for Billy to have a queue of disenchanted players outside his office every Friday but that day, it was just me. I challenged his decision forcibly, he reacted angrily and called for a back-up of troops – his entire back room staff – from whom he sought individual verifications of my performance. It was unnecessary and humiliating. Two of his six staff thought no one player was worse than another. The rest sort of toed the line. A total red mist suddenly descended over me and when he pushed me too far, I simply opened the office door and slammed it forcibly in his face. Close to tears, I grabbed my belongings and charged towards the marble halls and the exit. As far as I was concerned my professional playing career was over once and for all. My dad had been proved right. Football as a career was too precarious. One of Billy's back room staff ran after me. Alf Fields was a great Arsenal servant as player, coach and advisor to successive

49

managers. Alf grabbed me, told me to calm down and made me sit on the little bench seat in the corner of the old hall. 'Alf he can stuff it, I've had enough, I'm off', were more or less the words that I directed at this tall man, whose bravery in war time had earned him a British Empire Medal. Alf set about rebuilding whatever faith I had left in myself, honing my ability to dive headlong at opponents' feet, which he considered unique and a match winning-talent. Above all he told me what I already knew about my club. 'This place is the best son. I've told you that many times. You'll make it. You're a fool to give it all up now.'

I thanked Alf as best I could in the emotional tearful state I was in, shook his hand, walked past Herbert Chapman's bust and there and then resolved to prove Billy Wright wrong.

Billy was not the sort of man who enjoyed rows. I eventually felt sorry for him as he succumbed to the pressures of management failure with a drink too many and a loss of enthusiasm. In 1966 came the ignominy of the sack. How difficult that must have been for a man who had only ever known success and idolatry as a player.

I will remember him more for that genius he possessed and the way he would go out of his way to meet and greet any guests or family that I was showing around Highbury. That was the real Billy Wright and one who was genuinely fulsome of his praise for me a few years later when it was my turn for a touch of glory. Without that first meeting with Billy at Highbury in 1963 who knows what fate may have held in store for me. I will forever be in his debt.

❀ ❀ ❀

William Ambrose 'Billy' Wright

Born:
6 February 1924, Ironbridge, Shropshire
Died:
3 September 1994, London

Position:
Centre half

Clubs as player:
1939–59 Wolverhampton Wanderers, 541 games (16 goals)

Internationals:
1946–59 England, 105 caps (3 goals)

Clubs as manager:
1962–66 Arsenal

Honours as player with Wolverhampton Wanderers:
1949 FA Cup
1954 First Division
1958 First Division
1959 First Division

Awards:
CBE 1959

– Disasters and tragedies –

In 1964 the Liverpool manager Bill Shankly was quoted as saying, 'Football's not a matter of life and death. It's much more important than that.' He was talking about his passion for the game and how his life would have been less fulfilling without it. That his own club, Liverpool should be involved in two of the worst footballing tragedies is immensely ironic.

The first big disaster in the game came during the 1901–02 season. Part of a new stand at Ibrox Park, Glasgow collapsed. The stadium was supposed to hold 80,000 people but on that day it staged a Scotland–England international and there were an estimated 100,000 fans present. As the eastern terrace became full to overflowing, the latecomers headed for the new West Stand, constructed of wooden planks set on pylons of steel at a cost of £20,000. The game had only been played for six or seven minutes when the timber collapsed, with the spectators plunging some 40 feet to the ground below, many on top of each other. In all, seven rows collapsed exposing a 30-yard wide gap. The majority of the crowd inside Ibrox were oblivious to the scenes under the stand. Twenty-five people died and hundreds were injured. The date was 5 April 1902.

Burnden Park, Bolton was the scene of the next dreadful tragedy for the game of football. Bolton met Stoke City in a 6th round FA Cup tie, which at that time was played on a home-and-away basis. Bolton had already won the first leg 2–0. The gates were closed with 65,000 fans inside but many of the 20,000 who were left outside managed to force their way in. The big attraction was the appearance of Stanley Matthews. Sheer weight of numbers then led to two crush barriers collapsing. Horrific scenes followed as spectators piled up on top of each other in the ensuing panic with many trodden underfoot. The match still kicked off, was halted for a short time and, on the advice of the police to avoid panic, resumed. It was concluded with no halftime break and no score. The total dead numbered 33 with more than 500 injured. The date was 9 March 1946.

The next two football related tragedies both involved plane crashes. In the 1948–49 season many of Italy's best players died when the plane carrying the Torino team back from a match in Portugal hit a hillside at Superga, just outside Turin and close to a monastery. Eighteen players were lost including the bulk of the Italian national side. One of them was Valentino Mazzola, the captain and father of Sandro, who was to become as famous as his dad in his footballing career.

In all 31 people perished on 14 May 1949 and I recall, while on tour with Arsenal in the 60s, going to the scene of the crash and laying a club wreath in memory of a side that had won four consecutive league titles and were four points clear on the day of the crash. Their youth team completed Torino's last four games against the youth teams of their opponents, winning all four.

The Munich air crash on 6 February 1958 claimed the lives of more than half of the 40 passengers. Of the 23 who died, eight were Busby Babes, the name given to Manchester United's brilliant young side who were returning home after a thrilling 3–3 draw against Red Star Belgrade. At the time of the crash I was a fifteen-year-old schoolboy whose name was on the books of Manchester United. Nobby Stiles and I were the two chosen from the 1957 England schoolboys' team. My professional career was destined for Arsenal and Highbury, not Old Trafford, but I will always carry both a permanent scar and feeling of pride as a result of my relationship at that time with Manchester United. Matt Busby survived as did Bobby Charlton but wonderful players like Roger Byrne and Duncan Edwards were less fortunate.

There was a second Ibrox Park disaster on 16 September 1961 when two people died and several were injured when crush barriers failed. Incredibly it was not to be the last tragedy at this famous Glasgow venue.

All such disasters are tragic but the blackest day in football history came on Sunday 24 May 1964 when 318 people died in Lima following rioting after a Peru goal against Argentina was disallowed during an Olympic qualifying match in the National Stadium. Over 500 were injured when the crowd became incensed and rioted two minutes before the end of the game.

Four years later, on 23 June 1968, a stampede broke out following a game between River Plate and Boca Juniors in Buenos Aires, Argentina. Seventy-four people died and 150 were injured when spectators mistakenly headed towards a closed exit. The fans at the front of the melee were crushed to death against the doors by other fans at the back unaware of the closed passageway.

Ibrox Park was the scene of the worst disaster in the history of Scottish football on 2 January 1971, when 66 people were killed and more than 200 injured when crush barriers collapsed on a stairway which led out of the ground. The New Year's fixture between the auld enemies was in its closing stages, with Celtic winning 1–0, when hundreds of spectators started to make an early exit from the terraces. As they did so, Rangers' Colin Stein scored an equaliser. It was thought that the culmination of fans turning to get back into the ground meeting others who were still leaving caused the steel barriers to buckle. However a public inquiry discounted this theory and said the deaths were the result of the crush of fans pouring down stairway 13.

Similar incidents have occurred as fans and stadia continue to feature in painful stories that echo around the world. Cairo, Egypt experienced football tragedy on 17 February 1974 with 48 dead and 47 injured after a brick wall and iron fencing collapsed fifteen minutes before kick-off of a game between Zamalek SC and Dukla Prague. On 20 October 1982 a staggering 340 people were reportedly killed during a European Cup match in Moscow. Police were blamed for the incident because they were said to have forced fans down a narrow, icy staircase before the end of the match. But when a late goal was scored, exiting fans tried to re-enter the stadium, crushing the people caught in the middle. Russian officials attempted to claim the official casualty loss was only 61 and the police were not responsible for the disaster. And on 12 March 1988, Kathmandu, Nepal was the scene when at least 93 people were killed and 100 more were injured when fans attempted to flee from a hailstorm inside the stadium. They could not escape because the stadium doors were locked, causing a fatal crush at the front.

Between the 1984–85 season and the 1998–99 season English football reached an all-time low in relation to fans losing their lives. A fire killed more than 50 supporters at the Bradford City Valley Parade ground, sweeping through the main stand during the team's game with Lincoln City on 11 May 1985. What should have been a day of celebration for Bradford's newly won promotion to the Second Division turned into a horror story, the scenes of fans with clothes and hair alight terrifying. Thankfully at that time there were no anti-vandal security fences in place, as so many scrambled to safety over the barriers in front of the stand. Unfortunately a strong wind swept flames in all directions and the roof of the stand collapsed. Matters were made worse in that the wooden structure had years of litter beneath it and this had a tinderbox effect on the speed with which the fire ignited. How slow our footballing authorities were to recognise such danger, especially as similar fires had previously destroyed or caused severe damage to stands at Bristol Rovers, Brighton, Brentford and Norwich City, fortunately without loss of life in those instances.

Almost twelve months after Bradford came Heysel, when more than 40 people were killed, many of them trampled to death, when a wall and safety fence collapsed before the European Cup Final between Liverpool and Juventus. This disaster was so avoidable if rival fans had only behaved as normal human beings and not rioting enemies. The date was 29 May 1985. Most of the casualties were Italian. It would appear that Juventus fans provoked the first trouble by throwing missiles and fireworks at police, but it was Liverpool fans charging into some Italians that led to a wall collapsing and the subsequent death toll.

In truth the deaths were as a direct result of drunken rioting fans who used any piece of metal, whether it be barriers or cans of beer, bottles and flagpoles. A charge by Belgian police only inflamed the situation and lives were needlessly lost at another game of football. To prevent further trouble the match went ahead 85 minutes late and for the record, Juventus won 1–0 with a penalty scored by Michel Platini.

A long drawn out trial in Brussels relating to the Heysel Stadium disaster concluded with 14 of 24 Liverpool fans being found guilty of manslaughter and sentenced to three years' imprisonment, with half of each term suspended. The cases against the other ten were dismissed through lack of evidence. The local Brussels authorities and UEFA were all cleared without any form of censure.

Thirteen days before these verdicts were announced, English football and in particular Liverpool supporters were at the centre of another horror story, the worst soccer tragedy ever witnessed in Europe. The Hillsborough disaster claimed 96 lives with more than 150 people seriously injured. It was played out prior to an FA Cup semi-final between Liverpool and Nottingham Forest at Sheffield Wednesday's ground.

In simple terms, a senior police officer had allowed a gate to be opened in order to ease the frustration of Liverpool fans who were unable to access the Leppings Lane entrance with kick-off time imminent. The sudden surge of fans caused overcrowding on a terrace with bodies being pushed forward to the restraining barriers, some crushed and some buried under falling bodies. Easing the crush by opening certain gates only led to a greater volume of bodies pushing forward for a better view of the action, and the perimeter fencing at the bottom of the terraces, which was put there to prevent hooligans from invading the pitch, contributed to more deaths. Police at first failed to recognise the seriousness of the situation but when one did, he ran onto the pitch and ensured that the game was stopped just six minutes after it had begun.

I will never forget 15 April 1989 and the Hillsborough disaster. The tragic events of that afternoon unfolded as I was presenting BBC Grandstand. I had already handed over to the World Snooker Championships when the first indications of trouble at Hillsborough came through to us from the BBC production van in the ground. Very quickly we learned that a terrible disaster was unfolding. Our senior producer, John Shrewsbury, kept updating us but no live pictures were permitted. By the time of the scheduled kick-off, everyone within the Grandstand studio was aware that lifeless bodies had been taken to a makeshift mortuary close to where our TV vans and scanner were located. Every time the programme returned for an update to Hillsborough we withheld the real truth. The instructions delivered into my ear changed by the minute. A directive came from the head of sport, Jonathan Martin: 'Watch your tone, consider your words carefully, no mention yet of fatalities.'

For almost two hours the decision was upheld not to mention any loss of life, even though we knew that at least 50 people had been crushed to death. Many fans were still in the ground, anxious families were tuned in to their TV sets and Mrs Thatcher and her advisors were following progress at 10 Downing Street. In the last ten minutes of the scheduled programme we were advised to mention that there had been some fatalities. I could envisage the panic in hundreds of households in Liverpool alone. The lines I had to deliver were difficult and choosing my words carefully was demanding.

By the time Grandstand came off the air that Saturday afternoon, we had all been party to a terrible piece of history, one that we would never forget. There were many tears, the vast majority for the victims and their loved ones, but a few also for football, a game which should never, ever be embroiled in a matter as important as 'life and death'.

Since that time, lessons still have to be learned where crowds are gathered in a competitive atmosphere. On 16 October 1996, 84 people died and more than 150 others were injured during a stampede at an all-Central American clash between Guatemala and Costa Rica. And at the Ellis Stadium, Johannesburg, a stampede resulted in the deaths of 43 people during a match between the Kaizer Chiefs and the Orlando Pirates. The disaster, which occurred on 11 April 2001, was the worst in South Africa's sporting history.

Another stampede caused the deaths of fourteen people at a match between Lupopo and Mazembe in the Democratic Republic of Congo on 30 April 2001, while in Ghana, only ten days later on 9 May 2001, trouble started five minutes from time in a match where Asante Kotoko were 2–1 down to local rivals, Hearts of Oak – the country's two top clubs. Police over-reaction was blamed for what was thought to be the worst tragedy in African sporting history – the deaths of at least 126 fans at a football match – when supporters began tearing out the seats and throwing them onto the pitch. Witnesses blamed police for triggering a fatal stampede by firing tear gas in an attempt to quell violence.

So many lives that perished in the name of sport should not be lost in vain and world authorities should never shirk from their responsibility to make sure that the safety of stadiums and the policing of fans is the number-one priority on their agendas.

⚽ ⚽ ⚽

The years of patching up grounds, of having periodic disasters and narrowly avoiding many others by muddling through on a wing and a prayer, must be over.

Lord Justice Taylor, Taylor Report, 29 January 1990

Johnny Haynes

Johnny Haynes revolutionised the way I thought about the game. He gave me a whole new set of possibilities about how you could play and for me that way of playing creatively is as relevant today as it was forty-five years ago. Today we talk about power and speed and we ask if the great players of yesterday could operate in these conditions. Let me tell you something. If Haynes stepped into a game today he would be seen as someone from another planet, a man from Mars. Nutrition, training practices, physical development, all these things change. But some things don't and they include speed of thought and technique, sheer technique.

John Giles, Manchester United, Leeds United
and Republic of Ireland

They said Johnny was slow, but over ten yards he was greased lightning. He also saw everything so quickly. He made his own time, his own space. It was the same with Bobby Charlton. Over the short and vital distances, he too was blinding.

George Cohen, Fulham FC and
England World Cup-winner

He was the only reason I went to Fulham as a young boy of 15 leaving school. He was my hero, the captain of England and Fulham. The word 'great' rolls off the tongue quite easily these days but he really was. He was the best passer of a ball I've ever seen. I don't know anyone who could pass a ball as accurately.

Alan Mullery, Fulham and England

⚽ ⚽ ⚽

In every respect Johnny Haynes was years ahead of his time on the field and off it. As a player he changed the thinking of how the game should progress in England. His game was based on great technical ability, which included long and short passing that was admired by everyone who witnessed it. He became the first footballer to appear for England in every class of football – under-15, under-18, under-23, B-level and full international status. Johnny also followed footballer/cricketer Denis Compton onto the advertising boards, his thick black hair perfect for a Brylcreem campaign. Loyalty is a rarity in the modern game but Haynes played his entire English career at Fulham notching up 658 appearances, still a club record. He captained England in 22 of his 56 appearances. His footballing brain was such that he regularly controlled a game but was famously short of patience with his Fulham teammates when they failed to read his intentions.

It was a privilege to have played against him and he set up Fulham's winner for Graham Leggatt in a New Year's Day encounter against Arsenal in 1966. It was a game in which I dislocated my elbow in the opening minutes and played the rest of the match in agony. Leaving the pitch at the end of the game Johnny saw the severe bleed that had left my arm deeply bruised and was generous with his concern and walked me to our dressing room.

All those who knew him will tell you how much of a gentleman he was. He was the sort of guy you respected and looked up to. All footballers owed him a debt when he became the first professional to earn £100 a week, following the abolition of the £20 wage cap in 1961.

Just months before Johnny's tragic death from a brain haemorrhage while driving his car near his Edinburgh home, 'the Maestro' as Fulham fans named him, told me that he was quite happy to have spent his entire domestic career at Craven Cottage. He felt he was fully respected there, handsomely rewarded in monetary terms and, even when plying his trade in the Second Division and not the top flight, was never in danger of losing his place in the England team.

He admitted that the possibility once of a move to AC Milan had appealed, but not because of the £80,000 transfer fee which would have doubled the world-record fee at that time and made him the best-paid player in the world. Johnny thought that the Italian style of passing play would have suited him perfectly, but he was happy enough to accept the Fulham board's rejection of the deal. He considered that a signed contract and your word should always be honoured. The only time he plied his trade on foreign soil was when he was close to retirement in 1970. He joined his former Fulham pals Johnny Byrne and a larger-than-life character called Bobby Keetch at Durban City in South Africa. Ironically the national title that was won in his time there was Johnny Haynes' only winner's medal in club football.

There are naturally those who attacked Johnny Haynes' loyalty to Fulham as lack of ambition and fear of leaving a comfort zone. Those same people should take note of the quotes that precede this profile.

⚽ ⚽ ⚽

John Norman 'Johnny' Haynes

Born:
17 October 1934, Kentish Town
Died:
18 October 2005, Edinburgh

Position:
Inside forward

Clubs as player:
1951–70 Fulham, 658 games (158 goals)
1970–71 Durban City

Internationals:
1954–62 England, 56 caps (18 goals)

Honours as player with Durban City:
1971 National Football league

– *The Cottagers* –

In 1780, William Craven built a cottage where the centre circle of the Fulham pitch currently resides. The cottage was surrounded by woodland which made up part of Anne Boleyn's hunting grounds. It was lived in by a number of people for the next century until destroyed by fire in 1888. Following the fire, the site was abandoned.

Fifteen years later, it was discovered by representatives from Fulham FC who were looking for a site on which to establish a permanent home for the club. The land was so overgrown that it took nearly two years to make it suitable for football. The pitch saw its first match in 1896 and the team's new home was named Craven Cottage.

In 1905, the club called in Glasgow-born engineer and factory architect Archibald Leitch to construct a stadium. He built what's known today as the Johnny Haynes Stand, a listed building that remains one of the finest examples of football architecture, making the ground one of the most picturesque settings in league football today. However, Leitch forgot to accommodate some changing rooms in his final plans and so built the famous cottage that still stands in the corner of the ground today. Nevertheless it cemented the ground's name as Craven Cottage, and over time the team became known as the Cottagers.

Bertie Mee

Bertie's big saying was 'Let's get on with it'. He felt that if he spent too much time talking about things it was not productive.

Don Howe, former Arsenal coach

I have been motivating people in one way or another all my life, whether they are troops, sick people or professional footballers. Basically, people are the same whether they are footballers or factory workers.

Bertie Mee

If you study the history of the club, the person who made Arsenal is Herbert Chapman. People following in his wake like George Allison and Tom Whittaker did fine and deserve their place, but then there were 17 long years when the club who set all the standards, with things like dress and travel and tradition, did not win a trophy. Bertie was the guy who knew the history of the club and had this military bearing about him. He brought us back. He should get a bust at the club like Herbert Chapman. Arsene Wenger will get one – actually he'll probably get a bloody great statue – but Bertie deserves his place in history. Little Bertie Mee brought Arsenal back from the dead.

Bob Wilson

All quotes for Bertie Mee from
Bertie Mee: Arsenal's Officer and Gentleman by David Tossell

⚽ ⚽ ⚽

The first meeting I had with Arsenal FC was brokered by the club's physio, Bertie Mee. Having seen me play for the British Universities XI, in his capacity as physiotherapist to that team as well, he had passed on my name to the management at Arsenal, recommending they take a look at me. During the next eleven years Bertie continued to have a vested interest in my wellbeing. Initially he just encouraged me as I struggled to convince anyone at the club that I was not just a good amateur goalkeeper. Ultimately, and as a total surprise to all but the Arsenal board of directors, he became manager, achieving greatness when it wasn't expected and helping me fulfil every last dream I had ever held of playing for and winning trophies and international honours at a famous club.

He was an officer and a gentleman, never suffered fools gladly, was a brilliant organiser and the best physiotherapist of his time. After setting up my first visit to Highbury to meet their manager, Billy Wright, he took it upon himself to secure my interest in the club by inviting my fiancée Megs and me to his Southgate home. Part of the idea was to convince the two of us that housing in the London area could back on to green areas as his did. Over supper he sold the club and the possibilities that would open up for us if we joined. The four of us chewed the cud over supper and I complimented Bertie on the perfect temperature of his red wine. 'There is an art to that,' he told us in his most knowledgeable tone and promptly stood up from the table, reached towards a nearby radiator and raised a second bottle in the air with gusto. That was one of the rare occasions when Bertie let his normally serious mask slip.

Both as physio and manager he ruled with a rod of iron. When Billy Wright was sacked in the summer of '66 not one member of the playing staff anticipated the contents of a letter from the club secretary, Mr Bob Wall. 'The directors have appointed Mr Bertie Mee as acting manager and I am sure the directors and I can rely on your wholehearted loyalty to the new manager.'

The appointment was not without precedent. Arsenal had promoted Tom Whittaker in similar vein in 1947 from physio to manager and he had success. But very few of our squad anticipated anything other than a stopgap role in Bertie's case. He clearly thought different. From day one he brought in stringent rules regarding training, punctuality and above all behaviour. 'Gentlemen, remember at all times who you are and what you represent.'

Immaculate club suits had to be worn when travelling to and from games and the beautifully gold embossed gun on the breast pocket was a constant reminder that you were an employee of a historically established football club.

Bertie chose his backroom staff brilliantly, especially his coaching staff. First Dave Sexton began to build a winning team and when he left to manage Chelsea, Don Howe began his outstanding coaching career and, in tandem with Bertie, cemented a side that for six seasons from 1968–73 finished first or second in a major competition. Steve Burtenshaw played his part as well in charge of the reserves, ensuring that they were always ready and enjoying, as best they could, life in the 'stiffs'. Our medical staff was outstanding. Salary negotiations were conducted with Bertie face-to-face. You would be summoned to his office and told of the club's new offer for the next two or occasionally, three seasons. Daring to challenge Bertie's stern approach demanded bravery. He could put you down very easily and usually tempted everyone with a loyalty bonus that was linked to winning leagues and cups. The set win bonus for a game was £4, a draw added £2 to your payslip but the longer you stayed at Arsenal the more you were rewarded. Set alongside today's wage structure it was peanuts: the Double-winning squad of '70–71 earned, with all bonuses for lifting the League and FA Cup, around £17,500 each for the season.

On pre-season and close-season tours he insisted that travelling by air would be conducted in two separate flights carrying half the squad in each. For Bertie the Manchester United Munich disaster emphasised the risk taken in all being together.

On tour he would lecture us all about the burning possibilities of the sun and imposed a £50 fine, which was a lot of money then, should any player breach the rule and show blistering. 'There's a lot of ultra-violet around gentleman', would be his warning call and generally he would get the right reaction. He was totally professional and committed to doing the job to the utmost of his ability.

Unlike other managers of the time, Bertie laid down rigid rules when it came to speaking to the media. He refused to give any interviews in the immediate aftermath of a game, on the basis that it was too close to the heat of battle when emotions tend to run amok. It was easy to get carried away and say something that would be regretted an hour or more later. So Bertie left all reaction to the following day, giving journalists a set time to call him at home or in his office. These were strictly regimented and carried out with an efficiency befitting such a controlled and organised man. Nowadays of course, he or a close member of his staff would be forced, by Premier League rules, to answer questions immediately post-match. I cannot imagine Bertie would agree willingly and, based on the early instinctive and emotional comments that Arsene Wenger made, which he later withdrew as 'excessive', following his player Eduardo's sickening double compound fracture at Birmingham, suggest that the Mee way was a better way.

The happiest I ever saw him was in the week beginning 3 May 1971. On that Monday night we had to either beat Spurs at White Hart Lane or draw 0–0 to be champions of England. Any other scoreline would see Leeds United lift the league title. We won 1–0 and Bertie let his hair down, as we had never seen previously. We couldn't believe our eyes when he returned to our dressing room, tie-less and without a jacket. 'They're all mad out there,' he cried with total happiness. Five days later he repeated his actions after Liverpool were beaten in the FA Cup Final to give us the second double of the last century and ensure his own immortality.

As I followed skipper Frank McLintock and the glistening trophy down the Wembley steps and back onto the pitch, there was Bertie, as near to tears as I'd ever seen him, rushing at me and expressing his congratulations. He knew the long journey I had undertaken from Loughborough to Wembley after getting me to sign as an Arsenal player eight years earlier.

There were players who couldn't handle Bertie's style, notably Ray Kennedy and Charlie George, but then he in turn was not cut out to understand the excesses of many of the youngsters of that time. He recognised the crucial role Don Howe had played in the winning of that double and the Inter-Cities Fairs Cup in the previous year, but he should perhaps have done more to try and keep Don at Highbury when West Bromwich Albion sought his services as manager in that summer of '71. Although we returned to Wembley for the centenary FA Cup Final in '72 and finished close runners-up in the league to Liverpool in '73, there were no more trophies won by Bertie and his teams.

In 1974 a mixture of injury and disillusionment with events at the club led me to consider retirement from my beloved Arsenal. BBC TV had made me an offer to present sporting programmes. I was 33 years old, but a serious knee injury was only just holding up and enabling me to play at the top level. In my heart I knew I only ever wanted to be considered an Arsenal man. Bertie and I met and in deep discussion he pleaded with me to give him one more year. It would ensure that I got my testimonial game. If I decided on TV then I would not be given that reward. It was a difficult choice for me and a harsh ultimatum from a club I'd served for over 300 first-team appearances. There was genuine disappointment but also respect from Bertie when I told him I had decided to forgo the testimonial and go out at the top. He had always been a good listener as well as advisor and clearly trusted my intelligence and judgement by allowing me, in 1970, to work on a part-time basis for BBC TV Sport. I specialised in analysis items on teams or individuals and created a little niche for myself by logging every match covered by the Beeb. Only once did he threaten to take away this privilege after I had self-analysed the five Stoke City goals I had conceded in Arsenal's drubbing at the Victoria Ground halfway through our Double season.

'Talk about others by all means, but never about us' was Bertie's admonishment to me, probably the only time he gave me a good telling off.

On my final appearance in 1974 he paid me a huge compliment when he wrote in the match programme the following:

Bob Wilson has all the hallmarks that place him above his fellow keepers. First of all, he has a very high standard of consistency. Of course he makes mistakes sometimes, but I can say, in all honesty – and I mean every word of it – that during our Double year, I do not remember Bob making one mistake. This must have been worth 14 points to us over the season. He is a player with great courage and his enthusiasm for the game has never wavered. For a manager he is the ideal team man. He certainly takes his place in the Hall of Fame with the great Arsenal goalkeepers of the past and will be very difficult to replace.

I never received a kinder assessment of the part I have played in Arsenal's history than that written by my diminutive manager, but it is still not what I will most thank or remember Bertie Mee for. Rather, an extraordinary Churchillian-type speech he made in the Highbury dressing room several weeks before the end of the 1970–71 season. I sat very close to where Bertie stood and noticed his hands were shaking nervously as he addressed our entire seventeen-man squad. The gist of what he said centred on the opportunity we had created for ourselves to make history and follow our rivals and neighbours Spurs into the history books by achieving the second Double of the twentieth century:

Gentlemen, under normal circumstances I would never ask you to do what I now ask of you. Your family should always be the most important thing in your life, but until this campaign is over I am now asking you to put the club, the team and the fans first. Don't throw away the chance that we have worked so hard for.

It was Bertie Mee at his best. Never a coach but a thinker and a truly outstanding man-manager. After seventeen years in the cold he led Arsenal back from the wilderness, recreating so much of the vision and style that Herbert Chapman had begun in the thirties and restoring foundations which successors like Terry Neill, George Graham and Arsene Wenger built upon.

❀ ❀ ❀

Bertram 'Bertie' Mee

Born:
25 December 1918, Bulwell, Nottinghamshire
Died:
22 October 2001, London

Position:
Winger

Clubs as player:
1938–39 Derby County
1939 Mansfield Town, 13 games

Clubs as manager:
1966–76 Arsenal

Honours as manager at Arsenal:
1970 Inter-Cities Fairs Cup
1971 First Division and FA Cup

Awards:
OBE 1984

– *FA Cup Roll of Honour* –

1872	Wanderers
1873	Wanderers
1874	Oxford University
1875	Royal Engineers
1876	Wanderers
1877	Wanderers
1878	Wanderers
1879	Old Etonians
1880	Clapham Rovers
1881	Old Carthusians
1882	Old Etonians
1883	Blackburn Olympic
1884	Blackburn Rovers
1885	Blackburn Rovers
1886	Blackburn Rovers
1887	Aston Villa
1888	West Bromwich Albion
1889	Preston North End
1890	Blackburn Rovers
1891	Blackburn Rovers
1892	West Bromwich Albion
1893	Wolverhampton Wanderers
1894	Notts County
1895	Aston Villa
1896	Sheffield Wednesday
1897	Aston Villa
1898	Nottingham Forest
1899	Sheffield United
1900	Bury
1901	Tottenham Hotspur

1902 Sheffield United
1903 Bury
1904 Manchester City
1905 Aston Villa
1906 Everton
1907 Sheffield Wednesday
1908 Wolverhampton Wanderers
1909 Manchester United
1910 Newcastle United
1911 Bradford City
1912 Barnsley
1913 Aston Villa
1914 Burnley
1915 Sheffield United
Not held from 1916–19
1920 Aston Villa
1921 Tottenham Hotspur
1922 Huddersfield Town
1923 Bolton Wanderers
1924 Newcastle United
1925 Sheffield United
1926 Bolton Wanderers
1927 Cardiff City
1928 Blackburn Rovers
1929 Bolton Wanderers
1930 Arsenal
1931 West Bromwich Albion
1932 Newcastle United
1933 Everton
1934 Manchester City
1935 Sheffield Wednesday
1936 Arsenal
1937 Sunderland

1938   Preston North End
1939   Portsmouth
Not held from 1940–46
1946   Derby County
1947   Charlton Athletic
1948   Manchester United
1949   Wolverhampton Wanderers
1950   Arsenal
1951   Newcastle United
1952   Newcastle United
1953   Blackpool
1954   West Bromwich Albion
1955   Newcastle United
1956   Manchester City
1957   Aston Villa
1958   Bolton Wanderers
1959   Nottingham Forest
1960   Wolverhampton Wanderers
1961   Tottenham Hotspur
1962   Tottenham Hotspur
1963   Manchester United
1964   West Ham United
1965   Liverpool
1966   Everton
1967   Tottenham Hotspur
1968   West Bromwich Albion
1969   Manchester City
1970   Chelsea
1971   Arsenal
1972   Leeds United
1973   Sunderland
1974   Liverpool
1975   West Ham United

1976   Southampton
1977   Manchester United
1978   Ipswich Town
1979   Arsenal
1980   West Ham United
1981   Tottenham Hotspur
1982   Tottenham Hotspur
1983   Manchester United
1984   Everton
1985   Manchester United
1986   Liverpool
1987   Coventry City
1988   Wimbledon
1989   Liverpool
1990   Manchester United
1991   Tottenham Hotspur
1992   Liverpool
1993   Arsenal
1994   Manchester United
1995   Everton
1996   Manchester United
1997   Chelsea
1998   Arsenal
1999   Manchester United
2000   Chelsea
2001   Liverpool
2002   Arsenal
2003   Arsenal
2004   Manchester United
2005   Arsenal
2006   Liverpool
2007   Chelsea
2008   Portsmouth

Denis Law

Denis was in the class of Alfredo di Stefano because he could do everything, organise a side and score goals. Matt Busby knew how important he was.

Harry Gregg, former United keeper,
The European Cup 1955–80

⚽ ⚽ ⚽

The greatest aspect of my time as a professional footballer was that I played in a 'golden era'. In monetary terms we earned very little but generally above the national average salary. In playing terms it was a level field with no year-in-year-out domination by wealthier clubs.

All the First Division teams contained wonderful players. Clubs like Burnley, Ipswich Town, Everton, Leeds United, Derby County and Manchester City all became league champions. Even Manchester United could be relegated and indeed were in 1974.

The goal that guaranteed their relegation was scored by a Manchester City player. To make matters worse it was Denis Law, one of the greatest of the Red Devils' heroes, nicknamed 'The King' and 'The Lawman' by the United faithful during his eleven years at Old Trafford. If the fans were devastated, it was an equally desperate moment for Denis. He wouldn't celebrate the goal and was substituted within seconds, leaving the pitch with head down, despondent.

The game became the last of his eye-catching career as retirement beckoned. Denis Law is another of my favourite footballers, one whom it has been a privilege to face, a joy to know. He is the brightest of bright individuals, fun and a huge personality. He has always reminded me of an old famous comedian and film star called Danny Kaye. Same shock of fair hair, same open dazzling smile.

On the field he was a jack-in-the-box – popping up all over the place, quick, inventive and lethal. I love the story of his career and how he came to be recognised in 2003 by the Scottish Football Association as the greatest Scottish footballer of the previous 50 years. He was the son of an Aberdeen fisherman who regularly had to visit the local pawnbroker and lived in a council tenement, a kid with no proper shoes but whose emerging talent earned him a gift of some football boots from a neighbour. Any chances of him making the top grade were slim though as he had an eye problem, a serious squint. As always great talent won through and once he was recognised as an inside left rather than a full back he was selected as a reserve for the Scotland schoolboys' team. It led to an interest from Huddersfield Town but the chances of a contract again seemed slim when he learned of manager Andy Beattie's assessment of him.

'The boy's a freak. Never did I see a less likely football prospect; weak, puny, bespectacled.' But Huddersfield took a chance; an operation corrected the squint and meant he didn't have to play the game with one eye closed any more. It didn't take long before the big clubs came hunting. First Matt Busby and United, whose £10,000 offer was rejected, and then Liverpool who had taken the then Huddersfield manager Bill Shankly away from Yorkshire and who wanted in turn to acquire young Denis Law.

At that time they couldn't afford him. Manchester City decided they could and he went to Maine Road in March 1960 for a British-record fee of £55,000. Crazy to think many players are earning twice that amount each week today. Back then Denis never got a penny from the deal; there was no 5 per cent or more of the transfer fee given to the player. The highs and lows of being a pro continued apace: two Law goals kept City in the First Division in 1960, a year later as a Scotland full international he endured his blackest day when England beat the 'auld enemy' at Wembley 9–3. That summer of '61 he was sold to Torino but the ultra-defensive systems of play in Italy meant less scoring opportunities and he was clearly unhappy with life on the continent.

Lucky to survive a bad car crash with teammate Joe Baker, Denis more or less walked out of Torino, who tried to renege on a second British transfer record fee which took him to Manchester United, by telling him he had to sign for Juventus. You didn't threaten Denis Law. That's when the bubbly personality turns to one of steel. United or nothing was his reaction and Torino decided they needed the transfer money. The record fee paid by United was £115,000; the date was 10 July 1962.

Initially it was by no means plain sailing at Old Trafford. Although the FA Cup was won in 1963 it took another three seasons for United to become champions for the first time since the Munich disaster in 1958. The next season Denis became the first and still the only Scot to be named European Footballer of the Year. Twenty-eight goals made him the top scorer in the First Division. A serious knee injury prevented him from repeating the feat the next season but in 1967 United again won the league and, more satisfyingly for Denis, he scored in Scotland's 3–2 win over England at Wembley which was the first defeat inflicted on the new world champions.

Denis loves talking about that game in particular and also about the greatness of his United manager Sir Matt Busby. He believed that there was no secret, nothing extra-special about Busby. He just understood footballers, their needs and quirks and consequently treated them like normal people. The manager was not just concerned about talking football matters. He cared about life off the field, asking constantly about a player's family and his home. Matt Busby always had his players' interests at heart, being a calm, softly spoken father-figure. The more Denis got to know Busby the more he would give for him and his club. There was a stern side to the manager if a player ever stepped over the mark, was regularly late or dressed down. The Matt Busby belief was that a player was an ambassador for Manchester United Football Club. Collar and tie and club suits are still a part of Alex Ferguson's policy today.

As United won the European Cup for the first time in 1968 my own career at Arsenal was, at long last, promising brighter things. It was a huge irony that in the next six seasons, as Arsenal won or were runners-up in a major competition each year, United's fortunes faltered with relegation to the Second Division, the ultimate ignominy.

I wish that my appearances for Scotland had coincided with two of his 55 appearances in the national jersey. To have been in goal behind Kenny Dalglish and Denis Law would have been quite something. His fame lives on at Old Trafford where a statue of him sits at the Stretford End. Everyone in football was happy that a successful operation treated his prostate cancer, including Dennis Bergkamp who was named after Denis Law by his parents, at that time fans of Manchester United (albeit 'Dennis' with two 'n's). Now there's a thought – 'God' and 'The King' in the same team!

Denis Law's career reads a little like a comic-strip hero's. Boy from poor home, with a dodgy eye attains greatness. Targets achieved and records set but sometimes at a price and with a touch of sadness at heart. None more so than that famous back heel he scored for Manchester City to condemn United to the Second Division. It would never have happened had Manchester United and their manager Tommy Docherty not broken a promise made to Denis a year earlier. A place in the United coaching staff upon retirement had been discussed, alongside a testimonial as reward for eleven years of great service.

Denis had been happy with the proposal but, on holiday in Aberdeen during the close season, was shocked to see banner headlines declaring that United had given him a free transfer. A visit to Matt Busby, who was now on the board, for clarification did nothing to help alter the decision United had taken. Within weeks Denis was offered the chance to return to another old club, Manchester City. He decided he still had something to give as a player and signed a contract. Instead of bowing out quietly with a testimonial game and a place on the United coaching staff, Denis spent a season reclaiming his Scotland place and going to the World Cup finals, playing in yet another Wembley final and, of course, reminding United, in the most painful of ways, what a mistake they had made.

⚽ ⚽ ⚽

Denis Law

Born:
24 February 1940, Aberdeen

Position:
Striker

Clubs as player:
1956–60 Huddersfield Town, 91 games (19 goals)
1960–61 Manchester City, 50 games (23 goals)
1961–62 Torino, 27 games (10 goals)
1962–73 Manchester United, 393 games (236 goals)
1973–74 Manchester City, 26 games (12 goals)

Internationals:
1958–74 Scotland, 55 caps (30 goals)

Honours as player with Manchester United:
1963 FA Cup
1965 First Division
1967 First Division
1968 European Cup (missed final through injury)

Awards:
1964 European Footballer of the Year

– *English champions* –

1889	Preston North End
1890	Preston North End
1891	Everton
1892	Sunderland
1893	Sunderland
1894	Aston Villa
1895	Sunderland
1896	Aston Villa
1897	Aston Villa
1898	Sheffield United
1899	Aston Villa
1900	Aston Villa
1901	Liverpool
1902	Sunderland
1903	Sheffield Wednesday
1904	Sheffield Wednesday
1905	Newcastle United
1906	Liverpool
1907	Newcastle United
1908	Manchester United
1909	Newcastle United
1910	Aston Villa
1911	Manchester United
1912	Blackburn Rovers
1913	Sunderland
1914	Blackburn Rovers
1915	Everton

Not held from 1916–19

1920	West Bromwich Albion

1921	Burnley
1922	Liverpool
1923	Liverpool
1924	Huddersfield Town
1925	Huddersfield Town
1926	Huddersfield Town
1927	Newcastle United
1928	Everton
1929	Sheffield Wednesday
1930	Sheffield Wednesday
1931	Arsenal
1932	Everton
1933	Arsenal
1934	Arsenal
1935	Arsenal
1936	Sunderland
1937	Manchester City
1938	Arsenal
1939	Everton

Not held from 1940–46

1947	Liverpool
1948	Arsenal
1949	Portsmouth
1950	Portsmouth
1951	Tottenham Hotspur
1952	Manchester United
1953	Arsenal
1954	Wolverhampton Wanderers
1955	Chelsea
1956	Manchester United
1957	Manchester United
1958	Wolverhampton Wanderers

1959	Wolverhampton Wanderers
1960	Burnley
1961	Tottenham Hotspur
1962	Ipswich Town
1963	Everton
1964	Liverpool
1965	Manchester United
1966	Liverpool
1967	Manchester United
1968	Manchester City
1969	Leeds United
1970	Everton
1971	Arsenal
1972	Derby County
1973	Liverpool
1974	Leeds United
1975	Derby County
1976	Liverpool
1977	Liverpool
1978	Nottingham Forest
1979	Liverpool
1980	Liverpool
1981	Aston Villa
1982	Liverpool
1983	Liverpool
1984	Liverpool
1985	Everton
1986	Liverpool
1987	Everton
1988	Liverpool
1989	Arsenal
1990	Liverpool

1991	Arsenal
1992	Leeds United
1993	Manchester United
1994	Manchester United
1995	Blackburn Rovers
1996	Manchester United
1997	Manchester United
1998	Arsenal
1999	Manchester United
2000	Manchester United
2001	Manchester United
2002	Arsenal
2003	Manchester United
2004	Arsenal
2005	Chelsea
2006	Chelsea
2007	Manchester United
2008	Manchester United

Bill Nicholson

I did not enjoy dancing around, waving trophies in the air. I'm sure he didn't like it either. His comments regarding success were always cold ... I was embarrassed by the boasting around us but I escaped it with humour. He gruffed his way out of it. Our satisfaction was in doing the job.

Danny Blanchflower,
1961 Spurs Double-winning captain

⚽ ⚽ ⚽

Bill Nicholson was the greatest manager in the history of Tottenham Hotspur Football Club, one of the game's finest. Spurs, of course, will always remain Arsenal's traditional rivals. Curious then that I should enjoy writing about the man we all know as Bill Nick and that I cherish a friendship which began in the intense heat of battle between two very proud North London clubs. The game was a 1969 League Cup semi-final in which Arsenal had taken a slender 1–0 lead to White Hart Lane after the first leg at Highbury.

Without question it was the most violent game of football in which I had taken part. Only Spurs' magnificent goalkeeper Pat Jennings and I seemed to be on the periphery of what was simply a pitched battle. There were disgusting tackles, wild swings of arms and fists and the use of heads to cause damage. Both teams were guilty. It's amazing that all 22 players remained on the pitch for 90 minutes. Similar scenes today would result in at least eight of the players being dismissed.

It was a horror story long before Jimmy Greaves had put Spurs ahead on the night and level on aggregate. Nothing improved before or after John Radford had then equalised with a goal that would take us to Wembley. For me it got much worse, as I became the target of a very untypical piece of play from Spurs' elegant striker Alan Gilzean. As I beat 'Gilly' to a loose, bouncing ball the Scot simply volleyed my lower left leg. It is the only time when I lay on a pitch convinced that a limb was broken. Around me all hell had broken loose, a free-for-all as my teammates set out for retribution aimed at every, and any Tottenham player, but especially Gilzean.

My instinct was to just give in and take the stretcher back to the haven of the dressing rooms en route to hospital. Instead competitive spirit kicked in. In those days you didn't just lie down. Although fuming and in considerable pain I could see the Twin Towers of Wembley looming if we could survive the closing minutes. Several moments later I was back on my feet, hobbling and determined to get through to the final whistle helped by a serious adrenalin rush. It stayed at 2–1 on aggregate. The old enemy were beaten. Bragging rights went to the men in red.

Instead of returning to the away team dressing room for a shower or bath, I was helped to an area beyond where the Spurs lads changed. Within a few moments, while our physio George Wright and the Spurs doctor Brian Curtin worked on me, Bill Nicholson appeared. He looked concerned and spent ten minutes talking about my injury and expressing, as best he could, an apology for Gilly's tackle.

From that moment the respect I already had for Bill Nicholson grew into admiration for his belief in fair play. This was, of course, the man who was a cornerstone of Arthur Rowe's famous 'push and run' side that won the Second and First Division Championships in successive seasons. Then he had taken over the managerial reigns in October 1958, guiding Tottenham to the first domestic Double of the twentieth century in 1960–61, with a brilliant team that scored 115 goals in their 42 league games. It was a side I would try to get to see, as a Loughborough College student, as much as possible. I will always appreciate the time Bill took to ensure that there was no broken leg for me, wishing me well and offering good luck for the final.

Bill Nicholson resigned as Spurs manager as I retired from playing in 1974, but our paths continued to cross. For many years he was special guest at the London Football Coaches' annual dinner, an association of which I was chairman. No dinner went by over a decade and more without our members giving Bill Nicholson a standing ovation. My wife Megs and I had then got to know Bill better, together with his remarkable wife Darkie who was a driving force behind his success. She made us laugh and always brought a twinkle to her husband's eye, even during a sad but thankfully short period of time when his old club didn't treat him the way they should have done. Happily the Spurs board soon saw sense. An approach road to White Hart Lane was named Bill Nicholson Way in his honour in 1999 and he was club president from 1991 right up to his death on 23 October 2004.

His funeral was a wonderful celebration with Spurs Double-winner Cliff Jones providing a brilliant and fitting eulogy. There were very few dry eyes, with the indestructible Dave Mackay visibly moved by the funeral of his own boss. I was proud to represent Arsenal Football Club on that sad day, to say goodbye to an old adversary, to give Darkie a kiss and a hug and to be accepted in among the different generations of Bill Nick's Tottenham players.

The 'Battle of White Hart Lane' in 1969 and Bill Nicholson's concern for me came to mind and will remain forever, another of those memories that have enhanced my life.

✪ ✪ ✪

William 'Bill' Nicholson

Born:
26 January 1913, Scarborough, Yorkshire
Died:
23 October 2004, Hertfordshire

Position:
Right half

Clubs as player:
1938–39 and 1946–54 Tottenham Hotspur, 341 games (6 goals)

Internationals:
1951 England, 1 cap

Honours as player:
1951 First Division

Clubs as manager:
1958–74 Tottenham Hotspur

Honours as manager at Tottenham Hotspur:
1961 FA Cup, First Division (the first Double of the twentieth century) and FA Charity Shield
1962 FA Cup and FA Charity Shield
1963 UEFA Cup Winners' Cup
1967 FA Cup and FA Charity Shield
1971 League Cup
1972 UEFA Cup
1973 League Cup

Awards:
1975 OBE

– *Football League Cup Roll of Honour* –

1961	Aston Villa
1962	Norwich City
1963	Birmingham City
1964	Leicester City
1965	Chelsea
1966	West Bromwich Albion
1967	Queens Park Rangers
1968	Leeds United
1969	Swindon Town
1970	Manchester City
1971	Tottenham Hotspur
1972	Stoke City
1973	Tottenham Hotspur
1974	Wolverhampton Wanderers
1975	Aston Villa
1976	Manchester City
1977	Aston Villa
1978	Nottingham Forest
1979	Nottingham Forest
1980	Wolverhampton Wanderers
1981	Liverpool
1982	Liverpool
1983	Liverpool
1984	Liverpool
1985	Norwich City
1986	Oxford United
1987	Arsenal
1988	Luton Town
1989	Nottingham Forest

1990	Nottingham Forest
1991	Sheffield Wednesday
1992	Manchester United
1993	Arsenal
1994	Aston Villa
1995	Liverpool
1996	Aston Villa
1997	Leicester City
1998	Chelsea
1999	Tottenham Hotspur
2000	Leicester City
2001	Liverpool
2002	Blackburn Rovers
2003	Liverpool
2004	Middlesbrough
2005	Chelsea
2006	Manchester United
2007	Chelsea
2008	Tottenham Hotspur

Henry Cooper

Henry Cooper hit me so hard that my ancestors in Africa felt the blow.

Muhammad Ali (alias Cassius Clay) on that
Wembley knock-down, 1963

☙ ☙ ☙

Mutual respect is a real bond between all sports people. Whatever the athletic discipline, there is an understanding of what it takes to succeed and achieve. Making the dream come true requires ambition, enthusiasm, natural talent, manufactured ability, determination and dedication.

The only link between Henry Cooper and me was Arsenal. The British, European and Commonwealth boxing champion supported the Gunners. I played for them.

From the low point of injury and the long road to recovery, Henry and I forged a friendship that remains 42 years on. Henry, arguably England's best-loved sportsman alongside Bobby Charlton, had a damaged knee cartilage and I had a broken wrist. His need for a quick mend was more important than mine. A return World Heavyweight title fight against Cassius Clay, who became Muhammad Ali, was on the horizon. I was still making slow progress as an Arsenal keeper. The club offered the physiotherapy and training ground facilities to the Cooper camp so that he could re-build his fitness. Two injured athletes became firm friends, working the gym, walking or jogging the Hertfordshire fields. Henry, who has never let his great fame change his personality, enjoyed the daily contact with his footballing heroes. In turn our squad embraced him totally and I was lucky enough to spend a lot of time with him.

It was fascinating enough hearing about the boxing fraternity and some of the illegalities that took place. Henry's huge fame had been cemented by a left hook with which he had dumped Cassius Clay on his pants in a non-title fight at Wembley in 1963. Angelo Dundee, Clay's trainer, famously cut his fighter's glove to buy time although subsequently the mythical three minutes extra time gained was proved to be far less. What was totally illegal was the use of the unknown substance that Dundee broke from a small phial and used to help revive a dazed Clay. Listening to Henry's version of events and just how close he came to beating the reigning world champion was enthralling. Clay went on to win the bout and now was offering a second opportunity to Henry, a return world title fight that was to be held at Highbury.

Our conversation was by no means restricted to sport. Henry's stories of growing up in Southeast London alongside his identical twin brother George embraced a shadowy world of gang warfare and the infighting between the infamous Kray and Richardson families. When it came to quizzing the fighter about the essentials of making the grade at any sport he taught me a solitary lesson:

Always look after number one.

Believe in your own ability; polish the strengths; work on the weakness.

Openly practise the art of humility, because in sport you will face the twin impostors of success and failure, winning and losing, triumph and despair.

It was despair that 'Our 'Enery' again had to deal with when his return with Clay ended with the Highbury fight being stopped as the Cooper achilles' heel of cutting too easily struck again.

Since our recuperation spell together, Henry and I have stayed in touch, charity events also bringing us into contact. He has raised substantial sums for many charities and remains as popular as ever throughout the UK.

❊ ❊ ❊

Sir Henry Cooper

Born:
3 May 1934 London

British and Commonwealth Heavyweight Champion:
1959–71

European Heavyweight Champion:
1964–71

Awards:
1967 and 1970 BBC Sports Personality of the Year
2000 Knighthood

– *Floodlights* –

Playing football in artificial lights is today accepted without complaint or question. It wasn't always that way, although the earliest record of such an occurrence was treated as a novelty and certainly not the norm.

On 14 October 1878 Bramall Lane, Sheffield – which is still home to Sheffield United – staged a game between two teams drawn from the local area. The sides were captained by two brothers, J.C. and W.E. Clegg, both of whom had made appearances for England.

In each corner of the ground 30-foot wooden towers were erected, upon which were perched four electric lights. Portable generators powered the bulbs. The game attracted around 20,000 spectators. It was very experimental and continued to be so as Accrington, Birmingham and London followed suit, with varying degrees of success. The London match took place at the Oval, scene of so many great moments from different sports, and not just cricket for which it is now known.

Strong winds caused havoc that night with the floodlighting flickering unevenly throughout the game. The experiments did not lead to any adoption of the idea and although Herbert Chapman, Arsenal's legendary manager of the late 20s and early 30s, was a strong advocate of floodlit football, the FA remained immovable until 1951, some 73 years later. Then on 19 September the first official match under floodlights took place at the late Chapman's club, Arsenal, who entertained the Israeli team Hapoel from Tel Aviv. A 44,000 crowd saw the Gunners win 6–1. Amazing that Chapman, who had seen floodlit football on the continent around 1930, had insisted on having them fitted to the new West Stand at Highbury, despite an FA ban on their use in major games.

Evidently the FA feared that clubs would run the risk of bankruptcy if they spent a lot of money on lights. It was one of Chapman's protégés, Tom Whittaker, who decided to show the public what they were missing and the game subsequently received a unanimous thumbs up from the media, fans and the Football Association.

Don Howe

It was like finding Miss World was free and asking for a date.

Bobby Gould, 1986, after Howe agreed to coach his
Bristol Rovers team

⚽ ⚽ ⚽

Mention this man's name to any West Bromwich Albion or Arsenal fan and there will be glowing testimony and huge respect. Don Howe made his mark initially at the Hawthorns as a full back who played nearly 350 games for the Baggies and won 23 England caps. Billy Wright and Arsenal signed him in 1964 and he arrived as new club captain at the same time as I arrived as a new full pro following my year's probationary teaching in London.

The twelve months in which I had played for Arsenal as an amateur schoolteacher had not exactly excited the squad of players or management at Highbury. There was an uneasy feeling between them and me as I reported for my first full day's training. Only one man went out of his way to help my discomfort. It was Don Howe who sensed my embarrassment and took me on one side to have a chat. I didn't have many early opportunities to play behind him and within two years his playing career was finished by a horrific compound fracture of the leg.

It was a truly sickening injury and a complete accident as Don burst into the Blackpool penalty area and was met by the huge diving frame of their keeper Tony Waiters, my predecessor in the Loughborough College goal. The sound of the crack could be heard all around Highbury and as soon as Don was placed on the stretcher, I was given the task of trying to find his wife Pauline. The plate and screws which brought the broken tibia and fibula back together remain in Don's shin to this day. It's an example of how precarious a footballer's life can be.

Weaker characters than Don would struggle to cope with the disappointment and dejection of a playing career cut cruelly short. Not Don Howe. If he was unable to play the game then why not teach the game? That was his approach and one which led him to real greatness as a coach, arguably the finest and most knowledgeable of his generation. Even now, into his seventies, advice is asked of him at every level of the game in every country around the world.

His earliest coaching was with an Arsenal reserves team and manager Bertie Mee was inspired in giving Don the role while Dave Sexton coached the first team. Dave was also a wonderful coach but was soon tempted to try his hand at management with Chelsea. Don took over the reins and faced a rebellious bunch unhappy to have lost someone they loved. Don identified the unrest and answered the challenge, at first with fierce discipline and extra training, and then he won total respect by making a significant tactical change in defence. The team had been well drilled in man-to-man marking. Don started advocating a zonal system and spent hours and days and months perfecting it with the players. As the Arsenal defence stopped leaking goals, Don turned his attention to midfield and then attack, working diligently with the players until they could almost do what he wanted in their sleep. His personality was perfect for a squad who desperately craved success. Bertie Mee allowed him to have a free hand while he concentrated on man-management skills and all other areas necessary for the boss.

A League Cup Final defeat at Wembley in his initial year as first team coach led immediately to Arsenal's first ever European trophy the following year in 1970. The much coveted League Championship and FA Cup Double followed twelve months later. In the dressing room he never held back. If he thought someone had made a silly error he was in their face telling them so. If and when he was challenged, Don would listen but still make his point. He was tactile when he thought a player had turned the game in the team's favour, grabbing them and patting them on the back. His pre-match talks were simple and inspirational. For the second leg of the Fairs Cup Final against Anderlecht, Bertie Mee allowed a reporter into the dressing room at Highbury. His writing gives an example of the relationship between manager and coach:

> Mee sticks to general points. 'You know what this game means to you, your careers and this club.' Then Howe talks over the game as he wants them to play it. 'First 15 minutes I want you forward, either you or the ball. Their best two forwards can be bullied. Well bully them. Hit them hard and do it quick. And when you've done it pick 'em up. Let the crowd see it was an accident. I don't mean any messing with the offside trap. I want cover at the back. Don't let Jan Mulder start running at you. He can take four on and go straight past the lot of you. I've got a lot of respect for him.' Howe talks quickly, using gestures, pacing out attacks, living the moves he is describing. The team watch him intently. It is part of the weekly confidence trick that coach and

players work on each other. It does not matter who they are playing, if it is a home game they are the better team. That is why they are going to win. Simple.

That night in 1970 Arsenal overcame a 3–1 first leg deficit to win 4-3 on aggregate. The following season things simply got better and Don's delight at Wembley as the Double was won was uncontrolled. He'd missed out himself through injury but he'd got the next-best-thing in coaching and converting a good team into a great one. His success was bound to attract other people's attention and his old club, Albion, tempted him back to the Hawthorns and into management. It's a mystery why Don Howe did not have the success in management he always had as a coach. Perhaps his 'hands on' style on the training field was difficult to bring into the mix while dealing with players' contracts and the like. More likely he never had the right funding and backing from the board of directors, or was just unlucky.

His sheer brilliance as a coach has taken on many challenges – Galatasaray in Turkey, Leeds United and a return to Arsenal where the team reached four finals in three years during his work alongside manager Terry Neill. When Neill was sacked, Don became manager of Arsenal in 1983 only to resign on a point of principle in 1986 when his position was undermined by a member of the board. Almost immediately he was masterminding the greatest FA Cup Final shock of all time as a coach alongside Wimbledon manager Bobby Gould.

Don's ability to improvise and adapt his coaching skills, whatever the talent available was evident on one of his first days at Wimbledon. After taking over Wimbledon from Dave Bassett, Bobby and Don took the squad to Sweden. A flip chart was in place for Don to explain some of his coaching ideas and thoughts. Before he could use it the 'Crazy Gang' asked to have the first say. They believed in the old saying 'if it ain't broke, don't fix it'. The players' philosophy was straightforward. To win games they needed to launch 174 balls into the attacking third during 90 minutes play plus a minimum 44 crosses in the same duration. As long as Don appreciated this essential tactic they would entertain his own coaching ideas. He admits it provided the greatest of challenges and was therefore far more challenging than his spells with the England teams alongside Bobby Robson at the World Cup in 1990 and Terry Venables at Euro '96, both of which fell short after penalty shootouts at the semi-final stage.

There were also spells at QPR and Coventry before Don Howe returned for one more time to Arsenal to help develop the young players at the club in line with Arsene Wenger's thinking, tactics far removed from those employed by the 'Crazy Gang'. A triple heart by-pass operation failed to slow this son of Wolverhampton down or lessen his enthusiasm. Following his official retirement from coaching in 2003 his views have been constantly sought by newspapers, television or young aspiring managers. That's Don Howe, master coach.

❀ ❀ ❀

Donald 'Don' Howe

Born:
12 October 1935 Wolverhampton

Position:
Right back

Clubs as player:
1952–64 West Bromwich Albion, 342 games* (17 goals)
1964–66 Arsenal, 74 games (1 goal)

Internationals:
1957–59 England, 23 caps

Clubs as manager:
1971–73 West Bromwich Albion
1974–75 Galatasaray SK
1983–86 Arsenal
1989–91 Queens Park Rangers
1992 Coventry (caretaker manager)

– FA Cup Final players' pool –

During the 60s, 70s and 80s it became increasingly popular for the two teams contesting the FA Cup Final to cash in on their good fortune by having a 'players' pool'. This pool enabled the teams to arrange interviews with the media, sponsorship deals and advertising opportunities, the payments for which could supplement whatever bonus they might receive from their clubs for reaching the final, winning it or finishing as runners-up.

In 1972 I missed the FA Cup Final through serious injury having been carried off in the semi-final at Villa Park when Arsenal met Stoke City. The squad decided that my frustration at missing what was the centenary final, against Leeds United, could be eased by my assisting in running the players' pool. Recently I came across a copy of the agreements I had helped set up for the Arsenal squad and it makes interesting reading as well as giving an insight into how commercial activities have multiplied in the 37 intervening years.

⚽ ⚽ ⚽

Agreements – Firm and Agreed

ITV – through London Weekend TV	£500.00
(This is the stipulated TV payment to players as laid down in the ITV agreement)	
For semi-final	£250.00
BBC – certain requests e.g. interviews at banquet following match	
Estimated fee	£1000.00
For semi-final	£250.00
Esso Petroleum – photo for posters in Garage forecourts	£1000.00
Evening News	£100.00
Evening Standard	£100.00
Daily Express	£100.00
Goal Magazine	£50.00
Press Photo call	£350.00
Adidas/Umbro – boots and strip	£2000.00
The People – feature on George Armstrong	£250.00

Liverpool Echo – some interviews and photos	£50.00
Daily Mirror – to choose a song. Judges – McLintock and Armstrong	£75.00
Evening Standard – 20 page 'Go With Golden Gunners'	£1000.00

Pye Records

Tie-up between *Daily Express*, LWT TV, on a dreadful mutilation of 'Rule Brittania'. And a lively 'Marching Through Georgia'. Recording session on Sunday 10am, 5% of selling price (i.e. 5 pence a record) Estimated yield on 50,000 records £1050.00

RAC Records

1% sale of 'On The Ball'. No recording session. Nothing to do on our side. £200.00

Various press features:

The *Sun* – group of wives photo	£140.00
The *Daily Mail* – Feature on Frank McLintock (Dialogue with Tommy Smith)	£100.00
Feature on Charlie George	£150.00
Feature on wives and girlfriends	£300.00

Inside the Gunners

Booklet to be self-supporting on production costs – three ads London Co-op will sell in Wood Green, Highgate and Camden branches plus sellers at Stoke City home game and supporters' clubs. Sell at 15p £600.00

Souvenirs

Autographed ties, ice-container etc	£200.00

After Match

Drinks – Milk offer	£350.00
Trying Coca Cola – should get better deal – say	£500.00

Extra to *Evening Standard* Supplement

Certain advertisers may want to identify with
a player. Maybe they will give cash in hand   £350.00

Autographed footballs

17 leather balls *Evening Standard* will buy
for awards   £500.00

Firm expectation to date   **£11,515.00**

Trying to bring off the following:

'Double' Diamond and commercial
    winners   £5000.00
    losers   £1250.00

Projected overall target for Cup Final pool is   £17,765.00

Sir Alf Ramsey

He's the most patriotic man I've ever met.

Sir Geoff Hurst, 1966 World Cup-winner

He is more careful of his aspirates than his answers.

Arthur Hopcraft, 1968, author of *The Football Men*, after
Ramsey received elocution lessons

*It seems a pity Argentinian talent is wasted. Our best football will
come against the right type of opposition – a team who come to play
football and not act as animals.*

Sir Alf Ramsey, quarter-final vs. Argentina

*You've won it once. Now you'll have to go out there and do it
again.*

Ramsey team talk, prior to World Cup Final extra-time

☺ ☺ ☺

England's greatest manager was in charge of the national
team from 1963 until 1974, which spans exactly the same
period of time that I played for Arsenal FC. Other than
the odd nod of acknowledgement at football grounds
around the country, I only spoke privately to Sir Alf on two
occasions, so I do not claim to know him well. Both meetings
were significant in their own way. The first one followed an
evening game in 1970 at Highbury, not long into our Double
season. I enjoyed a lot of good form and luck that campaign
and that night had played particularly well.

While passing through the marble halls after the game, I walked straight into the England manager. In that very unusual clipped accent that he had cultivated since his boyhood days in Dagenham, he congratulated me on my performance, discussed briefly the match itself and wished me well. My manager Bertie Mee arrived to talk to Alf as I left. A couple of days later, Bertie told me that Alf had been enquiring about several of our team with a view to international recognition. Bob McNab, George Armstrong and Peter Simpson had all caught Ramsey's eye. So too it seemed had I, but Bertie soon quashed any lingering ambitions I might have held of playing international football for England. This meeting came just under twelve months before rules were changed regarding eligibility for my selection for Scotland. At that time, I could only represent the country in which I was born, which was England, and not the country of my parent's birth, which was Scotland.

Alf had asked Bertie whether I was still eligible to play for the England under-21 team. Our manager quickly informed a surprised Alf Ramsey that I had in fact just turned 30! England had so many great keepers in 1970, including Gordon Banks, Peter Bonetti and a young Peter Shilton.

A second meeting with Alf was longer in duration and gave me a complete insight into this much-discussed personality. In 1991 I had been asked to chair a charity dinner to celebrate the 25th Anniversary of England's World Cup Final victory. Our committee managed to bring together Sir Alf Ramsey and his entire squad with one notable exception, that of Jimmy Greaves who had missed out on the final itself following injury and Alf's decision to retain Geoff Hurst in the side. Greavsie's absence was a source of much discussion on that day when the squad gathered at the Royal Garden Hotel in Kensington, which is where they had celebrated victory in 1966, and later at the old Wembley Stadium for a dinner attended by the Duke and Duchess of Kent.

As chairman, much of my day was spent ensuring that Sir Alf was happy and comfortable. He was never less than polite, but not easy to converse with. At times he seemed aloof and defensive, especially when I talked about his enlightened and effective tactics for his team in 1966, who were described as 'Ramsey's Wingless Wonders'. Alf had been a very accomplished full back for Southampton and Spurs and he told me that that position had given him an insight into the lack of any defensive responsibilities of wingers he was asked to mark, like Stan Matthews or even Tom Finney. He preferred a system that provided for good attacking midfielders being able to double up, so that once the ball was lost they would be able to defend much better than attack-minded wingers. Essentially it was a 4-4-2 system that created problems for opponents used to facing wide players, rather than a midfield-backed forward line that attacked through the centre of the field.

However reserved Alf was as a person, and remember he and Jimmy Greaves were the only two people not to jump up in excitement at the final whistle on 30 July 1966, he had the total respect of his players. None had a bad word to say about him. I could claim I once played under Alf. That was the time that the late Emlyn Hughes and I were signed for Melchester Rovers, in the *Roy of the Rovers* comic. Alf became caretaker manager when Roy suffered a coma for a short spell of time.

Sir Alf was a proud man, and England should be proud of him. One of his successors as Ipswich Town manager, Sir Bobby Robson, was big enough to declare Ramsey 'the greatest British football manager', and that despite his own glorious times in Suffolk and with England. It is often mentioned that Alf was a little jealous of Bobby, but ultimately any airs and graces he might have possessed were put aside in thanking Bobby and his wife Elsie for helping pay for hospital bills incurred by him towards the end of his life.

☺ ☺ ☺

Sir Alfred Ernest 'Alf' Ramsey

Born:
22 January 1920, Dagenham
Died:
28 April 1999, Suffolk

Position:
Right back

Clubs as player:
1944–49 Southampton, 96 games (8 goals)
1949–55 Tottenham Hotspur, 250 games (25 goals)

Internationals:
1948–54 England, 32 caps (3 goals)

Clubs as manager:
1955–63 Ipswich Town
1977–78 Birmingham City

International teams as manager:
1963–74 England

Honours as manager at Ipswich Town:
1962 First Division

Honours as manager at England:
1966 World Cup

Awards:
1967 Knighthood

– *The Little Tin Idol* –

The current FA Cup trophy is in fact the fourth in the history of the competition. The first, less than 18 inches tall and much smaller than the one in use today, was made by Martin, Hall & Co. at a cost of £20. It was first awarded in 1872 and remained in use until its theft in 1895. Holders Aston Villa had decided to exhibit the trophy in the window of a football outfitters shop in Birmingham, but the first night of its display, the shop was broken into and the Cup stolen. In spite of a £10 reward, it was never recovered and was assumed to have been melted down. Before its disappearance and despite it being made of solid silver, it had become popularly and affectionately known as the 'Little Tin Idol'.

Although the trophy was never recovered, the story has an intriguing final twist. In 1958, 63 years later, an 83-year-old resident of a Birmingham hostel for the homeless named Harry Burge claimed that he had stolen it and used it to produce counterfeit half-crown coins. Although impossible to prove Burge's story, it remains the only plausible explanation for the Little Tin Idol's fate.

Pat Jennings

Big Pat is not big physically but his reputation is huge. Pat's a one off. The majority of keepers over the years have been trapeze artists. Pat is the complete opposite. He has great composure. Like his voice, it comes from way down near his feet. He does things in his own way.

George Best

Nobody ever won the hearts of Irishmen of every hue more than Pat Jennings. He unites the community in a province where thankfully, sport has avoided becoming embroiled in the traumas of the last 16 years.

Malcolm Brodie MBE, *Belfast Telegraph*

Pat would always be one of the first people in any football Hall of Fame. He's never got involved in anything that lessened his dignity.

Don Howe, Arsenal manager

⚽ ⚽ ⚽

'The Big Man' was my early professional hero, the perfect follow-up to Bert Trautmann who I had idolised as a kid. It helped in one way that I could go and watch him regularly at close quarters, a few miles away from Highbury or my first London home. The fact that he played his football at White Hart Lane for Spurs was more of a problem. Not that I was a recognisable opponent in those early days at Arsenal. Although almost four years younger, Pat was already establishing himself at the top level while I was buried in the Arsenal reserve team.

His style of goalkeeping was in many ways unique, then and throughout his illustrious career. He had amazing presence in his goal, huge hands that enabled him to catch a ball one-handed in flight when, in reality, he had slightly misjudged its flight, and was the first keeper in modern times to completely master the ability to save with feet, rather than plunge headlong into flying boots at the risk of serious injury.

I tried like mad to emulate Pat's way of goalkeeping for a period of time early in my Arsenal days, but it took a fine journalist to help me recognise that although my style could never be like Pat Jennings', if it still worked for me then go with it. Eric Todd wrote for the *Guardian* newspaper. After a supreme Jennings performance for Tottenham at Leeds he perfectly described Pat's style and display when he wrote:

> If Jennings had been available on that memorable day when the Romans met the Etruscans, Horatius surely would have had to have been happy with a seat on the substitutes' bench.

The following week the same scribe wrote about me following a half-decent game I'd played, also against Leeds. Eager to see if my way of keeping goal bore comparison to the elegant Jennings style, I was confronted with the following less flattering but highly accurate description:

> To play the way Wilson plays, you need courage, speed of thought, determination and an IQ of 20!

Little did I think in those formative times, that I would eventually be at the other end to Pat on many occasions,

113

become his coach for the latter part of his career and, best of all, get to know him as a really treasured pal.

There was little to choose between the Arsenal and Spurs teams when Pat and I were at opposite ends of the field. We won some, they won some, occasionally there would be a draw. For me the night at White Hart Lane when Ray Kennedy's header beat Pat to give us the 1–0 victory we needed to be champions of England was the highlight. Typically Pat was generous in his congratulations. It should have been the moment when I told him that he had been my inspiration but words failed me, such was the awe in which I held Pat Jennings.

Three or four years later I had barely left Highbury as a player before I was asked back by manager and former teammate Terry Neill, to develop my ideas on specialised goalkeeping with his new signing – Pat Jennings. Terry had pulled off a masterstroke; Spurs had committed *hari-kari* by letting their keeper leave for the old enemy. Pat was to tell me how hurt he had been by Spurs' attitude, especially on the day that he collected his boots and left White Hart Lane en route to Highbury. Various Spurs directors walked past him without a 'good morning' or 'good luck'. After his service to the club Pat described it thus: 'If someone had stuck a knife in me at that moment, it couldn't have hurt more.'

Being asked to coach my hero was one of the greatest challenges of my footballing life. Pat had never had a coach in his entire career. Such individuals simply didn't exist at football clubs. My approach to Pat on his first day was carefully thought out, and one I would normally never contemplate with any other keeper. He was 32, almost as modest and unaware of his greatness as when he burst on the footballing scene as a teenager at Watford in 1963. For the one and only time as a coach, I told Pat that he alone must guide me on when he wanted to work hard and for how long. I based my thinking on the fact that I couldn't teach him anything new.

Age wasn't a factor for me but it was, increasingly, for him. I insisted that if he wanted little or no work, he must still help me by giving the other keepers words of advice as well as serving the balls alongside me. In our eight seasons together I taught him little other than how to coach, but as he questioned his age and ability more and more, I think my enthusiasm and encouragement helped keep him going. More than once he told me, 'I think John Lukic is better than me now.' Time and again he surprised himself and as the sun rose over the city of Guadalajara on the morning of 12 June 1986, Pat was still there at the very top. It was a momentous day, his 41st birthday and he was making his 119th and final international appearance for Northern Ireland against, of all opponents, Brazil. The South Americans won 3–0 but it would have been six without the genius of Pat Jennings.

Typically the Irishman has given back to the game since retiring – as a fine coach of goalkeepers. He is in demand throughout the UK, remembered with affection for his play and his modesty. Although he found success and was hero-worshipped at Arsenal, he remains at heart a Spurs man, the club which recognised his raw talent and, despite early moments of despair, developed his potential to the full.

If you ask him out of all the tributes and compliments he has received, which is the best, he will tell you that it came from Jimmy Greaves. The legendary striker had clashed heads with Pat during training one day. Both needed urgent treatment when Jimmy told the Spurs doctor, 'Look after Pat first; he's far more important to tomorrow's game than me.'

Today his greatest relaxation comes from playing golf. He has a single-figure handicap and wins many pro-ams. He still makes time for others and lends his name and time as a patron to the Willow Foundation charity. A great man ... my hero.

✪ ✪ ✪

Patrick Anthony 'Pat' Jennings

Born:
12 June 1945, Newry, County Down, Northern Ireland

Position:
Goalkeeper

Clubs as player:
1963–64 Watford, 48 games*
1964–77 Tottenham Hotspur, 590 games (1 goal)
1977–85 Arsenal, 326 games

Internationals:
1964–86 Northern Ireland, 119 caps

Honours as player with Tottenham Hotspur:
1967 FA Cup
1971 League Cup
1972 UEFA Cup
1973 League Cup

Honours as player with Arsenal:
1979 FA Cup

Awards:
1973 FWA Footballer of the Year
1976 PFA Players' Player of the Year
1987 OBE
1999 KSG

– *Goalkeeping asides* –

1865   Tape to be stretched across the goals, eight feet from the ground.

1871   Goalkeepers first mentioned in laws of the game.

1875   The crossbar replaces tape on the goalposts.

1890   Goal nets invented by Mr Brodie of Liverpool and used for the first time.

1891   Penalty kick introduced.

1894   Goalkeeper can only charge when playing the ball or obstructing an opponent.

1895   Goalposts and crossbars must not exceed five inches in width.

1905   Goalkeepers are ordered to stay on goal-line, for first time, at penalties.

1909   To assist referee, goalkeepers must play in distinctive colours of scarlet, royal blue or white. Green was added three years later.

1912   Goalkeeper not permitted to handle the ball outside the penalty area.

1929 Goalkeeper compelled to stand still on his goal-line at penalty kick.

1936 Defending players not permitted to tap the ball into goalkeeper's hands from a goal-kick.

1937 Defending players not permitted to tap the ball into goalkeeper's hands from free-kick inside the penalty area.

1992 Back-pass rule introduced to discourage time-wasting. Prohibits the goalkeeper from intentionally handling the ball when a teammate uses his/her feet to intentionally pass them the ball, or from intentionally handling the ball when receiving directly from a throw-in.

1997 In own box, goalkeeper can hold or bounce ball for maximum of six seconds from moment ball is controlled by hands. Ball must then be released into play.

1997 Goalkeeper to remain on his own goal line, facing the penalty kicker, between the goalposts until the ball has been kicked. The phrase 'without moving his feet' deleted.

2000 Goalkeeper cannot take more than six seconds while controlling the ball with his hands before releasing it from his possession.

Bobby Moore

He was my friend as well as the greatest defender I have ever played against. The world has lost one of its greatest football players and an honourable gentleman.

Pele

If people say England would not have won the World Cup without me as manager, I can say it would have been impossible without Bobby as captain. In so many ways he was my right-hand man, my lieutenant on the field, a cool calculated footballer I could trust with my life.

Sir Alf Ramsey

There should be a law against him. He knows what's happening 20 minutes before anyone else.

Jock Stein, 1969, Celtic manager

⚽ ⚽ ⚽

England's only World Cup-winning captain. You would expect him to bear the title 'Sir Bobby', not just for his captaincy but for his contribution to the great game. Sadly there was no knighthood for this supreme player, a man who was popular with everyone with whom he came into contact. I still get asked whether I ever played against Bobby Moore. It's hard to shut me up once I start relating the matches against West Ham, the interviews I conducted with him and especially the precious times when we were in the same Old Internationals XI on tour in Brazil and South Africa.

By the time I had established myself as first-choice goalkeeper for Arsenal, Bobby had earned his immortality by lifting the Jules Rimet trophy after the 4–2 World Cup Final victory against West Germany. In fact one game against Bobby's Hammers had a huge psychological benefit for me. The game ended in a draw and, in the dressing room after the game, I studied the programme and the team line-ups. Glancing down the opposition names I read Bobby Moore, Martin Peters and Geoff Hurst, the three Hammers who had played such a massive part in England's route to being world champions. The value to me came in the fact that I had played really solidly and, arguably, as well as the three heroes during the 90 minutes. After such a long and rocky journey from amateur schoolteacher to Arsenal keeper, that performance did more for my confidence and morale than any other I remember. It made me feel that I could belong among the elite. As always, Bobby was gracious at the final whistle, that gentle firm handshake and genuine 'well done' which meant so much to me.

If asked to pick out one game that typified his genius, it would be England's 1–0 defeat to Brazil in 1970 in Guadalajara. The South Americans were unstoppable in that World Cup. They would have beaten the then reigning world champions by more, had it not been for Gordon Banks' 'impossible save' from Pele and Bobby Moore's unforgettable brilliance breaking up numerous attacks from Tostao, Jairzinho and co.

Moore's captaincy was different from so many other leaders. No animated screaming from Bobby, he simply led by example with the occasional aside that was invariably positive in nature and rarely, if ever, negative. I experienced his style up close and very personal during two tours when a group of ageing former internationals travelled first to Brazil and then South Africa. The way he handled himself made you want to impress him in return, to try and get a complimentary little nod, or even a look that said, 'well done, mate'.

It would be hard to find anyone who dealt with fame better than Bobby. After reaching our hotel in Rio de Janeiro and collecting our room keys, 'Mooro' asked me if I fancied getting the long flight out of my system by joining him for a run on the famous Copacabana beach which fronted our base. I didn't have to think very hard to accept such an invitation. Ten minutes later, wearing very short shorts and some trainers we hit the beach running on the firmest sand we could find by the water's edge. What you have to bear in mind is that all Brazilian football fans – which is 99 per cent of the population – always remember an iconic photo from the 1970 World Cup finals in which their own hero Pele exchanged shirts with the England captain Bobby Moore – a photo of two smiling athletes in their prime, bare to the waist, showing huge respect for each other.

After a few hundred yards of the training run with Bobby I suddenly became aware of a lot of shouting and excited bodies closing in on us. I knew they weren't chasing me, that they had no clue I had ever been a professional footballer even, but the great Bobby Moore they recognised instantly. Suffice to say that for the next twenty minutes or more, I stood in the water and watched in admiration as he signed bits of paper, body parts, t-shirts and swimming attire. Never hurried or flustered, but polite, smiling, appreciative of the Brazilians' love for him. It's a special story and an equally great memory.

The later tour to South Africa was also memorable. Our team was helping break down the awful barriers that had been put there as a result of apartheid. Most of the teams we faced were made up of six black and five white players, or the reverse. In the township of Soweto we faced the famous Kaiser Chiefs in which the only white faces among a 30,000-seat stadium were the visiting tourists' team. As we were on a goodwill mission Bobby decided that should we score first, we would then allow the Chiefs to equalise before halftime. Then, if all went well, we would score again before 'gifting' the opposition a late chance, so that the game would be drawn. And that is exactly what occurred, leaving everyone in the stadium very happy, especially our diplomatic skipper.

At the start of that tour I played a notable part in introducing Bobby to one of the BA aircrew who had helped transport us to Africa. Her name was Stephanie. I left them in animated conversation. Several months later, back in the UK, I came out of a lift at the Wembley Conference Centre, prior to watching an England international. From the adjoining lift Bobby appeared with a lady. After hugs and handshakes he said, 'You remember Stephanie?' 'No, nice to meet you,' I replied. At that moment Bobby laughed and gently reminded me that I had indeed introduced them! Some time later, Bobby and Stephanie were married and although their time together was all too brief because of his tragic battle with cancer, his wife has kept his spirit and memory alive brilliantly with her tireless work for the Bobby Moore Fund which supports Cancer Research UK. Stephanie's work and the efforts of my wife Megs and me for the Willow Foundation has maintained the link between us.

I heard about Bobby's death at the age of 50 while in the Caribbean on the island of Antigua. The news hit me just as hard as if it was a brother. Almost immediately I began to call on all the great times I had spent in his company, including the final months of his life when, despite his own fight for life, he would always put others ahead of himself. 'All is well Bob? Good, keep well.' 'All is well' became his favourite saying.

A knighthood is the title he most deserved and although it's one that eluded him, to everyone who played with and against him or knew him he will always be 'Sir Bobby'.

❖ ❖ ❖

Robert Frederick Chelsea 'Bobby' Moore

Born:
12 April 1941, Barking
Died:
24 February 1993, London

Position:
Defender

Clubs as player:
1958–74 West Ham United, 642 games (27 goals)
1974–77 Fulham, 150 games (1 goal)
1976 San Antonio Thunder, 24 games (1 goal)
1978 Seattle Sounders, 7 games

Internationals:
1962–73 England, 108 caps (2 goals)

Clubs as manager:
1980 Oxford City
1981–82 Eastern AA
1984–86 Southend United

Honours as player with West Ham United:
1964 FA Cup
1965 Cup Winners' Cup

Honours as player with England:
1966 World Cup

Awards:
1964 Footballer of the Year
1966 BBC Sports Personality of the Year
1967 OBE

– *The Hammers* –

In 1895, the foreman of the shipbuilding department of Thames Ironworks suggested to the managing director, Arnold Hills, the possibility of the company forming its own football club. Hills – keen to improve morale in his workforce in the wake of a bitter industrial dispute with his employees – thought it was a good idea and established Thames Ironworks FC. By 1898, they had turned professional and been elected to the Southern League.

In 1900, having acquired another engineering firm, Hills and the board decided to make Thames Ironworks a public company. Consequently, with shareholders to consider, they could no longer carry on pumping the company's money into the football club. Thames Ironworks FC was subsequently disbanded but, in its place, West Ham United Football Club Company Limited was formed.

By that stage Thames Ironworks FC had become known simply as the Irons, a name that carried over to the formation of West Ham and the name by which fans still refer to their club today. Over time, journalists created the name Hammers as another reference to their Ironworks origins, not as an extension of the word Ham, as is sometimes thought.

Bill Shankly

Shankly – He Made the People Happy

Inscription on statue of Shankly at Anfield

First is first. Second is nothing.

Bill Shankly, 1971

*I was managed by the best sports psychologist the world has ever seen.
Bill Shankly made us feel we were super-human.*

Ray Clemence, 2002, former Liverpool keeper

*I remember a speech he made in which he talked about retirement.
That word, he said, should be removed from the dictionary. When
he went from Liverpool he said he'd had enough, but in the end,
he found that the close involvement with football was the thing he
missed most. I tried to persuade him to stay, but he told me he wanted
to make a complete break from the whole thing. He was adamant.*

Bob Paisley

⚽ ⚽ ⚽

'Shanks' will always remain one of my favourite men. His
captivating manner of speech enthralled everyone with whom
he came into contact, not just the many players who raised
their games as a result of the inspiration he gave them.

I doubt that the true greatness of Liverpool FC and the
dynasty that occurred would have taken place without the
proud Scot that was Bill Shankly. Paisley, Fagan, Dalglish,
Souness all took a bit of Shankly into their managerial

locker and then added their own touch. I'm certain that the continental managers like Houllier and Benitez would have been educated in the Shankly legend and laughed along with all who have been given an insight into his beliefs and enthusiasm.

A visiting team to Liverpool would leave the coach and walk the few yards to the Anfield dressing room. Invariably the Liverpool manager would be standing somewhere en route. Catching his eye could be a mistake. Looking directly at you he would express a threatening sort of greeting, 'Aye, hello son, welcome to Anfield.' It would be delivered in that slightly aggressive Scottish drawl, every syllable expressed with meaning.

Nowadays we talk about the importance of psychology in sport. It's always been there and Brian Clough of old and Jose Mourinho of new are two of the greatest exponents of this tactic. However Bill Shankly would make them look like novices with his cutting remarks and perfectly timed asides. On more than one occasion I was on the receiving end of his tongue.

Imagine my nerves as an amateur schoolteacher heading towards professional status but still green behind the ears, spotting Shankly in the marble halls at Highbury before playing a game. Star-struck, I wondered if he knew who I was, so that maybe I could ask him for an autograph. He glanced my way several times, as I proceeded to put tickets on the front door for my family. Shanks never said a word until I turned to head for the dressing room. Then in a loud voice that seemed to echo around the marble walls and floor, I heard him ask the doorman, 'Aye, excuse me. Are Arsenal at full strength tonight, or is that Bob Wilson playing?' It was a dagger through the heart, a direct blow to my belief and confidence.

By the time Arsenal were due to meet Liverpool in the 1971 FA Cup Final I was thrilled to know I had won Shankly over and had his respect. After losing 2–0 at Anfield in a league game he went totally overboard in his praise for the Arsenal keeper: 'Bob Wilson deserves the George Medal for bravery. Without him we'd have won 6 or 7.' It was flattering and great for my self-belief, despite the fact that I'd been on the losing team.

Before any game Bill Shankly still looked for a moment to instil fear in the opposition. The day before any FA Cup Final of yesteryear the teams would visit Wembley separately and view the pitch and facilities. We did that on Friday 7 May 1971. As we walked up the tunnel from the dressing rooms I spotted Shanks at the top overlooking the stadium. No other Liverpool person was in sight. The familiar growl met me. 'Aye, hello son' was enough to remind me who we were meeting and what a tough time we would have against his young, emerging side. The Liverpool manager watched as we all inspected different areas of the sacred turf. I concentrated on my goalmouths, constantly feeling the wet surface. All I could think about was how my one-inch studs (which I preferred in order to make my 6' 1" into 6' 2") would stick in the soft, lush Wembley turf. Shankly must have sensed my concern because as we left, he uttered his gracious goodbyes to all our team but as I reciprocated he added, 'Aye, Bob Wilson, nightmare pitch for goalkeepers, eh? Aye!'

Twenty-four hours later, despite my positional error at the near post, which allowed Steve Heighway to put Liverpool ahead, Arsenal came back to win 2–1 and lift the FA Cup and the Double. Bill Shankly knew we had been the better team and a huge hug from him together with his congratulations was worth almost as much to me as my winner's medal.

One of my last meetings with Bill Shankly came after I had finished my playing career and started in the TV business. The Liverpool boss had bought my old teammate Ray Kennedy as a forward but the early indications were not good and Big Ray looked lost without his Arsenal striking partner John Radford beside him. I arrived at Liverpool's training ground to do an interview with Bill for my *Football Focus* programme. As we were setting up cameras a worried-looking Shankly invited me to his office. He told me he had bought badly, that Ray Kennedy was not what he had expected. He was genuinely upset and concerned. We talked and talked and I kept telling him what a great talent Kennedy was, how he was brilliant with back to goal, had a great potential to create as well as score goals. Shankly thanked me and seemed to be reassured, if only slightly. Ultimately Ray Kennedy, Bill's last signing, proved to be a brilliant acquisition for Liverpool, not as an out-and-out goalscorer but as a creative left-sided midfield man. Domestic and international honours flowed his way. After the chat, on that day many years ago, I left Melwood with a Liverpool tracksuit under my arm – a gift from one of the greatest footballing men in the game's history.

⚽ ⚽ ⚽

William 'Bill' Shankly

Born:
2 September 1913, Glenbuck, Ayrshire.
Died:
29 September 1981, Liverpool

Position:
Right half-back

Clubs as player:
1932–33 Carlisle United, 16 games*
1933–39 Preston North End, 297 games (13 goals)

Internationals:
1938–44 Scotland, 5 caps (+ 7 wartime internationals)

Clubs as manager:
1949–51 Carlisle United
1951–54 Grimsby Town
1954–55 Workington Town
1956–59 Huddersfield Town
1959–74 Liverpool

Honours as player with Preston North End:
1938 FA Cup

Honours as manager at Liverpool:
1964 First Division
1965 FA Cup
1966 First Division
1973 Cup Winners' Cup and First Division
1974 FA Cup

Awards:
OBE 1974

– *The Kop* –

Whenever I was asked which opponent's ground was a favourite to play on I would always say Anfield, home of Liverpool. It's quite sad that it is unlikely to exist for many more years as plans for a new 71,000-seat stadium have been accepted and it is due to be built at Stanley Park in time for the start of the 2011–12 season.

The reason that Anfield pips somewhere like Old Trafford is the Kop, that amazing area behind one goal which in my time contained a swaying mass of humanity numbering 28,000 dedicated fans but which today is restricted to an all-seated capacity of 12,499. Generations of Liverpool managers have spoken about the Kop's capability to 'suck the ball into the back of an opponent's net'. The banners proclaiming loyalty remain today, even if the number of fans under the famous roof has reduced. 'You'll Never Walk Alone' is an iconic Liverpool song that retains the ability to affect opponents while rallying the Liverpool players.

It's fair to say that the noise from the Kop can either impede or inspire an opposing goalkeeper. I loved it and can instantly recall the run from the dressing rooms to the Kop end, which is considerably further than getting to the opposite goal. Whether playing well or poorly, winning, losing or drawing, the Kop would greet any arriving goalie with wonderful applause. I'm delighted to see that the new ground, will be anchored by an expanded 18,500-seat stand-alone Kop, an increase of more than 5,000 seats.

1884   Anfield Stadium built in Liverpool.

1906   New brick and cinder banking installed at Walton Breck Road end, originally called the Oakfield Road Embankment, then the Walton Breck Bank, before being christened 'Spion Kop' in memory of the many soldiers from Liverpool who died on a battle over a hill of that name in South Africa during the Boer War.

1928   Kop altered to terracing for 28,000 supporters, and a massive roof added.

1975   Health and Safety regulations reduce maximum capacity of the Kop to 22,000.

1994   Kop changed from terrace to all-seated Kop Grandstand with capacity of 12,499.

Frank McLintock

He was as important an influence on the Arsenal Double team as fellow Scot Dave Mackay had been on the Super Spurs side ten years earlier. Like Mackay, he was a tremendously inspirational captain who could make his teammates willing to run through brick walls.

George Graham, former Arsenal teammate

⚽ ⚽ ⚽

The importance of a captain's role within the structure of any football team cannot be overstated. The definition of captain reads, 'a chief, a leader'. They are the individuals who, once a game starts, take over from the manager and coach. In truth a good captain also leads off the pitch as well as on it, brokering disputes between management and players. Football has embraced many different styles of skipper, those who quietly lead by example and sheer excellence as a player, like Bobby Moore, and those more vocal characters like Tony Adams and Dave Mackay.

The best captain I ever knew was Frank McLintock. He fell into the second category – extremely vocal, daringly confrontational, a Braveheart whose leadership qualities were nurtured within an area in a city that, when Frank was a kid, was known as the Chicago of Europe. The Gorbals in Glasgow had a reputation for being 'tough and rough, angry but warm, a city of extremes, a place where brutal hardship was commonplace and violent men thrived'. These are Frank's words and his description of life on the ground floor of a tenement block are equally powerful, almost shocking:

Our flat had two small rooms, known as a 'room' and a 'kitchen'. Most of our time was spent in the larger room that doubled-up as bedroom and living area. There was a curtained-off bed recess in the wall where my parents slept and I shared the pull-down settee with my sister. We didn't have electricity but still relied on gas lamps for light. We shared an outside toilet with two other families.

Out of this challenging environment emerged a terrific footballer, outstanding man and a great, great captain. The secret of Frank McLintock's leadership lay in his durability to survive great highs and great lows, and to react to them better than any of those around him. Victory and trophies created a laughing, tub-thumping person who could party all night long. Defeat and coming second had an initial depressive despairing effect on Frank but he was always the first to bounce back, the most famous occasion following a 3–1 first-leg defeat for Arsenal in the 1970 Inter-Cities Fairs Cup Final against Anderlecht.

Arsenal had been taken apart in Brussels by a clever team who contained a genius of a striker called Jan Mulder. As shirts and boots were torn off our bodies in disgust and desolation in the dressing room, the most visual dejection was on our captain's face. He'd already played in four Wembley finals and not been on a winning side for either Leicester City or Arsenal. Frank's emotional state initially impacted on those around him and for once, the dressing room went eerily quiet. At that moment there was no chance of a second-leg comeback and it stayed that way for a good ten minutes. Then the silence was broken in the most inspirational way as Frank emerged from the shower and began a diatribe delivered in that broad Glaswegian accent of his. 'Aye, you know, they're rubbish really. If we get at 'em next week at Highbury, they'll cave in. We'll effing murder them.' By the time he'd finished some minutes later we were all believers again. Frank's secret lay in his impulsive nature – he could love an item of clothing one moment and dismiss it as awful a short time later. He would be abusive over an error you'd made and within minutes be hugging and encouraging you to do better. The kid who had battled his way out of the Gorbals scenario had a hatred of getting beaten and couldn't wait for the next game to come around.

Anderlecht were indeed undone in the second leg, beaten 3–0 and left convinced that the running power of the Arsenal team they had faced could only have come from taking drugs. It was the greatest night ever witnessed at Highbury. The fans were amazing; a 55,000-sell out, helping to lift both the team and the first trophy for seventeen years. Frank acknowledges the importance of those supporters but as other players went to thank them, after he had lifted the trophy he just headed for the dressing room, wanting to be with his teammates, waiting to slap them on the back and start talking about what this triumph could lead to next.

One year later he led his men to the League and FA Cup Double but only following another remarkable halftime rant that helped bring the team back from the dead and 2–0 down against Stoke City in a Hillsborough semi-final. His leadership that season earned him the Football Writers' Footballer of the Year award and the honour of an MBE. It should have been the best time of his life, the most memorable at least, but even now he struggles to recall the days surrounding the events:

People don't realise how difficult it was to win the Double then. Only Spurs had won it in the first 61 years of the century. Ten years later it was us. Sixty-four competitive games and ten friendlies; a squad of seventeen of which only sixteen played – having to go to Spurs to win the League on a Monday and five days later beat Liverpool to win the FA Cup in 90 degrees of heat at Wembley that day. I was gone at the end, totally gone, elated but exhausted. It's easier for the big clubs to win the Double now. I didn't enjoy it. Crazy, but I'd given it my all.

Frank only just recalls my pulling him back on his way up the steps to receive the cup, telling him to slow down and enjoy the moment. It is such a shame that at the moment of true greatness and glory, it remains a blur for Frank McLintock. Two years earlier after Arsenal had lost to Swindon Town at the same Wembley, but on a quagmire of a pitch, I stood close to him as he threw his runners-up trophy into the mud that had resulted from heavy rain after the staging there of the Horse of the Year Show. 'Not another bloody tankard,' he had groaned. We retrieved it for him as Frank disconsolately wandered off by himself into the middle of the marching band only to get hit on the head by a trombone player's instrument.

I've always been great at getting up and getting on with things. Even after losing my savings in a business venture, I'd be straight up and at it. I have a terrific determination that surprises me at times.

In all he played over 700 times for his three clubs, Leicester City, Arsenal and QPR and loved his time at each one of them. At Leicester he reached two FA Cup Finals, both lost. With

Arsenal there were four more cup finals, a championship title and a runners-up medal in the league. At QPR, the Hoops grabbed a UEFA Cup place and missed out by the narrowest of margins to Liverpool in the league.

Being resilient and having a hard streak doesn't mean he is without emotion. When Bertie Mee called him into his office in 1973 to tell Frank that his services were no longer required he admits that 'there were tears bouncing off my blazer. I was that heartbroken. Arsenal were somehow different, an establishment, a bit like royalty. They had more class than any other club.'

Bertie was the same man who Frank had doubted when he had been made manager following the departure of Billy Wright. He immediately asked for a transfer telling Bertie, 'I don't know where I'm going or you're going.' Frank had expected the new boss to be either Don Revie or Alf Ramsey. He was 'gob-smacked' by Mee's appointment, a wonderful physio, but not a coach or manager. He thought Bertie pompous and 'a bit of a Mr Mainwaring character'.

However Frank soon changed his view. Bertie's organisation and discipline plus a combination of Dave Sexton and Don Howe's coaching brilliance led to his conversion from a marauding, out-of-control midfielder, to a central defender who struck up a remarkable partnership with Peter Simpson: 'I had become a headless chicken. My make-up meant I wanted to change everything in order to win things and I tried stupidly to do everyone's job.'

There is a wonderful loyalty about Frank, whether it is for his pals or his three clubs. Davie Gibson remains his biggest mate from Filbert Street days and Leicester and likewise George Graham from their time together as roommates at Arsenal. The biggest shock for Frank was to see George attain such great heights as a manager. 'If you'd bet me £100,000, I'd never have thought George Graham would become a good manager, let alone a great one. He was a mickey-taker, life was never too serious for George. He was the last person in the whole club I would have ever thought would make it.'

Frank's own managerial career back at Leicester and Brentford fell surprisingly short of all expectations, but when it went wrong he turned his talent to after dinner speaking, punditry on radio and TV and currently in developing a fast-growing security business. He admits that he would like the sort of money that is earned by today's guys but that he wouldn't enjoy playing golf seven days a week. Keeping active is important for this amazing captain who insists, 'At heart, I'm still the seventeen-year-old that I was.'

⚽ ⚽ ⚽

Francis 'Frank' McLintock

Born:
28 December 1939 Glasgow

Position:
Wing half/centre half

Clubs as player:
1957–64 Leicester City, 200 games (28 goals)
1964–73 Arsenal, 403 games (32 goals)
1973–77 Queens Park Rangers, 127 games* (5 goals)

Internationals:
1963–71 Scotland, 9 caps (1 goal)

Clubs as manager:
1977–78 Leicester City
1984–87 Brentford

Honours as player with Leicester City:
1964 League Cup

Honours as player with Arsenal:
1970 Inter-Cities Fairs Cup
1971 First Division and FA Cup

Awards:
1971 FWA Footballer of the Year
1972 MBE

– *FWA Footballer of the Year* –

The Football Writers' Association Footballer of the Year Trophy is an annual award which goes to the player who, in the opinion of approximately 400 of England's football writers, has consistently produced the best performances during a season.

I was only seven years old when the inaugural award went to Stanley Matthews. It is an award that originated from Charles Buchan, former footballer-turned-journalist and one of the FWA's founding members.

The closest I came to winning this hugely prestigious trophy was in 1971 when I was nominated in the top six. My teammate at Arsenal, Frank McLintock won deservedly for his extraordinary captaincy during that season, when he was also honoured with an MBE. Today there is a second Player of the Year Award voted for by the PFA members, who are the players in all divisions.

⚽ ⚽ ⚽

1948	Stanley Matthews	Blackpool
1949	Johnny Carey	Manchester United
1950	Joe Mercer	Arsenal
1951	Harry Johnston	Blackpool
1952	Billy Wright	Wolverhampton Wanderers
1953	Nat Lofthouse	Bolton Wanderers
1954	Tom Finney	Preston North End
1955	Don Revie	Manchester City
1956	Bert Trautmann	Manchester City
1957	Tom Finney	Preston North End
1958	Danny Blanchflower	Tottenham Hotspur
1959	Syd Owen	Luton Town
1960	Bill Slater	Wolverhampton Wanderers
1961	Danny Blanchflower	Tottenham Hotspur
1962	Jimmy Adamson	Burnley
1963	Stanley Matthews	Stoke City
1964	Bobby Moore	West Ham United
1965	Bobby Collins	Leeds United
1966	Bobby Charlton	Manchester United
1967	Jack Charlton	Leeds United
1968	George Best	Manchester United
1969	Tony Book	Manchester City
	Dave Mackay	Derby County (joint winners)
1970	Billy Bremner	Leeds United
1971	Frank McLintock	Arsenal
1972	Gordon Banks	Stoke City
1973	Pat Jennings	Tottenham Hotspur
1974	Ian Callaghan	Liverpool
1975	Alan Mullery	Fulham
1976	Kevin Keegan	Liverpool
1977	Emlyn Hughes	Liverpool
1978	Kenny Burns	Nottingham Forest

1979	Kenny Dalglish	Liverpool
1980	Terry McDermott	Liverpool
1981	Frans Thijssen	Ipswich Town
1982	Steve Perryman	Tottenham Hotspur
1983	Kenny Dalglish	Liverpool
1984	Ian Rush	Liverpool
1985	Neville Southall	Everton
1986	Gary Lineker	Everton
1987	Clive Allen	Tottenham Hotspur
1988	John Barnes	Liverpool
1989	Steve Nicol	Liverpool
1990	John Barnes	Liverpool
1991	Gordon Strachan	Leeds United
1992	Gary Lineker	Tottenham Hotspur
1993	Chris Waddle	Sheffield Wednesday
1994	Alan Shearer	Blackburn Rovers
1995	Jürgen Klinsmann	Tottenham Hotspur
1996	Eric Cantona	Manchester United
1997	Gianfranco Zola	Chelsea
1998	Dennis Bergkamp	Arsenal
1999	David Ginola	Tottenham Hotspur
2000	Roy Keane	Manchester United
2001	Teddy Sheringham	Manchester United
2002	Robert Pirès	Arsenal
2003	Thierry Henry	Arsenal
2004	Thierry Henry	Arsenal
2005	Frank Lampard	Chelsea
2006	Thierry Henry	Arsenal
2007	Cristiano Ronaldo	Manchester United
2008	Cristiano Ronaldo	Manchester United

Gordon Banks

At that moment I hated Gordon more than any man in soccer. But when I cooled down I had to applaud him with my heart for the greatest save I had ever seen.

Pele, 1970, Brazil vs. England, World Cup finals

⚽ ⚽ ⚽

Until England win the World Cup for a second time, Gordon Banks will retain the glorious title of England's greatest goalkeeper. Week in week out, wearing his club colours he may not have had the consistency of a Pat Jennings, David Seaman or Peter Schmeichel, but with the three lions emblazoned on his international jersey he was close to perfection, faultless.

It is a miracle that I eventually found myself in goal at the other end to Banksy, including two memorable FA Cup semi-finals in 1971 and '72, which both ended in victory for Arsenal and left Stoke totally frustrated until they won the 1973 League Cup – the great keeper's only domestic triumph.

The miraculous aspect relates to my youth when I stood close behind Gordon Banks' goal when he was at his first club in my home town of Chesterfield. Rarely if ever have I seen a goalie with such natural spring in his feet. Even as he ran out before a game I would marvel at that bounce which gave him not just fast feet, but great elasticity and gymnastic ability when attempting to save. He quickly established himself and his confidence was very apparent to the keen student who eyed him enviously from the terraces behind his goal. What surprised me is that he could make some saves look so 'flash'. Later he would laugh when I mentioned this aspect of his game, never denying it, but usually joking that the fans paid good money to be entertained. What I have always found with Gordon on the occasions we have met off the field is that he has an instant smile to go with a rare humility for one so famous.

The only time I recall this not being the case was when a photographer captured the two of us shaking hands at the end of our 2–2 semi-final draw in the FA Cup at Hillsborough. Goalkeepers do not have to run the distances of outfield players. Their work, when called upon, is instinctive and explosive. Few observers understand the mental torture that accompanies following a move towards your goal, the preparation you make to save and then, invariably, the relief that the attack has broken down. Total concentration for 90 minutes is essential, the fatigue factor draining in the extreme. On that semi-final day in 1971 the strain that showed on our two faces was quite extraordinary. In Gordon's case the disappointment at Arsenal equalising with a late penalty was etched on his features. For me the relief from the reprieve we had earned was never more apparent.

On more than one occasion in my TV career it has been a privilege to interview Gordon alongside Pele, against whom he made that 'impossible save'. That is the Brazilian's description of Banks' unforgettably dramatic stop during the 1970 World Cup meeting between Brazil and England: 'I was actually shouting "Goal!"' Pele explained, 'and then there was this body and a salmon's leap.'

The loss of an eye in a car crash towards the end of his career only added to the legend that is Gordon Banks. What is almost unforgivable is that the FA failed to use his expertise to further the cause of goalkeeping in the UK. The modern game is awash with foreign custodians, sacrilege for the one position on the field of play that used to be dominated by the best of British and in particular, a man called Banks.

⚽ ⚽ ⚽

Gordon Banks

Born:
30 December 1937, Sheffield

Position:
Goalkeeper

Clubs as a player:
1955–59 Chesterfield 23 games*
1959–66 Leicester City 356 games
1966–72 Stoke City 194*
1967 Cleveland Stokers 12 games
1977 St Patrick's Athletic 1 game
1977–78 Fort Lauderdale Strikers 39 games

Internationals:
1963–72 England 73 caps

Honours as player with Leicester City:
1964 League Cup

Honours as player with Stoke City:
1972 League Cup

Honours as player with England:
1966 World Cup

Awards:
1970 OBE

143

– *European Championship Roll of Honour* –

1960 USSR
1964 Spain
1968 Italy
1972 West Germany
1976 Czechoslovakia
1980 West Germany
1984 France
1988 Netherlands
1992 Denmark
1996 Germany
2000 France
2004 Greece
2008 Spain

Jimmy Greaves

He was always very calm, very collected and, where scoring goals was concerned, he was a Picasso.

Clive Allen, 1987, Spurs striker

⚽ ⚽ ⚽

Whenever I am involved in a question-and-answer event and asked about the strikers I feared facing most during my playing days, I instantly name Jimmy Greaves. He was a goalkeeper's nightmare, a predatory goalscorer the likes of which I doubt I will ever see again. He retired, for the first time, in 1971, having created an all-time record of scoring 357 goals in just 516 Football League games. On top of that he found the net 44 times during his 57 England appearances.

Today his value would be priceless. He would have been capable of earning a fortune. There seems to be an irony in Spurs manager Bill Nicholson's insistence that Jimmy's transfer from AC Milan to White Hart Lane should be capped at £99,999 in order to avoid him bearing the burden of being the first £100,000 transfer, the fee the Italian club were asking.

Sheer bad luck prevented him from being a member of the England team who won the 1966 World Cup Final against West Germany. He started the tournament as first-choice striker but sustained a leg injury in the game against France and although regaining fitness, was controversially left out of the side by manager Alf Ramsey in favour of Geoff Hurst, who had scored England's winner in the quarter-final against Argentina and who went on to score a hat-trick in the final.

Day after day in training, keepers dedicate themselves to perfecting positional play and angles in order to make the goal as small as possible for the opponents to shoot at. Yet however much keepers reduce the size by the position they take up, they cannot entirely cover every square inch of the eight yards by eight feet which makes up the space between and under the posts and crossbar. Therefore all keepers are vulnerable, however good they are, if faced by an individual who can instantly size up the situation, recognise the part of the goal a keeper has not covered and then hit that spot. That is what James Peter Greaves could do, and do it better than anyone else. He drove me mad, as I faced him with confidence and assurance making myself 'big', shutting off all but the far top corner of my goal and then – wham – the ball would curl into that very spot and Greavsie would wheel away nonchalantly as if I'd left a cavernous hole for him to score.

Would England have won the '66 World Cup had they been playing Greaves rather than Geoff Hurst? Some might suggest not. I would suggest England would not have needed extra-time had Jimmy been playing. At least his part in Alf Ramsey's squad has now been recognised with a belated winner's medal being awarded to him and the ten other reserves. He and Alf Ramsey were the only two to remain seated as the Swiss referee, Herr Dienst, blew his whistle. He was asked the question about his inner feelings when we shared a stage in the Channel Islands a decade or so later following a charity football game in which we'd appeared. Jimmy made light of it, insisting that he was as thrilled as the rest of the squad. He also acknowledged that no player, whatever his reputation, should be guaranteed a place in a team.

It's difficult for me to state definitely that Greavsie was telling the total truth on that evening, because it was at a time when he was battling the demons of a well-documented alcohol problem, which he overcame thankfully in the late 70s. Anything he said during the event created laughter because he was under the influence and he, and I as host, fought constantly over the one microphone available to us. That had been a suggestion of mine in order that I held some degree of control over events. Jimmy failed to make the airport for our return to London the next day and sadly he was the one absentee when I chaired the 25th Anniversary Dinner honouring the '66 squad in 1991.

People have their own opinions on how badly Jimmy was affected by his World Cup experience. I think that when you know you are as brilliant a player as he was, it must be difficult to accept missing out on the greatest moment in the history of English football.

'Funny old game, football' is a phrase coined by Jimmy after he became a popular television presenter sitting alongside Ian St John in a Saturday lunchtime show called *Saint and Greavsie*. For a while their TV programme was in direct opposition to *Football Focus* on BBC TV. There were many arguments as to who claimed most viewers but eventually the ITV show was put on a little later than *Focus*, which left all football fans happy. For seven years Jimmy provided the light-hearted dry humour in the programme while Ian became his sparring partner, punchbag and sensible co-host.

Jimmy Greaves ensured his continuing value to the media. *Sporting Triangles* was one show he co-hosted, as well as a radio talk-show and working as a newspaper columnist. His humour has never dimmed and he remains in great demand as an after dinner speaker.

Occasionally when I dream about my time in football I wake up with a start, the dream having become a nightmare as I'm back in goal facing Jimmy Greaves.

⊛ ⊛ ⊛

James Peter 'Jimmy' Greaves

Born:
20 February 1940, East Ham

Position:
Striker

Clubs as player:
1957–61 Chelsea, 169 games (132 goals)
1961 AC Milan, 14 games (9 goals)
1961–70 Tottenham Hotspur, 381 games (268 goals)
1979–81 West Ham United, 40 games* (13 goals)

Internationals:
1959–67 England, 57 caps (44 goals)

Honours as player with Tottenham Hotspur:
1962 FA Cup
1963 UEFA Cup Winners' Cup
1967 FA Cup

Honours as player with England:
1966 World Cup

– *Spurs* –

In 1882, boys from Haringey's Hotspur cricket club and the St John's Presbyterian local grammar school got together and decided to form a football club. Reputedly in a meeting under a street lamp on Tottenham High Street, close to the current ground, they decided to retain the cricket club name and simply call it Hotspur FC.

The cricketers among them had initially chosen the name Hotspur after the fourteenth century's Sir Henry Percy, or Harry Hotspur as he was otherwise known – the eldest son of the 1st Earl of Northumberland. By the nineteenth century, the Northumberland dynasty had significant ties with Haringey, owning large tracts of land in the area. Harry Hotspur was a great warrior and had acquired his new name as a result of the large riding spurs on his armour and fiery devil-may-care bravery in battle against the Scots towards the end of the fourteenth century. In 1403 he led a rebellion against Henry IV but was killed in the Battle of Shrewsbury when hit in the mouth with an arrow. Something that your average Tottenham fan will forget to tell you at this point is that after his death Henry IV had his body quartered and sent to different corners of England and his head stuck on a pole at York's gates. However, his bravery and fiery temperament were later immortalised in William Shakepseare's *Henry IV, Part I*.

Throughout 1883, Hotspur FC were playing their matches on Tottenham marshes but it soon became apparent that they had to distinguish themselves from another team in the area going by the name of London Hotspur. So in 1884, they renamed themselves Tottenham Hotspur Football and

Athletic Club, but before long, like the large, sharp spiked wheels on the heels of their hero's armour, they were simply known as the Spurs.

Bobby Charlton

The World Cup in 1966 wasn't won on the playing fields of England. It was won on the streets.

Bobby Charlton, 1966 World Cup-winner

☺ ☺ ☺

In the couple of years I spent on Manchester United's books, from 1957 to 1959, he was a hero to me. He was a survivor of the Munich air crash that had made such an impact on my understanding of the fragility that exists between life and death. He had gone on to World Cup glory and, as I eventually broke through into the top echelons of football, he lifted the European Cup just before we became opponents and faced each other on the field of play.

I'm quite proud that on numerous visits to schools during my life, I have been mistaken for Bobby! Countless times I have heard head teachers or their staff ask their flock, 'Now children, hands up, who knows the name of today's special guest?' Often I cringed as I anticipated the response. 'Please sir, I know. It's Bobby Charlton.' If I wasn't mistaken for Bobby Charlton a fair proportion guessed that I was Bobby Moore! The two things we all had in common – being footballers that were all christened Robert – rather confused the younger generation.

I never could understand any resemblance I might have to Mooro, who had lots more hair than me, or even Bobby Charlton, who had a great deal less. However I do think Sir Bobby and I shared something else in respect of our natures and personalities. We both had strong minds of our own, were prepared to be loners off the field and led our lives in what was an untypical style to the vast majority of our teammates. It didn't stop us having empathy for the rest of our colleagues. On the contrary we were both, I believe, an integral part of the jigsaw that made our respective squads a winning unit. Had we not been able to play, at least in the minds of our colleagues, then we certainly wouldn't have survived. Ironically, by the time Bobby and I became regular opponents, Manchester United were in a steep decline.

United won the first of their European Cups in 1968 as I made my breakthrough and then they struggled almightily, even entering into relegation battles. Of course, it didn't stop the famous Charlton shooting skills from scaring me to death. Every time he received the ball near my goal, my mind would instinctively recall moments like the goal he scored against Mexico, on the run from distance, during the 1966 World Cup finals. As a keeper facing Bobby, you knew that there were only three possibilities when he faced you with the ball at his feet: a goal conceded, a great save made, or a 'bullet' that would fly high and handsome into the crowd behind your net. Any save from him boosted my confidence and the fact that he never scored against me is a source of great satisfaction.

Bobby's value to any broadcasting company was immense, particularly at World Cups. In the 1982 finals in Spain we were part of BBC TV's coverage, both of us attached to England: me as team reporter, Bobby as the ambassador and key to our gaining access to Ron Greenwood and his squad, or any other country that was taking part. Such was the Charlton fame and charisma that, regardless of any bans or locked doors, his appearance and face would secure instant admission.

I recall our standing together, outside Brazil's heavily guarded headquarters, film crew and producer in tow, but with no promise of an interview. On making ourselves known, the Brazilian press guy appeared and was quite clearly about to tell us where to go. Then he spotted our secret weapon! 'Ah, Mr Bobby Charlton! How are you, sir? It is an honour. Please come in.'

With that modest manner and renowned humility, Bobby then asked, on our behalf, if we could film the Brazilian squad training and perhaps be granted some interviews. Two hours later we had got everything, even more than we had ever anticipated. The worldwide fame of Bobby Charlton, 1966 World Cup-winner, had saved us.

During that tournament the BBC had a small light aircraft at its disposal. Sometimes Bobby and I would sit together and discuss the tournament or other issues. I also conducted an interview with him for a youngster's magazine and learned just how difficult it had been for him to step onto any aeroplane after February 1958 and Munich. Although philosophical about the necessity to travel by air in the modern day, he was clearly uncomfortable when it came to take-off. It showed on his face and his hands. I felt sorry for him, but at the same time an admiration that he was prepared to live his life to the full and not succumb to fear or even, what some observers thought was ever-present for Bobby, 'survivor's guilt'.

I will always owe Bobby a debt of gratitude for prolonging my broadcasting career, even saving it from self-destruction. During that 1982 World Cup in Spain I fell out with BBC Sport in a pretty dramatic way. As designated England reporter, I expected to be the one to conduct all interviews with England players. After being the only media person to reveal Kevin Keegan's injury problems early in the tournament, I felt I was certain to be the one to interview him on his return. Not so, I was told, and immediately responded by threatening to walk away from Spain and the Beeb. Several people tried to get me to change my mind, but I had booked a flight home when I bumped into Bobby Charlton. He understood, better than most, the often strange politics that will always exist in the TV world, but had an even bigger grasp on how my angst would rebound on my life and particularly my wife and children. 'Think of your family and not yourself,' was Bobby's firm instruction. He followed it up by calming me down and making me see sense.

My full-time TV career, which was in danger of ending after eight years, continued and still had twenty more years to run, thanks to Bobby. Conducting an interview with him on *Grandstand* following the award of his knighthood in 1994, I was able to speak for a nation in congratulating Sir Bobby for everything he had done in the name of football. His first manager at Manchester United summed up his value to the Red Devils. Sir Matt Busby said, 'The greatest thing for a manager is to trust the talent. Bobby Charlton never betrayed that trust. It was a privilege to have him play for you.'

The latest man in charge at United, Sir Alex Ferguson is even more succinct: 'Bobby Charlton's career was miraculous.'

⚽ ⚽ ⚽

Sir Robert 'Bobby' Charlton

Born:
11 October 1937, Ashington

Position:
Striker

Clubs as player:
1954–73 Manchester United, 758 games (249 goals)
1973–74 Preston North End, 38 games (8 goals)
1975 Waterford United, 31 games (18 goals)

Internationals:
1958–70 England, 106 caps (49 goals)

Club as player-manager:
1973–74 Preston North End

Club as caretaker manager:
1976 Wigan Athletic

Honours as player with Manchester United:
1956 FA Charity Shield
1957 First Division and FA Charity Shield
1963 FA Cup
1965 First Division and FA Charity Shield
1967 First Division and FA Charity Shield
1968 European Cup

Honours as player with England:
166 World Cup

Awards:
1966 European Footballer of the Year
1966 FIFA Football Writers' Footballer of the Year
1973 CBE
1994 Knighthood

– *The Red Devils* –

Manchester United football club was founded in 1878 by workers of the Lancashire and Yorkshire Railway Company. They named it Newton Heath LYR and the club was soon nicknamed the Heathens. In 1902, however, the club were declared bankrupt, which led to the formation of Manchester United. Following this, the team was simply known as the Reds or United.

In the early 1950s, United manager Sir Matt Busby assembled a young, exciting and brilliant team, which the media quickly labelled the 'Busby Babes'. Two league titles followed in 1956 and 1957.

The quality and success of the team meant Busby had entered the club into the European Champions Cup each year from 1956. Tragically, in 1958, when the team were returning from a game abroad against Red Star Belgrade, their plane crashed while trying to take off at Munich airport. Seven players were killed and Busby was severely injured. Another member of the team, the great Duncan Edwards, died a fortnight later and a further two were sufficiently injured to never play again. Although Busby recovered to rebuild and manage the team again, the Busby Babes moniker was now wholly inappropriate and was dropped.

At the beginning of the 1960s, Salford Rugby Club toured France and because of their red shirts, became known as the Red Devils. Busby liked it, as he thought that opposing teams would find the name intimidating, and he adopted it for his own side. Devil logos soon made their way into match programmes and onto club scarves, and in 1970, the official club badge was redesigned to incorporate a devil holding a pitch-fork. Manchester United have been the Red Devils ever since.

Tommy Smith

Tommy Smith wasn't born, he was quarried.

Tommy Smith would start a riot in a graveyard.

Bill Shankly

☻ ☻ ☻

There was a period during the 1960s and '70s when every top club had a hard man in their team. I played against them all and am glad I was in goal and not an outfield player. Ron 'Chopper' Harris of Chelsea, Norman 'Bite Yer Legs' Hunter of Leeds, Nobby Stiles of Manchester United and Peter Storey of Arsenal, all had reputations that went before them.

The hardest of the hard though played for Liverpool and he could threaten me with a look. From the time Bill Shankly signed him as a schoolboy in May 1960, Tommy gradually became an extension of his great manager; a passionate 'Red', a fierce competitor with a threatening psychological demeanour that intimidated even the best. Jimmy Greaves was once handed a piece of paper by Tommy as he ran out at Anfield. On enquiring of its contents he was told to just 'take a look'. It turned out to be the menu from the local Liverpool hospital!

Now aged 63 Tommy struggles to walk, the outcome of 638 games for Liverpool over an eighteen-year period, another 36 or more at Swansea City at the end of his career plus one England cap. He has two knee replacements, a new hip and elbow. His nickname is 'Anfield Iron'. In his mind there is no question that the sacrifices made were worthwhile. 'Of course it was worth it. For the camaraderie, the fans, for the success we had. I felt lost when I left Liverpool.'

Having lost his dad when he was only fourteen years old, Tommy turned to Liverpool and found father figures in the successive managers, Shankly, Paisley and Fagan. Had he played today, he would have huge wealth and far fewer health problems, but on the latter, he has argued that yesterday's players were real men compared to now.

In an interview with Sue Mott of the *Daily Telegraph*, he explains:

Now football is full of cheats who hit the deck and roll over three times when they haven't been hurt. If you watch games in the old days, players went down, got up and got hold of somebody. Now everyone goes down to get another player booked. I would send the divers off.

Of course, the game has changed, if not always for the better, especially in the area of simulation and diving. All players of our generation hate what we see and the inability of the game to deal more firmly with offenders, none more so than a player like Tommy Smith. When he captained Liverpool in the 1971 FA Cup Final, it was an honour to be on the same field as him, despite being a little scared!

⚽ ⚽ ⚽

Thomas 'Tommy' Smith

Born:
5 April 1945, Liverpool

Position:
Defender

Clubs as player:
1961–78 Liverpool, 638 (48 goals)
1978–79 Swansea City, 36* (4 goals)

Internationals:
1971 England, 1 cap

Honours as player with Liverpool:
1965 FA Cup and FA Charity Shield (shared)
1966 First Division and FA Charity Shield
1973 UEFA Cup and First Division
1974 FA Cup
1976 UEFA Cup and First Division
1977 European Cup, European Super Cup, First Division and
FA Charity Shield

Awards:
1978 MBE

– *World Cup Roll of Honour* –

1930 Uruguay
1934 Italy
1938 Italy
1950 Uruguay
1954 West Germany
1958 Brazil
1962 Brazil
1966 England
1970 Brazil
1974 West Germany
1978 Argentina
1982 Italy
1986 Argentina
1990 West Germany
1994 Brazil
1998 France
2002 Brazil
2006 Italy

Charlie George

Charlie had talent almost beyond compare. He could ping the ball like Franz Beckenbauer and it would zip forty yards right on target. He had unbelievable shooting ability, was good in the air, strong, quick and brave. Charlie had every attribute. At 19 years of age he was a genuine superstar.

Frank McLintock, Arsenal captain

It doesn't concern me that current top players are earning millions when players of my generation earned in units of thousands. I spent mine – and enjoyed doing it.

Charlie George

⚽ ⚽ ⚽

Anyone who has scored an FA Cup-winning goal is guaranteed a place in football history. Legendary status is then attached by the supporters of the winning club. Roger Osborne of Ipswich, Ian Porterfield of Sunderland, Lawrie Sanchez of Wimbledon, just three of the more unlikely heroes that spring to mind. Charlie George was not an unlikely hero. From the moment he signed for his local team, Arsenal, great things were expected of him. This kid's talent was exceptional, the fact that he supported the Gunners simply added to the story.

I got to know him first during the 1963–64 season. I was on Arsenal's books as an amateur, training with the club twice a week in the indoor centre behind Highbury's Clock End. Among the schoolboy hopefuls who trained alongside me on those evening sessions were Pat Rice, who became club captain, and Charlie George, who won the 1971 FA Cup Final for us with a dramatic strike. You didn't need to be a brain surgeon to realise young Charlie had a rebellious streak in him. Thirty-seven years on I reckon it's still there. It's not the only thing that has remained constant in his makeup. He still loves Arsenal as much today as when he was a fourteen-year-old Holloway schoolboy. The fans in turn adore him. His rapport with them is as electric as it was all those years ago and his daily tours of the Emirates Stadium are full to overflowing.

Back in 1963 Arsenal were quick to secure Charlie's services. He was that good, a natural. It was a racing certainty that Charlie George would succeed. With Bob Wilson and Pat Rice there was much more of a gamble involved. He was a little cautious of me in those early days. After all, I was a PE teacher, and Charlie hated school. He found it amusing that once I'd signed full professional forms a year later, I still kept my hand in teaching at, of all places, Holloway School, situated about three miles from Highbury, where Charlie was a pupil. He just about tolerated PE and games lessons but was a constant source of trouble to the rest of the teaching staff. Charlie's final year was cut short when, three months from the end of the summer term, he was expelled.

His genius lay not in his head but in his talented feet. The brushes with authority would continue with his various managers, from Bertie Mee at Arsenal all the way through to Don Revie and England. I loved the guy, not for his rebellious nature, but for his talent, his humour and a vulnerability that he has tried to hide with a cocky, brash exterior, but one that existed nonetheless. In the dressing room before games, Charlie could often be found being physically sick but he would then go out and produce moments of sheer magic, even during his less effective performances. In the six-year spell between 1968 and 1974, we were a team in the best possible sense, close-knit, together, ambitious. We possessed only one true free spirit: Frederick Charles George.

He was the one we turned to for a flash of inspiration during a dour or dogged display. Very rarely did he fail to find a killer pass that would set up victory or a shot of real venom that would nestle in the opposing rigging. He grew his hair long much to his manager Bertie Mee's dismay. It was one of many aspects of behaviour in which manager and star player were at total loggerheads, two people who simply held opposite perspectives on how life should be lived. Thankfully Bertie never failed to recognise Charlie's talent which resulted in important contributions on the run to glory in the Inter-Cities Fairs Cup of 1970 and the Double triumph a year later.

After breaking his ankle at Everton in the opening game of this season and missing five months of action, Charlie came roaring back by scoring in the fourth, fifth and sixth rounds of the FA Cup, as well as claiming that decisive strike in the final against Liverpool. He famously celebrated by falling to the Wembley turf and lying flat on his back with arms aloft. Some say he was milking the moment; others suggested time-wasting; I think he was knackered. But what a moment, what a shot to beat Ray Clemence! Iconic status guaranteed for the local-boy-made-good.

Charlie should have been an Arsenal player for his entire career, but his fallouts with his manager eventually became terminal and he was transfer-listed by the club in the Christmas of 1974. Seven months later he was on his way to Derby County having played just 179 games for Arsenal. The fee was £100,000. These days it would have been nearer £20 million. At the Baseball Ground he scored a memorable hat-trick against Real Madrid in a European Cup tie and won his one and only England cap, immediately falling out with manager Don Revie for playing him totally out of position in a left wing role. Sadly his career petered out at a variety of clubs at home and abroad, while knee injuries also hindered his cause. His potential suggested he should have achieved more than he did but characters like Charlie George are their own men. They don't have regrets. They live for the moment and accept what today brings them.

Essentially Charlie is happy with his lot, content in the warmth of affection that thousands of Arsenal fans bestow upon him for starting out as one of them, a fan on the Highbury North Bank terraces who dreamt of fame and found it with his local team.

❂ ❂ ❂

Frederick Charles 'Charlie' George

Born:
10 October 1950, Islington

Position:
Forward

Clubs as player:
1968–75 Arsenal, 179 games (49 goals)
1975–78 Derby County, 117 games (36 goals)
1978 Minnesota Kicks, 18 games
1978–81 Southampton, 44 games* (11 goals)
1980 Nottingham Forest (on loan), 2 games*
1982 Bournemouth, 2 games*
1982 Derby County, 11 games (2 goals)

Internationals:
1976 England 1 cap

Honours as player with Arsenal:
1970 Inter-Cities Fairs Cup
1971 First Division and FA Cup
1980 UEFA Super Cup

– *The Monkeyhangers* –

According to local legend, a large French ship was wrecked off the Hartlepool coast during the Napoleonic Wars. The only survivor was a monkey, who was washed ashore clinging to some wreckage and dressed in a French military uniform – presumably to amuse the ship's crew. The locals quickly held an impromptu trial on the beach. Being a monkey, it obviously didn't respond particularly well to their questioning and so, with its supposed refusal to give up any information, the locals came to the conclusion that it was a spy and should be sentenced to death. The unfortunate creature was promptly hanged, the mast of a fishing boat providing the makeshift gallows, and ultimately giving rise to Hartlepool United's nickname as the Monkeyhangers.

The Hartlepool United FC mascot is called H'Angus the monkey. In 2002, the man in the monkey costume stood for Hartlepool mayor 'for a laugh', dressed as H'Angus and offering free bananas for schoolchildren if he won. He did, and with his victory quickly found himself overseeing a £106 million budget and over 3,000 staff.

George Best

Arrogance is an important weapon in his armour. How can he be better than the other players if he does not believe that he is and show that he is? But he must beware that arrogance. In a sense, it represents his confidence in his own judgment – the style takes over the effect. His style is his witness; George's football talent has such sweet style that it has captured the adoration of most fans.

Danny Blanchflower, Spurs and
Northern Ireland captain

When I look back on a life that was too brief, too troubled, I share that sense of wonder, sometimes disbelief when I think of how good he was and all those improbable things he achieved under such immense pressure.

Sir Bobby Charlton, Manchester United

When I die, they won't remember who I dated, the fights and car crashes because they're not important. They will remember the football.

George Best, 2005

In 1969 I gave up alcohol and women. It was the worst twenty minutes of my life.

George Best, 2003

☻ ☻ ☻

A lot of things and a lot of people needled George Best. I'm quite proud to be on the offending list, especially as it's for a positive rather than negative reason. 'Besty' is one

166

of the greatest footballers the world has ever seen – quick, two-footed, balanced, a great, skilful dribbler, a fine header of the ball and a lethal goalscorer. On top of that he had devastating good looks. He was the first superstar of the modern footballing era and it was my dubious privilege, if not pleasure, to face him on many occasions and once, memorably for me, to take the ball off his toes in a one-vs-one situation from which he would normally have ended up scoring.

By himself George was terrific company. He was friendly and impish with strong opinions. In a crowd he could become a different animal, seemingly trying to live up to his superstar image, a boozer, brash and boastful.

The world of celebrity was only in its infancy when Besty gate-crashed the party. Manchester United scout Bob Bishop had set the ball rolling with his famous telegram to Matt Busby: 'I think I've found you a genius.' Chief Scout Joe Armstrong then set up a trial and immediately signed him. The rest of the footballing story of George Best is well-documented. So too are the problems he encountered with alcohol, gambling and girls. I have always believed that United could and should have done more to ensure George didn't go off the rails. Sir Matt was no longer the strong man that he was pre-Munich. Had Sir Alex Ferguson been in charge the George Best story would have been much more fulfilling and, almost certainly, would have had a happier ending.

From a distance, all his opponents and fellow pros looked on in awe of his talent and amazement at his antics. We understood how he needed to be shackled and not given a free rein. Whenever I was asked for an autograph I imagined what it must be like multiplying the requests by 50 or 100 and still trying to cope. With his ability and fame, Besty should have been the first footballer in history to be able to retire fully at the end of his playing days with Manchester United. Instead the club were prepared to let George go and he was away from Old Trafford at the age of 27 and then he scuttled hither and thither in an ever-downward spiral towards a tragic end. Look at the clubs that followed his glorious time and achievements with the Red Devils and, Fulham days excluded, it tells a sorry story. During a decade of decadence and beyond, George would happily tell you that he had no regrets, had experienced everything worth living for and would not change a thing. Too often drink clouded his judgement.

It offered a sharp contrast to the beauty of his football, that ability to thrill spectators everywhere, to lift them out of their seats, to be proud to say that they saw George Best play. Imagine then, facing him on the pitch, in a situation where he was put clean through with just the opposing goalkeeper to beat. That was the dilemma facing me at Highbury in the opening home game of our Double season. Arsenal were winning 1–0 when Besty came towards me, ball seemingly tied to his toe in complete control. Diving at opponents' feet was my speciality. I looked for a slight mis-control and, at that moment, went hand and head first, hoping the element of surprise might put the enemy off. But this was George Best and I knew that nine times out of ten he would score. How the ball finished in my hands and not the back of the net was a shock to me and an even bigger shock for George. He described the moment in one of the Best biographies, this one written by Sir Michael Parkinson:

I still wake up at night even now reliving some of the awful things that happened to me on the field. Once we played Arsenal and I get the ball, thread through their defence and I've only got Bob Wilson to beat. He comes rushing out, dives at my feet and takes the ball from me. Now I still get the raving needle when I relive that moment. I always reckoned that when I got through with only the goalkeeper to beat, you could put a million quid on me scoring and you'd be right a hundred times out of a hundred. I still can't fathom out what went wrong that game and it still worries me.

Years later George still found it difficult to credit me. Over a sequence of photos showing the save he wrote, 'Kind regards Bob. Sooner or later you get a lucky one. George.'

Similarly on my *This is Your Life* programme, George recognised what the save had meant to me, laughingly saying 'Bob probably still remembers the date, time, weather and state of the pitch.' Well of course I do – a magical moment for me and one that I can proudly relay to my grandchildren.

He nearly got his own back a year later after the Highbury save when Arsenal met Manchester United at Anfield, the result of an FA punishment incurred by United after crowd problems at Old Trafford. I was aware of how George had 'nicked' the ball away from Gordon Banks as the England keeper released the ball from his hands to kick, in an international against Northern Ireland. It was a fabulous, famous moment but Besty's goal was disallowed for dangerous play or ungentlemanly conduct. At Anfield, he did the same to me. Where he came from I'll never know. It was like a magician's sleight of hand, except it was achieved with his feet and at great speed. My embarrassment was saved by a desperate dive to stop the ball crossing the goal line.

I will always prefer to discuss the headlines created by George Best's footballing genius rather than the equally well-publicised frailties which ended with the abuse of a life-saving liver transplant and his eventual death. One hundred thousand mourners were said to have lined the route as the cortege travelled the short distance from George's home in Belfast to Stormont where the Grand Hall service was relayed live on BBC 1, UTV, RTE, ITV News, BBC News24, Sky News, Sky Sports News, Euro News and MUTV. Among the many banners lining the route, one expressed how his countrymen looked upon their favourite son: 'Maradona good, Pele better, George Best.'

☻ ☻ ☻

George Best

Born:
22 May 1946, Belfast
Died:
25 November 2005, London

Position:
Winger

Clubs as player:
1963–74 Manchester United, 470 games (179 goals)
1974 Dunstable Town (loan), 5 games
1975 Stockport County, 3 games (2 goals)
1975–76 Cork Celtic, 3 games
1976 Los Angeles Aztecs, 23 games (15 goals)
1976–77 Fulham, 47 games (10 goals)
1977–78 Los Angeles Aztecs, 32 games (12 goals)
1978–79 Fort Lauderdale Strikers, 28 games (6 goals)
1979–80 Hibernian, 22 games (3 goals)

1980–81 San Jose Earthquakes, 56 games (21 goals)
1983 Bournemouth, 5 games
1983 Brisbane Lions, 1 game
1984 Tobermore United, 1 game

Internationals:
1964–77 Northern Ireland, 37 caps (9 goals)

Honours as player with Manchester United:
1965 First Division
1967 First Division
1968 European Cup

Awards:
1968 European Footballer of the Year and
FWA Footballer of the Year

– *European Footballer of the Year* –

Year	Player	Nationality	Football Club
1956	Stanley Matthews	England	Blackpool
1957	Alfredo Di Stéfano	Argentina/Spain	Real Madrid
1958	Raymond Kopa	France	Real Madrid
1959	Alfredo Di Stéfano	Argentina/Spain	Real Madrid
1960	Luis Suárez	Spain	FC Barcelona
1961	Omar Sivori	Argentina/Italy	Juventus
1962	Josef Masopust	Czechoslovakia	Dukla Prague
1963	Lev Yashin	USSR	Dynamo Moscow
1964	Denis Law	Scotland	Manchester United
1965	Eusebio	Portugal	SL Benfica
1966	Bobby Charlton	England	Manchester United

Year	Player	Nationality	Football Club
1967	Flórián Albert	Hungary	Ferencváros Budapest
1968	George Best	N. Ireland	Manchester United
1969	Gianni Rivera	Italy	AC Milan
1970	Gerd Müller	Germany	Bayern Munich
1971	Johan Cruyff	Netherlands	Ajax
1972	Franz Beckenbauer	Germany	Bayern Munich
1973	Johan Cruyff	Netherlands	Ajax/FC Barcelona
1974	Johan Cruyff	Netherlands	FC Barcelona
1975	Oleg Blokhin	USSR	Dynamo Kyiv
1976	Franz Beckenbauer	Germany	Bayern Munich
1977	Allan Simonsen	Denmark	Borussia Mönchengladbach
1978	Kevin Keegan	England	Hamburger SV
1979	Kevin Keegan	England	Hamburger SV
1980	Karl-Heinz Rummenigge	Germany	Bayern Munich
1981	Karl-Heinz Rummenigge	Germany	Bayern Munich
1982	Paolo Rossi	Italy	Juventus
1983	Michel Platini	France	Juventus
1984	Michel Platini	France	Juventus
1985	Michel Platini	France	Juventus
1986	Igor Belanov	USSR	Dynamo Kyiv
1987	Ruud Gullit	Netherlands	PSV Eindhoven/ AC Milan
1988	Marco van Basten	Netherlands	AC Milan
1989	Marco van Basten	Netherlands	AC Milan
1990	Lothar Matthäus	Germany	Inter Milan
1991	Jean-Pierre Papin	France	Olympique Marseille

Year	Player	Nationality	Football Club
1992	Marco van Basten	Netherlands	AC Milan
1993	Roberto Baggio	Italy	Juventus
1994	Hristo Stoichkov	Bulgaria	FC Barcelona
1995	George Weah	Liberia	Paris St-Germain/ AC Milan
1996	Matthias Sammer	Germany	BV Borussia Dortmund
1997	Ronaldo	Brazil	FC Barcelona/ Inter Milan
1998	Zinedine Zidane	France	Juventus
1999	Rivaldo	Brazil	FC Barcelona
2000	Luís Figo	Portugal	FC Barcelona/ Real Madrid
2001	Michael Owen	England	Liverpool
2002	Ronaldo	Brazil	Inter Milan/ Real Madrid
2003	Pavel Nedved	Czech Republic	Juventus
2004	Andriy Shevchenko	Ukraine	AC Milan
2005	Ronaldinho	Brazil	FC Barcelona
2006	Fabio Cannavaro	Italy	Juventus/ Real Madrid
2007	Kaka	Brazil	AC Milan

Ray Clemence

I watched Ray Clemence at least eight times before I signed him, more than any other player I bought. That was because he was a goalkeeper. You have to check on little things with a keeper. We noticed that he possessed an unusual combination of being a strong left-footed kicker and yet good on his right-hand side. I don't like left-footed keepers especially if they are left-handed as well. I've always felt they are short of balance. Ray was left-footed but right-handed and that was good – a hell of a combination. The thing that impressed us above all was that he was hell-fire quick … moving in a flash. He also had that special kind of courage that good keepers must have … it's a desperate courage.

Bill Shankly, Liverpool manager

❂ ❂ ❂

The date was 8 May. I rolled a ball around my eighteen-yard box wasting time deliberately. As I kicked it from my hands upfield, Norman Burtenshaw put his referee's whistle to his mouth, gave it a long blast and brought to an end the 1971 FA Cup Final. Arsenal had won and completed an historic double triumph of league championship and FA Cup.

Hysteria took over my colleagues and me. Laughter, tears, backslapping, hugs. Somewhere in the haze of victory it dawned that our opponents were mostly sitting on the Wembley turf, dejected, desperate. Opposing goalies always look for each other at the end of the game. Bill Shankly's emerging young Liverpool team included a 22-year-old between the sticks by the name of Ray Clemence.

As I extended a hand and placed an arm around his shoulder I could see how close to tears he was. Searching for words of consolation I came out with, 'Don't worry Ray. You've got lots of time. I might never play here again.' The words were prophetic. The following season I missed playing in the '72 final against Leeds, having torn cartilage and ligaments in the semi-final. It was an injury which signalled the start of the end for me. In '73 I again missed the opportunity of a further Wembley visit, as eventual winners Sunderland knocked out Arsenal in the semi-final. I never did play at Wembley Stadium again. Ray Clemence returned to make almost 50 appearances in the grand old ground.

In a 23-year career 'Clem' collected twenty major medals. During the same period of time he also won 61 caps for England. Ray was long, lean and, as his first Liverpool manager Bill Shankly described him, 'hellish fast'. A good pair of hands, superb temperament, undisputed courage – he had it all.

He would have won a century of caps or more had it not been for the presence of Peter Shilton in the England squad as well. The arguments as to who was the better keeper still linger today. People who worked closely with Shilts choose him. Clem's compatriots favour his goalkeeping. Peter finished with 125 England caps. It suggests a variety of international managers plumped for him as best, but one, Ron Greenwood, decided there was no difference and played the two keepers alternately, until the 1982 World Cup finals, when I witnessed him tell Ray that he was going to stick with Shilts. The normal smiling face of the man born in Skegness, was a picture of misery, shoulders dropped, disappointment obvious. Clem always bounced back though. Any adversity, in football or in his fight with prostate cancer, was met with a wide grin.

He has an array of tales from his remarkable career, one of the best involving the promises made to him by Bill Shankly in persuading him to leave Scunthorpe for Anfield. Shanks told Ray that his current keeper Tommy Lawrence, was 30 and on the way out. Only when he signed did Ray learn that Tommy was only 27. Shankly had a way with words all right. At the end of his fourteen-year spell at Liverpool Ray took his brilliance to Spurs and more honours followed. He is one of a select group of footballers who have appeared in five or more FA Cup finals. For a short time I did some coaching of Ray, a privilege to be part of his career after our first real meeting in 1971. We will always remain friends and continue to promote the importance of goalkeepers. I'm glad he still has a part to play in the England backroom staff, but unhappy that his role as goalkeeping coach for the international team has been given to Italian Franco Tancredi by Fabio Capello. His second home, Wembley Stadium, will miss him.

⚽ ⚽ ⚽

Raymond Neal 'Ray' Clemence

Born:
5 August 1948, Skegness

Position:
Goalkeeper

Clubs as player:
1965–67 Scunthorpe United, 48 games*
1967–81 Liverpool, 665 games
1981–88 Tottenham Hotspur, 330 games

Internationals:
1972–84 England 61 caps

Clubs as manager (joint):
1992–93 Tottenham Hotspur

Clubs as manager:
1994–96 Barnet

Honours as player with Liverpool:
1973 UEFA Cup Winners' Cup and First Division
1974 FA Cup and FA Charity Shield
1976 UEFA Cup, First Division and FA Charity Shield
1977 European Cup, European Super Cup, First Division and
FA Charity Shield (shared)
1978 European Cup
1979 First Division and FA Charity Shield
1980 First Division and FA Charity Shield
1981 European Cup and League Cup

Honours as player with Tottenham Hotspur:
1981 FA Charity Shield (shared)
1982 FA Cup

Awards:
MBE 1981

– *FIFA World Player of the Year* –

Year	Player	Nationality	Football Club
1991	Lothar Matthäus	Germany	Inter Milan
1992	Marco van Basten	Netherlands	AC Milan
1993	Roberto Baggio	Italy	Juventus
1994	Romario	Brazil	CR Flamengo
1995	George Weah	Liberia	AC Milan
1996	Ronaldo	Brazil	FC Barcelona
1997	Ronaldo	Brazil	FC Barcelona
1998	Zinedine Zidane	France	Juventus
1999	Rivaldo	Brazil	FC Barcelona
2000	Zinedine Zidane	France	Juventus
2001	Luis Figo	Portugal	Real Madrid
2002	Ronaldo	Brazil	Inter Milan
2003	Zinedine Zidane	France	Real Madrid
2004	Ronaldinho	Brazil	FC Barcelona
2005	Ronaldinho	Brazil	FC Barcelona
2006	Fabio Cannavaro	Italy	Real Madrid/ Juventus FC
2007	Kaka	Brazil	AC Milan

Johan Cruyff

Cruyff calls the suit and nine times out of ten he draws the winning card. I really admire that. His style is tailored, his influence strong, his move to score fast and astute and his finishing is stunning. In other words, he's got the lot.

Gerd Müller, West German opponent,
1974 World Cup Final

Johan is 1974's model player. Perhaps just the best with his deceptive simplicity, his economy of movement, his determination. Yes, I would rank him above Pele.

Franz Beckenbauer,
1974 West German World Cup-winning captain

⚽ ⚽ ⚽

There are only two signed shirts hanging in my office at home. One is a Santos shirt worn by Pele. The other belonged to a player I believe ran the great Brazilian close when it came to all-round ability, Dutchman Johan Cruyff. I admit to a degree of bias in that I had the privilege of playing against this footballing genius on six occasions, four when he was captain of Ajax, once as he led out Holland in my last appearance in goal for Scotland and once as his new club Barcelona entertained Arsenal in a friendly at the Nou Camp Stadium. We got to know each other well on the field and off, as Johan's family and mine spent holidays at the same hotel and beach on Portugal's Algarve coast.

That is where I came to learn and appreciate the rarely seen dry humour of one of the greatest footballers the world has ever seen. In public, on camera during games, all you would be aware of was an intensity of look bordering on arrogance, that all the best talents seemed to portray. But there was a humorous side to him.

In the middle of my signed Cruyff shirt is a photo with a message:

Don't you wish you had a body like mine? It's impossible.
Your joking friend. Johan Cruyff.

The photo shows Johan in boots, socks and shorts juggling a ball. His top half is naked revealing the perfectly chiselled six-pack and perfectly honed physique that was the basis of his greatness. I have always likened his physique to a greyhound, the perfect machine. I have only seen one similar player in terms of physique and all-round technical ability and that is Thierry Henry.

Pele's greatness lies with his phenomenal goalscoring record during a career of more than 1,300 games and his World Cup-winner's medals. For most of his serious playing career an aura and myth grew up about the Brazilian because he simply smiled a lot and was unable to converse to the world's media other than in his native tongue.

The less popular image that Johan Cruyff received was as a result of his ability to speak several languages. The greatest player of his generation suffered from trying to accommodate the media scrum that surrounded him at club and country level. Everyone wanted a piece of him, an individual quote or interview. I watched as Johan attempted the impossible and could see his frustration and growing disillusionment at the portrait that was painted of him by the less understanding among the press corps.

It wasn't just as a linguist that Cruyff bettered Pele. He was a more complete all-round performer. Great technical ability embracing dribbling, shooting, tackling and heading skills all set within a perfectly balanced body capable of turning a taunting jog into an Olympic-standard sprint.

To have an individual footballing skill named after you is quite something. 'The Cruyff Turn' as it is known, came to public attention during the 1974 World Cup finals. With the ball at his feet and with his back to a Swedish opponent, the Dutch captain made to pass the ball one way but suddenly dragged it backwards, turning his body at the same moment and accelerating in the other direction to leave his unfortunate opponent for dead. It was a never to be forgotten moment for the fans and a skill which subsequent generations of footballer have sought to perfect.

I count myself lucky not to have been made to look similarly foolish when facing Johan. In fact I still relish the 1970 Inter-Cities Fairs Cup semi-final when my Arsenal team knocked out an emerging Ajax on the way to lifting the trophy. Less memorable was the European Cup quarter-final when a Cruyff-inspired Ajax knocked us out. For the Amsterdam club that season, 1971–72, saw them win the major European prize for the first of three straight triumphs. The consolation for me lay in the fact that he did not score in any of those games. I thought I had again got the better of Johan when, in my second appearance for Scotland, I enjoyed a good performance as we held Holland to a 1–1 scoreline right up to the closing moments, only for Barry Hulshoff to head the winner and set the famous orange scarves flying.

By the time I met Johan again, shortly after he had joined Barcelona, we had spent time together with our families on that Algarve beach. Even then his fame, not mine, led to the great Portugal star Eusebio joining us by the water, plus photographer and journalist. Apart from learning about Cruyff the dad, I also became aware of his brilliant waterskiing skills and his less inspiring passion for a cigarette. During that last friendly game in the Nou Camp in Barcelona, Johan twice faced me one-on-one. Twice he failed to score. Great saves? Hardly, because on both moments he beat me with his shot, only for my goalpost to come to my rescue ... great positional play on my part I reckon!

You can imagine the Cruyff reaction. He was even more frustrated as he emerged for the second half. Being a friendly game, our manager Bertie Mee rotated our squad so all seventeen players got a game. Geoff Barnett took my place in goal. When Johan realised I was on the bench, he ran over and, gesticulating at our manager, demanded he put me back on the field. Bertie didn't understand that Barcelona's great new signing wanted the opportunity to make it 'third time lucky' against his old adversary.

⚽ ⚽ ⚽

Hendrik Johannes 'Johan' Cruyff

Born:
25 April 1947, Amsterdam

Position:
Midfield/forward

Clubs as player:
1964–73 Ajax, 319 games (251 goals)
1973–78 FC Barcelona, 227 (85 goals)
1979–80 Los Angeles Aztecs, 27 games (16 goals)
1980–81 Washington Diplomats, 27 games (10 goals)
1981 Levante, 10 games (2 goals)
1981–83 Ajax, 46 games (16 goals)
1983–84 Feyenoord 44 games (13 goals)

Internationals:
1966-1978 Netherlands, 48 caps (33 goals)

Clubs as manager:
1986–88 Ajax
1988–96 FC Barcelona

Honours as player with Ajax:
1966 Eredivisie
1967 Eredivisie and KNVB Cup
1968 Eredivisie
1970 Eredivisie and KNVB Cup
1971 European Cup and KNVB Cup
1972 European Cup, UEFA Super Cup, Inter-Continental Cup,
Eredivisie and KNVB Cup
1973 European Cup, UEFA Super Cup and Eredivisie
1982 Eredivisie
1983 Eredivisie and KNVB Cup

Honours as player with FC Barcelona:
1974 La Liga
1978 Copa del Rey

Honours as player with Feyenoord:
1984 Eredivisie and KNVB Cup

Honours as manager at Ajax:
1986 KNVB Cup
1987 UEFA Cup Winners' Cup and KNVB Cup

Honours as manager at FC Barcelona:
1989 UEFA Cup Winners' Cup
1990 Copa del Rey
1991 La Liga
1992 European Cup, UEFA Super Cup and La Liga
1993 La Liga
1994 La Liga

Awards:
1971 European Footballer of the Year
1973 European Footballer of the Year
1974 European Footballer of the Year
1999 Voted European player of the century

– *The Clockwork Orange* –

Although the Dutch national flag of red, white and blue is the oldest tricolour still in use today, the country's national football team play in bright orange. This comes from the coat of arms of William I of Orange – or Father of the Fatherland as he is known in the Netherlands – the main leader of the Dutch revolt against the Spanish in the 16th century.

From nowhere, the 1970s saw the emergence of Holland as a true footballing superpower, reaching consecutive World Cup finals in 1974 and 1978. This was largely due to their perfection of Total Football, or *totaalvoetbal*, a system pioneered by legendary coach Rinus Michels. In this system, if a player moves out of position, their role is immediately filled by a teammate leaving the team formation intact. Holland became so proficient in using total football that the side became known as the Clockwork Orange.

Tommy Docherty

I talk a lot. On any subject. Which is always football.

Tommy Docherty, 1967, Chelsea manager

☺ ☺ ☺

'The Doc' and I first met in May 1957. I was representing England against West Germany in an under-15 international. He was preparing to play for Scotland in a full international. The venue was Stuttgart's Neckar Stadium. At the moment I asked for his signature, he could never have dreamed he would one day become manager of his country and that his first team selection would include me as his goalkeeper. Tommy was very gracious when he signed his autograph and so too were his teammates like keeper Tommy Younger, little striker Jackie Mudie and the centre half and skipper George Young. There were lots of smiles and laughs as the Scots encouraged the English boys for the curtain-raiser before their game.

Tommy Docherty enjoys a joke and in recent years has become a master of the one-liners as he tours the country with his after dinner speeches. As a player, he had a reputation as a hard man whether it was at Celtic, a club he loved, Preston North End where he achieved most, Arsenal for whom he made 83 appearances, or latterly Chelsea where he wore the blue shirt just four times. As a manager he nearly ran out of clubs (sixteen in all) and he wasn't scared to discipline errant behaviour, famously sending eight Chelsea players home for breaking a curfew before a vital game at Burnley.

Whatever the Doc's strengths and weaknesses, I will always promote his genuine ability to motivate by finding the words that helped inspire his charges. At times his quotes for the media were over the top, even said with tongue in cheek, never more so than when he faced a barrage of questions and criticism when he selected me for Scotland. Tommy made Alex Cropley, who had a Scottish accent but was born in Aldershot, and myself the first English-born players to play for Scotland. In my case the Scottish press went crazy, not pleased that I was there, despite being recognised as one of the best goalkeepers at that time, and questioning my right to be called a Scot. Quite frankly it was a shocking campaign and one that infuriated my entire family, all proud Scots from dad and mum, grandparents, great-grandparents, uncles, the lot. If the same press corps had only delved a little deeper into the Wilson clan they would have found out that Hampden Park, the very stadium in which I was about to meet Eusebio and Portugal, was opened in 1903 by my great-uncle, Sir John Ure Primrose, Lord Provost of Glasgow and chairman of Rangers. Every milligram of blood that courses through my veins is Scottish, only the old ruling and the place of my birth designated that I was English.

Tommy Doc understood totally. He couldn't have cared less about what the press said, but he was wonderfully protective on my behalf. In response to headlines like 'The Doc picks MacWilson' and 'Docherty calls up Englishman Bob' he retorted with an outrageous claim stating, 'To hell with the man's accent, he's as good as Gordon Banks.' It wasn't exactly a totally accurate quote, but boy, it made me feel ten feet tall. Tommy understood the pressure that was being heaped upon me as I made a little bit of history. When my Arsenal teammate George Graham and I flew up to Glasgow to join the Scottish team, Tommy was waiting at the airport in a bus, which contained every member of the squad. Arsenal had just won the Double in England so there was great respect among the group who eyed me curiously. The 'ochs' and 'ayes' that I tried to insert in my conversation were, on reflection, a mistake. The couple of days training at Largs on the Ayrshire coast were made easy for me by Tommy's insistence that, with me in goal, Scotland now had a real chance to qualify for World and European tournaments.

By the time we reached Hampden Park, his enthusiasm and support for me had reached the previously wary Scottish FA officials and the fans. 'Welcome home, son', was one greeting and a huge chant of 'Bob Wilson, Bob Wilson' chorused as we broke from the national anthems.

The 2–1 win against Portugal was deserved. It was a European qualifier and, out of interest this was the Scotland team:

Bob Wilson (Arsenal); Sandy Jardine (Rangers); David Hay (Celtic); Billy Bremner (Leeds Utd, captain); Eddie Colquhoun (Sheffield United); Pat Stanton (Hibernian); Jimmy Johnstone (Celtic); Alex Cropley (Hibernian), John O'Hare (Derby County), George Graham (Arsenal); Archie Gemmill (Derby County)

Tommy's belief in me as a goalkeeper had no limits. Even when I received a career-threatening injury a few months after my second cap against Holland, he rang regularly to suggest I join the squad. He had the 1974 World Cup finals in mind and I should be fully fit by then. Fate conspired to tell a different tale. The Doc was lured to Manchester United and his successor Willie Ormond clearly did not believe in the new ruling which allowed players with Scottish parents to represent his country.

When on 2 November 1998 BBC TV sprung the *This Is Your Life* programme on me, Tommy Docherty was one of the main guests. Bright as a button, mischievous and entertaining, he told presenter Michael Aspel, 'The only problem I had selecting him was his name, so we called him Jock MacWilson!'

⚽ ⚽ ⚽

Thomas Henderson 'Tommy' Docherty

Born:
24 August 1928, Glasgow

Position:
Midfield

Clubs as player:
1944–49 Celtic, 11 games (3 goals)
1949–58 Preston North End, 349 games (5 goals)
1958–61 Arsenal, 90 games (1 goals)
1961–62 Chelsea, 4 games

Internationals:
1951–59 Scotland, 25 caps (1 goal)

Clubs as manager:
1961–67 Chelsea
1967–68 Rotherham United
1968 Queens Park Rangers
1968–70 Aston Villa
1970–71 FC Porto
1972–77 Manchester United
1977–79 Derby County

1979–80 Queens Park Rangers
1981 Sydney Olympic
1982 Preston North End
1982–83 South Melbourne Hellas
1984–85 Wolverhampton Wanderers
1987–88 Altrincham

International teams as manager:
1972 Scotland

Honours as manager at Chelsea:
1965 League Cup

Honours as manager at Manchester United:
1977 FA Cup

– FA Premier League –

The 1980s saw an all-time low in the history of English Football. Hooliganism, crumbling stadiums and the fact English teams were banned from Europe following the Heysel tragedy discouraged top foreign players from joining the English League. Lord Justice Taylor's report encouraged a change in the way football clubs were run and structured. In 1988 ten of the top clubs threatened to break away in order to take advantage of higher television revenues.

The FA Premier League was formed on 27 May 1992. It followed the signing of a founder member's agreement which had been created the previous year on 17 July 1991 by all the Division One clubs. It established the basic principles of a new commercially independent premier league, which would be free to negotiate its own sponsorship, television and radio deals. Sky TV paid £191 million over the first five seasons with the BBC's highlights deal and overseas contracts boosting the overall total to £304 million. This represented an extraordinary rise in the value of the product.

The Premier League kicked off on 15 August 1992, a day on which I presented *Football Focus* for the nineteenth season, and on which Gary Lineker would become a regular guest.

At the end of the 2005–06 season a new Premier League contract pumped even more money into football. The contract represented a 66 per cent increase on the previous deals and was worth £1.76 billion over three years. As a European Court ruling insisted that no one company could enjoy a monopoly, the Setanta Sports Channel paid £392 million for 46 matches alongside Sky's £1.3 billion, which gave them 92 live matches. Additional terrestrial highlights, overseas rights, online and mobile deals took the final total over £2 billion.

⚽ ⚽ ⚽

Premiership Main Statistics 1992–2008

Titles won
Manchester United (10), Arsenal (3), Chelsea (2), Blackburn (1)

Most Points in a season
2004–05 Chelsea (95 points)

Fewest points in a season
2005–06 Sunderland (15 points)

Most wins in a season
2004–05 Chelsea (29)

Fewest wins in a season
2007–08 Derby (1)

Fewest defeats
2003–04 Arsenal (unbeaten)

Most defeats in a season
1994–95 Ipswich (29)

Most goals scored
1999–2000 Manchester United (97)

Fewest goals scored
2007–08 Derby (20)

Most goals conceded
1993–94 Swindon (100)

Most clean sheets
2004–05 Chelsea (25)

Longest unbeaten run
7 May 2003–24 Oct 2004 Arsenal (49 games)

Most Championship medals
Ryan Giggs, Manchester United (10)

[N.B. seasons prior to 1995–96 comprised 42 matches;
subsequent seasons comprised 38]

Liam Brady

I've heard it said that you can't be a football manager and tell the truth. Well, I'm going to have a go at it.

Liam Brady, 1991, new Celtic manager

✿ ✿ ✿

I am regularly asked questions about the finest player I faced, the greatest footballer ever and the most brilliant of Arsenal teammates. I struggle choosing between Johan Cruyff and George Best as finest faced. Pele usually gets my vote for greatest ever, but there's little doubt in my mind about the most gifted and talented Arsenal colleague.

Liam Brady came from a footballing background. Both his great uncle Frank Brady and older brother Ray had been Irish internationals. Another brother, Pat, played with QPR. Liam though is the most famous. He won 72 Republic of Ireland caps, was twice a Serie A-winner in Italy with Juventus, and an Arsenal legend as the inspiration behind the team that reached three FA Cup finals in succession and a Cup Winners' Cup Final, between 1978 and 1980.

His debut for the Gunners came as a substitute in October 1973. It was followed by a full debut in a North London derby at White Hart Lane. Liam didn't have his best game; we lost and manager Bertie Mee decided to use the young Irishman sparingly. I played in both of his first two matches and, despite his nervousness, knew that Arsenal had on their books an exceptional talent.

Liam Brady was one of the great playmakers, favouring the left side of the pitch simply because he possessed a 'magic wand' of a left foot which enabled him to produce elegant technical skills including breathtaking passes, wonderful dribbling skills and a shot of venom. I can still visualise him dispossessing Spurs' Peter Taylor outside the box in a derby 48 hours before Christmas Day and hitting the White Hart Lane rigging with a powerful swerving shot. It made for a happy Christmas for all Arsenal fans who grew to idolise this quiet, reserved genius, who they knew as 'Chippy', after his love of fish and chips.

My career was almost at an end when we were in the same side but, as goalkeeping coach to Pat Jennings, I was able to watch Liam fulfil all the expectations held of him. Before long Arsenal fans were comparing him to Alex James of the 30s era and a similar player of legendary status.

It's a pity that the Arsenal team in which he flourished was more of a cup side rather than potential league champions. However it was appropriate that in the 1979 FA Cup Final, which proved to have a remarkable climax, it was Chippy who ran the game and set up Arsenal's two-goal lead against Manchester United, only for United to square the game in the closing five minutes. A betting man would have plumped for United at that moment, but almost directly from the re-start the ball found Chippy Brady. The familiar control, dropping of the shoulders and easy close control took him on a surge into United's defensive third. Then he slipped a pass to his great mate Graham Rix, wide on the left. 'Ricko' in turn delivered a teasing, searching cross, which United keeper Gary Bailey got totally wrong and Alan Sunderland's head won the match for Arsenal.

Watching from five yards away, in my capacity as post-match interviewer, I lost all sense of impartiality and could be seen punching the air in undisguised delight. When I put it to Liam, in the interview that followed the cup presentation, that it would forever be known as 'the Brady final', he reverted to type, refused the accolade and set about praising his teammates: 'Without them I would be nothing.'

The following season Arsenal and Brady were back at Wembley but lost to West Ham. Four days later they lost the Cup Winners' Cup Final on penalties to Valencia. It was the final act by Chippy in an Arsenal shirt. During the summer of 1980 he signed for Juventus in a deal worth £500,000. Juventus had been beaten by Arsenal in the semi-final of the Cup Winners' Cup and had been impressed by the Republic of Ireland star. The Arsenal fans were devastated and, as their own team struggled, the Italian giants with Liam on board won back-to-back Serie A championship titles. In Italy, he did what many other British players failed to do when moving abroad. He learned the language, encouraged by his wife Sarah. Consequently when he left Juventus he went on to spells at Sampdoria, Inter Milan and Ascoli before returning to England and West Ham United.

Management seemed a natural extension of his footballing career for this intelligent, thoughtful man, but his time in Scotland at Celtic and on the south coast of England with Brighton never touched the heights of his playing career, both clubs hindering their own progress with financial difficulties. There was a happy ending to the story though when in July 1996 Liam returned to Arsenal as head of youth development and academy director. He has done a tremendous job as Arsenal has set about recruiting some outstanding young talent from around the world. More recently he also added another role with the Republic of Ireland as assistant to manager Giovanni Trapattoni.

The amazing thing about the Liam Brady story is that it nearly didn't happen. His initial steps into the world of football were wobbly and he came perilously close to falling and not getting back up. Many young apprentices, George Best included, faced the dilemma that Liam faced: the choice of pursuing a career in the harsh reality that is football or returning to the safety of family and friends. He was just fifteen when he signed schoolboy forms in 1970, arriving the following summer at a club basking in the glory that goes with being champions of England and FA Cup winners.

The early days were exciting enough for Liam but homesickness soon created doubts in his mind. Negative thoughts about football as a profession and his own ability took just four months to emerge. The young Irishman found there was no comparison between the game he knew as fun back home and the football played for a living. Friday became his favourite day when the apprentices got paid all of £6. The excitement of cleaning boots, loading kit and equipment and being at the beck and call of the senior players rapidly wore thin. Liam also had concerns about his size and strength. In his own words he was 'trailing in the muscles department'. When his form on the field dipped he was suddenly facing a crossroads. His personality is such that he will always give very careful consideration to what is right and wrong, good and bad. When he was accused of feigning illness to miss a youth game, he decided football was not for him. In the Christmas of 1971, back home in Dublin for a short break, Chippy Brady told his mum he was not going to return to Arsenal. What he had imagined to be a great life as a footballer had turned into a nightmare of disillusionment and disappointment.

Being back with his family and friends in Dublin seemed a better option than life in London. Arsenal's concern at his non-return to the club was immediate and happily Liam himself soon resolved the crisis by realising that football, precarious career that it is, was still what he wanted most in his life. On his return he set about carving out a great career for himself and his first professional contract followed when he turned seventeen – two years at £20 a week were the terms agreed.

Liam was lucky he had a wise head on his young shoulders. What he learned from his early crisis was graphically expressed in his autobiography *So Far So Good*. It serves as a perfect template for all young talent who hope to make the grade:

> I learned that football as a profession makes a man of a boy more quickly than most professions. That without discipline you cannot hope to succeed as a player or indeed in any walk of life. That criticism is more than just an attack of a personal nature. Often it is helpful in the development of your career. I learned that no one player is bigger than his club. I learned that football is a game which you never stop learning. I advise every boy entering the game to listen to every scrap of advice given, chew it over, see what works for you as an individual and disregard the rest. Stand on your own two feet, make decisions for yourself never forgetting to listen to all that advice because from every dose you get, something will prove invaluable. But don't feel duty bound to swallow and agree with everything thrown your way. You have a mind and talent all of your own. Use them.

☻ ☻ ☻

Liam 'Chippy' Brady

Born:
13 February 1956, Dublin

Position:
Attacking midfield

Clubs as player:
1973–80 Arsenal, 307 games (59 goals)
1980–82 Juventus, 76 games (15 goals)
1982–84 Sampdoria, 57 games (6 goals)
1984–86 Inter Milan, 58 games (5 goals)
1986–87 Ascoli, 17 games (10 goals)
1987–90 West Ham United, 101 games (10 goals)

Internationals:
1974–90 Republic of Ireland, 72 caps (9 goals)

Clubs as manager:
1991–93 Celtic
1993–95 Brighton and Hove Albion

Honours as player at Arsenal:
1979 FA Cup

Honours as player at Juventus:
1981 Serie A
1982 Serie A

Awards:
1979 PFA Players' Player of the Year

– *Zebras* –

Juventus FC was founded on 1 November 1897, by a group of boys aged between fourteen and seventeen. They played in pink shirts because it was the cheapest material available. Although the club grew quickly, entering the Italian Football Championship in 1900, they continued to use their pink shirts. However, as the number of games increased, so did the need to wash the shirts and they faded too quickly. So in 1903 the club decided to find a new kit. John Savage, an English player at the club at the time asked his friend to send over some shirts from England. His friend, being an ardent Notts County fan, sent a set of his beloved team's black-and-white striped shirts to Turin. Juventus have worn them ever since, becoming the Zebras.

Jack Charlton

Jack makes out he's not really interested in football and tells the world he's going fishing. But we know what he's thinking about when he's fishing. Football.

Johan Cruyff, 1990, Barcelona coach

Jack is not always right, but he is never wrong.

Johnny Giles, 1991, ex-Leeds colleague and
Republic of Ireland manager

☺ ☺ ☺

The majority of top footballers have lots of good stories to tell. Few, if any, can tell them as well as 'Big Jack' Charlton. His angular 6' 3" ungainly walk undoubtedly adds to the overall effect when Jack entertains his audiences wherever he speaks. I had heard Jack talk at sporting dinners long before I had an intimate two-week personal show alongside him on a P&O cruise in which Jack and I were two of a trio of guest lecturers, Alan Mullery completing the set. In the evening at the dinner table with our wives, we covered every aspect of the game.

There were never many smiles, if any, when I faced Jack and Leeds United over a period of years. Every set piece against corners and free kicks were made doubly difficult by the Charlton physique, standing directly in front of me, twisting, turning and often getting to the incoming ball first. Most keepers would complain to the referees about obstruction or foul play. Jack invariably would score.

His presence was too much for my Arsenal predecessor Jim Furnell on 2 March 1968. A horrible League Cup final was won by a Terry Cooper volley after Jack Charlton had blocked Jim's route to the ball. It was the keeper's penultimate appearance in the Arsenal goal. An error a week later in the FA Cup against Birmingham presented me with the opportunity I had long sought. It's fair to say Leeds United employed every trick in the book to win games, fair means or foul. Don Revie's side could mix it with anyone. The shame was they didn't need to be an ugly side. At the time they were capable of producing amazing possession football. How Arsenal pipped them to the 1970–71 league title remains a mystery to some degree.

At one stage in the New Year they had a twelve-point lead over us. Every expert wrote us off, but eleven wins, a draw and one defeat in our last thirteen games meant that at the last game of the season at Tottenham we had not only closed the gap but held our destiny in our own hands. Nil–nil was enough or any win: 1–1 or worse and Leeds would be champions. Two or three games before our 1–0 win at Spurs it was Jack Charlton and Leeds who inflicted our only league defeat since Christmas. Even then we thought Jack was offside as he appeared in the box late in the game and swung a hopeful boot at the ball to score. I chased the referee Norman Burtenshaw around the back of the goal in protest, but it was proved he and his linesman were correct. Bob McNab out wide had played Jack onside.

Time spent together with Jack and his brother Bobby only confirmed how fond they are of each other despite family differences. I was so pleased that was the case especially when you recall the images of the two brothers at Wembley in 1966, World Cup-winners and crying their eyes out in the joy and emotion of the moment.

I applaud loyalty and Jack's loyalty to Leeds was outstanding – 733 appearances over a 21-year period. A one-club man as player, he went on to be manager at four clubs and one national side. He enjoyed success at Middlesbrough and Sheffield Wednesday but it was the nine years he spent guiding the Republic of Ireland to unprecedented heights that have made him a very proud honorary Irishman. Qualification for the 1988 European Championship in Germany was exciting. A 1–0 victory over the country he'd represented, England, was dreamland. Making the 1990 World Cup finals for the first time continued the fantasy, a quarter-final place against Italy proof of how good a team he'd built. His swansong with Ireland was qualification again for the 1994 World Cup finals in America. His pitch-side argument with a linesman for delaying a substitution added to the legend. On Ireland's return Jack received the Freedom of the City of Dublin. An OBE followed and then came honorary Irish citizenship, the highest honour Ireland can present to anyone.

During our two-week Mediterranean cruise spreading the word about football, Jack regaled us with stories of his Irish adventure especially the provision of a home in the Republic for which he was not allowed to pay for anything – roofing, carpentry, kitchens, bathroom, paintwork. Absolutely every tradesman gave services and products free of charge as a show of gratitude for his putting Ireland on the world football stage. Free fishing rights was the ultimate gift!

As a raconteur, 'Big Jack' was riveting and hilarious in equal proportions. While enjoying his company it is easy to forget the place he earned for himself in the history of English football, as a winner of the World Cup.

❂ ❂ ❂

John 'Jack' Charlton

Born:
8 May 1935 Ashington

Position:
Centre back

Clubs as player:
1952–73 Leeds United, 772 games (95 goals)

Internationals:
1965–70 England 35 caps (6)

Clubs as manager:
1973–77 Middlesbrough
1977–83 Sheffield Wednesday
1984 Middlesbrough
1984–85 Newcastle United

International teams as manager:
1986–95 Republic of Ireland

Honours as player with Leeds United:
1968 Inter-Cities Fairs Cup and League Cup
1969 First Division
1971 Inter-Cities Fairs Cup
1972 FA Cup
1973 FA Cup

Honours as player with England:
1966 World Cup

Honours as manager at Middlesbrough:
1974 Promotion to First Division

Awards:
1967 Footballer of the Year
1973 Manager of the Year
1974 OBE

– *Substitutions* –

On 21 August 1965, the opening day of the season, Keith Peacock of Charlton Athletic became the first player to appear as a substitute under a new ruling allowing one sub for an injured player. The game was a Second Division fixture at Burnden Park between Bolton Wanderers and Charlton Athletic. For the 1988–89 season the Football League agreed to allow two substitutes per team.

In more recent years the number of substitutes permitted in Football League matches has gradually increased. At present, each team is permitted to name five or seven substitutes, depending on the country and competition, of which a maximum of three may be used.

George Graham

If ever there was a player I felt definitely would not have what it took to be a manager, it was George Graham. Running a nightclub? Yes. A football club? Absolutely not.

Don Howe, 1999, Arsenal coach

I admit I'm single-minded. I think all of the great football managers have been single-minded.

Graham, 1991, after being nicknamed 'Ayatollah' and 'Gadaffi' by his players

⚽ ⚽ ⚽

There will always be a bond between George Graham and me. We have shared many special moments, initially as teammates for club and country, then as goalkeeping coach and manager at Arsenal respectively. There has been friendship both inside football and away from it.

'Stroller' was the nickname given to George. It suggests he wasn't blessed with real pace. That is accurate, but what he lacked in speed he made up with style and poise. That's also a fitting description for his daily appearance away from the football pitch. He has always been immaculately groomed and enjoys the best in clothing.

Elegant ball skills and a remarkable capacity to head and direct a ball delivered in the air were his strengths as a player. He was named the Man of the Match in the 1971 FA Cup Final. Initially he was also thought to have scored our equalising goal against Liverpool but after studying TV replays it was decided that George had not got a touch to Eddie Kelly's mishit shot. I remain one of the few people who believe that the Graham boot brushed the ball last. If it didn't then his run across the front of the Liverpool defenders created the indecision that allowed the ball to bumble its way beyond Ray Clemence.

As a player he won four major trophies and was a runner-up in four more. As a manager he exceeded that, winning a total of seven major honours, six at Arsenal and one at Spurs. In the process he amazed every one of his former teammates at Arsenal who, for the most part, would have considered him the least likely candidate to ever enter the cutthroat, demanding and dedicated world of management.

As a player George enjoyed a night out and a glass of champagne. He and our skipper Frank McLintock were buddies and roommates. They would drink together and sing together, Frank Sinatra songs in the main. Not always a pretty sound or sight!

I was hugely grateful for his company when I became the first English-born player to be selected for Scotland in October '71. Tommy Docherty picked George for the first of his twelve caps at the same time. The 'Doc' had been the Chelsea manager who sent George and seven other members of his team home in disgrace in 1965 for breaking a pre-match curfew.

My introduction and acceptance as a Scot with the media, the fans and especially my teammates was helped by the way George stayed close to me, sticking up for me, sharing a room at our Largs base. After the 2–1 victory against Portugal at Hampden on 13 October 1971 we were rushed to Glasgow railway station and happily boarded the overnight sleeper together on our way back to London.

After he was transferred to Manchester United in December 1972 I saw very little of George for more than a decade. His playing career took him from United to Portsmouth, then Crystal Palace and finally to California Surf. His greatest pal for many years has been Terry Venables and it was the influence of one of England's former managers that persuaded George to try his hand at coaching, first at Crystal Palace, then at QPR. I watched with surprise as George Graham took up his first managerial position at Millwall and instantly transformed the club, guiding it away from relegation and, within a season or two, winning promotion to the old Second Division. Within another two seasons Millwall made it to the First Division, but by then George Graham had got his feet well under the table back at Highbury.

When he arrived on 14 May 1986 I had already been coaching the club's goalkeepers for eleven years. It was an honorary role I undertook alongside my main employment with BBC TV. On his arrival I instantly discovered that the laidback George Graham I knew as a teammate had changed. Now in charge, he was very focused and sought loyalty from every member of his staff. I was slightly surprised when he asked me whether I had tried to help Graham Taylor, who was an innovative manager at Watford, to get the job at Arsenal. Taylor, whose goalkeepers I had also coached for a short time, did indeed ask me to let the Arsenal directors know he would be interested in the vacant manager's position at Highbury. It was as simple as that. I was a messenger boy passing on Graham Taylor's name to an Arsenal director, who thanked me for the info. That director must have in turn told George after his appointment and as a result I faced a grilling.

I wasn't angry that George should question my loyalty but I was unhappy with that member of the club's board.

George ruled with an iron rod. He was like Bertie Mee, the manager who had taught him the value of discipline and organisation.

From that initial uncomfortable moment, normal service was resumed and on many occasions he took me into his confidence. One of those was when he had contractual differences with one of my goalkeeping charges, John Lukic, an outstanding individual who had played a major role in the first two trophies George Graham brought to Arsenal. George asked me about David Seaman who was at Queens Park Rangers, another of the several clubs that I helped with keepers. I told the Arsenal manager that if he was thinking about buying David, he wasn't even taking a risk. I suggested he would soon be the England number one and had the potential to be as good as Pat Jennings.

So it was that John Lukic left for Leeds where he became the only keeper to win First Division titles with two different clubs. David Seaman arrived and began a glittering Arsenal career that saw him win nine major trophies, be a runner-up in seven more and collect 75 England caps.

George Graham's tactical genius was best illustrated in two games. The first was the night in 1989 when Arsenal won the league title at Anfield, the home of their closest rivals. Needing to win 2–0 at Liverpool, George told his team not to be too anxious in the first half, but to stay calm, remain tight in defence and be happy at halftime to be drawing 0–0. Then in the second, he told the team to exploit whatever opportunity came their way. He predicted Arsenal would score midway through the half and when panic set in for the Liverpool lads, to score a second and become champions. It was planned like a military campaign and executed in similar style. Staggering!

The 1994 European Cup Winners' Cup Final in Copenhagen surpassed even the amazing night on Merseyside. Riddled with injuries and facing a Parma side that included the talented Zola and Asprilla, George used a blackboard at the team hotel prior to leaving for the stadium to display his master plan: subduing the talented Italian side, defending heroically and taking what chance might fall his players' way. It was simple and brilliant, a truly outstanding and confidently expressed tactical plan which his players heeded as Alan Smith's strike won the day against all the odds.

It was the sixth and last trophy to which George led Arsenal, ensuring his place as one of the club's greatest managers. After all he had done for the club, the manner of his leaving Highbury was awful, sacked after accepting an 'unsolicited gift' from Rune Hauge, one of those football agents who didn't have the good of the game at heart, but who was prepared to risk giving it a bad name by entering the murky world of 'bungs'.

George was wrong and admitted as much. His error has not diminished my friendship with him, my liking of him, or the memories we shared and the kindness he has shown me. One of his last interviews as manager of Arsenal came on the first day I began work for ITV Sport in August 1994. It was conducted in one of Highbury's executive boxes. As it was concluding, my wife Megs, daughter Anna and her husband Mitchell burst into the box, desperate to tell me that the latest scans on Anna's life-threatening cancer were clear, that she was in remission, and that there was a chance we had hardly dared hope for.

George joined in the happiness and embraces and promptly found a bottle of champagne to celebrate. It was a moment when all of us understood a little more clearly what was and wasn't really important in our lives.

☻ ☻ ☻

George Graham

Born:
30 November 1944, Bargeddie, Lanarkshire

Position:
Forward/midfield

Clubs as player:
1961–64 Aston Villa, 10 games (2 goals)
1964–66 Chelsea, 102 games (46 goals)
1966–72 Arsenal, 308 games (77 goals)
1972–74 Manchester United, 58 games (4 goals)
1974–76 Portsmouth, 61 games* (5 goals)
1976–77 Crystal Palace, 44 games* (2 goals)

Internationals:
1971–73 Scotland, 12 caps (3 goals)

Clubs as manager:
1983–86 Millwall
1986–95 Arsenal
1996–98 Leeds United
1998–2001 Tottenham Hotspur

Honours as player with Chelsea:
1965 League Cup

Honours as player with Arsenal:
1970 Inter-Cities Fairs Cup
1971 First Division and FA Cup

Honours as manager at Millwall:
1985 Promotion to Second Division

Honours as manager at Arsenal:
1987 League Cup
1989 First Division
1991 First Division
1993 FA Cup and League Cup
1994 UEFA Cup Winners' Cup

Honours as manager at Tottenham Hotspur:
1999 League Cup

– *Agents* –

The word 'agent' within the world of football is more often than not greeted with suspicion. It is, at best, a necessary requirement for the vast majority of players to be attached to a reputable person who can act on their behalf in negotiations with a club, whether it is over a transfer fee or a salary agreement.

At worst the world of agents is considered a murky one with tales of bungs and illegal payments. Strangely, if a representative of a player is called a lawyer or accountant there is an acceptance of their honesty and fortitude.

Footballers, as a rule, are talented sportsmen and gifted athletes. They have little or no knowledge of business dealings and contracts and invariably need help. It's the same for film stars, musicians and the like. All concentrate on maximising their gifts, leaving legal documents and the negotiation of salary terms to others who are more familiar with the language of business. In short, agents are a necessity and down the years there have been good and bad. I recall a friendly rotund, smiling little Italian called Gigi Peronace in the 70s who was at the centre of the transfers of British players like Jimmy Greaves, Joe Baker and Denis Law. The success and fame of people like Gigi encouraged many other individuals to try their hand at being an agent. The role of helping players can be extended to assisting managers as well as keeping clubs informed of who is and is not available at any given time.

The basic premise when a footballer says 'you'll need to talk to my agent', means that when a club is making any payment to an agent it should always be on behalf of the player involved and part of any benefits he is legally due from the club. Because there have been so many grey areas in which agents can work, rules should be simple. The case which former Premier League Chief Executive Rick Parry made clear many years ago argued 'that procedures are drawn up which say what agents can and cannot do. Penalties have to be brought into force if the agent breaks the rules. These guys are here to stay, we have to accept that. It's now up to the Premiership and FA to draw up a set of proposals that are workable and achievable.'

Fourteen years on from that statement the authorities have still not totally closed the case on agents. The Stevens Inquiry was supposed to put things to bed when it issued its findings in December 2006. The nine-month inquiry covered 362 transfer deals being examined by Lord Stevens. Many agents simply failed to respond to any enquiry and only a limited number of bank accounts were investigated. Thirty-nine recommendations were made, including the creation of a specialist body to handle the audit of transfers in place of the Football Association. Any scant regard for rules laid down would be deemed 'unacceptable'. Relatives 'should not be paid' in deals and the PFA should not be able to act as agents.

There were specific suggestions regarding agents working in the UK. Previously agents' fees were always paid by the club that was dealing with the transfer. Now it is recommended that UK agents' commission should be paid directly out of the taxed income of the player, something that players are coming to resent. This rule does not, however, affect agents who work abroad. They cannot be challenged and players will most likely turn to them in order to protect their own income, thereby making it virtually impossible for UK agents to exist.

The overall conclusion was that criminal investigations were not endemic within the Premiership. I would ask, how does any investigation prove right or wrong over bungs when cash has been involved – the sort of 'bung' which cost George Graham his job at Arsenal in February 1995, despite his returning the £425,500 given to him by an agent, plus interest?

There is a fascinating chapter within Sir Alex Ferguson's book *My Autobiography* entitled 'Among the Agents'. Within it he recalls a variety of dubious incidents involving agents and the players they represent, including the methods whereby several agents would claim to be representing the same client and notably a 'gift' he was given once late at night from a Russian advisor to the former United player Andrei Kanchelskis. The present was within a beautifully wrapped box. Only when he got home did Sir Alex discover that the gift was not a bottle or two of Champagne or chocolates but 'piles of cash, bundles of the stuff'. The United manager and his wife Cathy counted the money before taking it to Old Trafford the next morning. There was £40,000 in notes. Sir Alex and United had to employ club and personal solicitors in order to cover themselves from any possible plot that might have materialised.

I would imagine there are many similar stories that the authorities have never and will never hear about and that there will continue to be good agents and dubious agents. I've got to know many personally, none more so than Dennis Roach, a former Barnet and Bedford centre half, who began his career as an agent representing Johan Cruyff in the UK. I never have discussed the intricacies of deals with him but used to benefit, in my role as a football presenter, from Dennis' phone calls informing me of the latest news. He has a renowned sense of humour which is best illustrated by a lunchtime call to me at the BBC *Grandstand* set, five minutes before I was due to present *Football Focus*.

'Bob, I've got some transfer news for you to put out. Brian Clough has just bought a Norwegian international centre half for Nottingham Forest.' I was excited and thanked Dennis, asking immediately for the player's name. He asked if I had a pen handy to write down both the spelling of the name and how it should be pronounced. 'Look his name is Aas, but it's pronounced Arse.' I checked that he was sure about the pronunciation and he confirmed adding, 'Now here's his Christian name. I'll spell it for you. Ready? It's s.i.l.l.y.' Without thinking and running out of time to going on air I repeated what I had written: 'So that's Silly Arse!' And then the penny dropped, followed by hilarious laughter at the other end of the line. The Norwegian's name was in fact Einaar Aas.

Somehow I think the moral of this story lies somewhere within the ability of some agents, over many years, to make an 'Aas' of the rules, regulations and governing bodies when supposedly representing footballers' interests.

Brian Clough

He's a kind of Rolls-Royce communist.

Malcolm Allison, 1973, rival manager

If God had meant football to be played in the air, he'd have put grass in the sky.

Brian Clough

I certainly wouldn't say I'm the best manager in the business, but I'm in the top one.

Brian Clough

I'd ask him how he thinks it should be done, have a chat about it for 20 minutes and then decide I was right.

Brian Clough, on dealings with his players

⚽ ⚽ ⚽

The real greatness of Brian Clough lies not in what he has achieved but where he achieved it. As a player at Middlesbrough and Sunderland his goalscoring record was nothing short of phenomenal. As a manager his success almost defies belief. Cloughie rightly takes his place as one of the best managers of all time. My contact with him has been memorable. Out and out confrontation, kindness, hilarity and friendship have marked the times I have been in the company of this unique character. Always, his initial look towards me was one of scorn. Invariably it melted into an impish grin. He was a master of the wind-up.

The best example in a match situation came in an FA Cup fifth round replay in front of 63,000 fans at Highbury. The score was 0–0 after 90 minutes. Extra-time team talks took place on the pitch and as the referee signalled managers and coaches to leave, the Derby manager walked straight into our Arsenal team group, deliberately headed for me and with even more purpose, knocked me flying. It was his way of rattling me, getting me to lose temper and focus. He succeeded initially as it took several teammates to hold me back from chasing him and punching him. I expect he walked away with a little grin on his face

By then we knew each other quite well, having been colleagues during the BBC's 1970 World Cup coverage. He had a habit of giving everyone a hug, even a kiss sometimes. Basically he thought I was a bit soft, an educated grammar-school boy who played for a 'posh' club in what essentially was a working man's game. Brian didn't 'do' posh and revelled in beating the big boys with teams from a less salubrious background and history. I'm not sure he could have handled an Arsenal or Manchester United, although he would have been a brilliant manager of England.

Television and his renowned caustic comments only added to his compulsive appeal, although I feel the powers that be at the BBC and ITV pushed him into trying to find definitive, shocking and provocative statements every time he appeared. How wrong he was to call goalkeeper Jan Tomaszewski a 'clown' after Poland had knocked England out of the World Cup at Wembley. He didn't like it when an upstart like me – goalkeeper though I was – challenged his view.

But underneath that brash exterior lay wonderful kindness and generosity. When my playing career had come to an end and my television career began at the Beeb, Brian would often give me the chance to interview him, albeit unexpectedly. Unexpectedly because he was so totally unpredictable. I would continually phone his loyal secretary Carol and she would chat away, always giving me hope that I would catch him at a good time, some day. It was often a drama to get him to say 'yes', then inevitably I would face a long wait to ask the questions.

Most memorable was an interview we undertook during the prolonged miners' strike when his love of politics and socialism led to a lecture the like of which I only received much later from one other manager, Sir Alex Ferguson. You took your life in your hands if you challenged Brian's beliefs too strongly.

'Expect you couldn't get round the roundabout because of the striking miners?' he asked. I had the audacity to reply 'Well most of them are now wanting to get back to work, Brian.' What a mistake! At least ten minutes later I was still on the receiving end of Cloughie's tongue. The vitriol he poured on the prime minister, Margaret Thatcher, and her government had to be heard to be believed. 'How can that upper-class shower ever understand what it's like [for miners] to go below ground and put their lives at risk for a pittance?' It was dangerous to argue against him because all thought of a football interview would be discarded until he thought I could see his point of view.

Cloughie usually insisted I match his consumption of whisky dram by dram as he raided the chairman's drinks cabinet. When the chat finally turned to football his views were invariably riveting. His personality was unique and, on his own admission, his arrogance reflected that of his great hero, possibly the only person he held in awe, singer Frank Sinatra.

I treasure a photo in which Brian is thrusting the league championship trophy in my face. Early in that brilliant campaign for Forest I had reported for *Grandstand* on their away win at QPR. Boldly I declared that 'Nottingham Forest were lucky to get all the points and although they are new favourites to win the title, I think their bubble will burst.'

Brian's response to my prediction made banner headlines in the local Nottingham paper two days later. He castigated me, even suggesting I should lose my job. I wasn't fired by the BBC but at the end of the season I was invited to interview him at the City ground, as long as the local paper could also take the gloating photo with the championship trophy to be accompanied by the words 'Now young man, what was it you said about our bubble bursting!'

Like almost everyone else I loved the man who called himself 'Old Big 'Ead' after receiving the honour of an OBE. Even now perhaps that put-down of his own award provides a continuing lesson for me.

Brian always had the last word, so that should be the case now with this excerpt from *Walking on Water*, his story:

> When I'm gone I want to be remembered as somebody who contributed good things to the English game – not least the winning of trophies with teams that played football with good manners, according to the rules imposed by referees, and with style and a bit of a swagger. Let them remember me as a bigheaded so and so, a conceited bugger who believed he was always right and sometimes said things he shouldn't. But don't remember Cloughie for any of the negatives of life – apart from having one drink too many too often.

⚽ ⚽ ⚽

Brian Howard Clough

Born:
21 March 1935, Middlesbrough
Died:
20 September 2004, Derby

Position:
Striker

Clubs as player:
1955–61 Middlesbrough, 222 games (204 goals)
1961–64 Sunderland, 74 games (63 goals)

Internationals:
1959 England, 2 caps

Clubs as manager:
1965–67 Hartlepool United
1967–73 Derby County
1973–74 Brighton and Hove Albion
1974 Leeds United
1975–93 Nottingham Forest

Honours as manager at Derby County:
1969 Promotion to First Division
1972 First Division

Honours as manager at Nottingham Forest:
1977 Promotion to First Division
1978 First Division, League Cup and FA Charity Shield
1979 European Cup, European Super Cup and League Cup
1980 European Cup and League Cup
1989 League Cup and Full Members Cup
1990 League Cup
1992 Full Members Cup

Awards:
1991 OBE

– *The Black Cats* –

There are various links between Sunderland AFC and the black cat stretching back over the last 200 years. In 1805, a nearby gun battery on the River Wear was renamed the Black Cat battery after a number of workers heard a mysterious wailing that turned out to be a black cat trapped inside the factory. Then there's a photograph from 1905, a hundred years later, of F.W. Taylor, the club chairman, with a black cat sitting on a football next to him – and three years later, in 1908, the black cat crept into a full team photograph.

Before long, black cats were featuring in the match-day programme and in club-related cartoons in the local paper. For the FA Cup Final in 1937, many fans wore a specially made black-cat tie-pin to hold their red-and-white buttonhole in place. After the same final, the press made much of twelve-year-old Billy Morris and his black kitten, which sat in his pocket at Wembley throughout that game – supposedly bringing the team sufficient luck to come from behind and beat Preston 3–1. For years, a black cat also lived at Roker Park, where it was looked after by the club, and its arrival sparked a long winning streak.

Despite all this, it's only recently that the name was properly adopted by the club. It has had a number of nicknames in its history, including the Roker Men and the Rokerites, but the move from Roker Park in 1997 left these redundant. It's only now, fully ensconced at the Stadium of Light – with their match-day mascots Samson and Delilah – that Sunderland have truly become known as the Black Cats.

Alan Ball

*The only thing that stops me being a world-class player is that I don't
score enough goals.*

Alan Ball, 1972

*Players' attitudes have changed because of money. Getting vast
amounts takes away the hunger, that little edge. Players of today
say, 'I go out and play with the same desire', but it can't be that way
when the comfort zone comes so quickly and easily.*

Alan Ball, 2002

☉ ☉ ☉

When I first heard that my club Arsenal had broken the
British transfer fee record to bring Alan Ball from Everton
to Highbury for £220,000, I was elated. Having won the
coveted League Championship and FA Cup Double the
previous season (1970–71), we were struggling to maintain
our standards. Manager Bertie Mee had gone for one of the
best.

We thought we knew what to expect. An England 1966
World Cup hero, arguably the finest player on view at
Wembley during the 4–2 victory over West Germany, a fiery
redhead, a tireless skilful little midfield genius who, with
Colin Harvey and Howard Kendall had inspired Everton to
the league title in 1970. Well yes, we got all that but within
weeks we also discovered another side to this character, an
individual who could drive us all mad, on and off the pitch.

We all knew from the moment he arrived that Bally was being paid more than the rest of us – a basic salary well in advance of our own £60–80 a week, plus bonuses, which we had earned as a result of three straight Wembley final appearances, a European trophy and the freshly acquired title of Champions of England. Alan always wore his heart on his sleeve and was never backward in coming forward. Imagine our reaction when he would collect his wage slip on a Friday, the day before a game, and then deliberately leave it on the Highbury dressing room table for all of us to view with interest and not a little anger. There were some of the squad who never came to terms with his belief in himself and his ability.

When results failed to improve much after his arrival, the dressing room atmosphere became even more volatile. His actions on the field could also stir the lads. Often when we had managed to take a slender 1–0 lead, Bally would taunt the opposition by either sitting or kneeling on the ball. Time and again after the game he would laugh as we tore him off a strip. 'The game's about entertainment; I'm an entertainer,' would be the squeaky response from those instantly recognisable vocal chords.

Why did Alan provoke the way he did? The effects of World Cup glory at nineteen years of age? I don't think so. No, more likely it came from Alan Ball senior, his dad and mentor, a man driven and determined that his boy could take on the world. Alan Jr told me on more than one occasion how, despite playing brilliantly and earning club and international recognition, his father refused to praise him too highly. Anyone who listened to Bally's after dinner speech, which was riveting and revealing, will know exactly who had motivated him – the hard disciplinarian that was his father.

We got on well because I genuinely liked him and he in return enjoyed engaging in an argument with a teammate who I hope he respected but who he knew he could provoke into heated discussion – the state of the game, great players and managers, his outright disgust that I claimed to be Scottish. You name it, Bally and I spent hours on journeys debating it.

He gambled too much and drank in excess, loved his wife Lesley and his three children to distraction and always drew a crowd wherever he went. Laughter, wonderful raucous joking laughter, went hand in hand with tears and uncontrollable and unashamed weeping when you were in Alan's company. Like me, he cried too easily. Take the night when at a party thrown at comedian and Arsenal fan Bernie Winter's house, he took to the dance floor by himself with a glass of champagne in his hand and wept as he acknowledged what was the impending end of his illustrious career by singing Perry Como's 'Catch a Falling Star'.

That was a difficult night for him and there were plenty more to come. Often on a Sunday evening my wife Megs and I would answer the knocking at our door and there would be Alan begging to come in and have a drink while discussing his future without the playing side of football.

He never let down those he liked and we were looking forward to him again gracing our Willow Foundation Annual Golf Day when, five days before it took place, the news of his heart attack and tragic death took a very unique character away from us all.

Only at his funeral at Winchester Cathedral could one appreciate Alan Ball's impact on his fellow man. As his coffin was borne aloft for the last time, spontaneous applause broke out and seconds later cheers, chanting and whoops. Evocative, emotional, extraordinary – that was Bally.

⚽ ⚽ ⚽

Alan James Ball

Born:
12 May 1945, Farnworth
Died:
25 April 2007, Warsash

Position:
Midfield

Clubs as player:
1962–66 Blackpool, 116 games (40 goals)
1966–71 Everton, 250 games (78 goals)
1971–76 Arsenal, 217 games (52 goals)
1976–78 Southampton, 234 games (13 goals)
1978–79 Philadelphia Fury, 34 games (5 goals)
1979–80 Vancouver Whitecaps, 38 games (10 goals)
1980–81 Blackpool, 30 games* (5 goals)
1981–82 Southampton, 63 games* (2 goals)
1982–83 Eastern AA, 12 games
1983–84 Bristol Rovers, 17 games* (2 goals)

Internationals:
1965–75 England, 72 caps (8 goals)

Clubs as manager:
1980–81 Blackpool
1984–89 Portsmouth
1989–91 Stoke City
1991–94 Exeter City
1994–95 Southampton
1995–96 Manchester City
1998–99 Portsmouth

Honours as player with Everton:
1970 Division One

Honours as player with England:
1966 World Cup

Awards:
2000 MBE

– *The Toffeemen* –

The Toffeemen or Toffees have been the established nicknames for Everton Football Club from its very early days and are likely to have come about as a result of the following story. Many early club meetings were held at the Queen's Head Hotel, which was near Ye Anciente Everton Toffee House run by a woman known as Old Ma Bushell. She produced Everton Toffees, which she sold in large numbers to the fans who came to watch Everton play in the new Football League. However, in 1892, the club moved from Anfield to Goodison Park, displacing her market and consequently reducing her sales to nothing.

Instead, near the new ground was Mother Noblett's Toffee Shop, but Mother Noblett couldn't take advantage of her new-found bit of fortune, as Old Ma Bushell had patented the Everton Toffee. So Mother Noblett created the Everton Mint, which – with the black and white stripes of an earlier Everton strip – was a huge success.

Refusing to be beaten by the creative Mrs Noblett, Old Ma Bushell successfully persuaded the club to let her distribute her Everton Toffees to the fans inside the ground before kick-off. She employed the services of her beautiful grand-daughter Jemima Bushell who, wearing her best hat and dress, went around the ground with a basket full of toffees. So the tradition of the Everton Toffee Lady – which remains to this day – was born.

Tom Finney

If all the brains in the game sat in committee to design the perfect player, they would come up with a reincarnation of Tom Finney.

Lancashire newspaper feature

Tom Finney would have been great in any team, in any match, in any age ... even if he'd been wearing an overcoat.

Bill Shankly, former Preston North End teammate

⚽ ⚽ ⚽

Loyalty is a word which means very little to the modern-day footballer. Money, agents and commercial possibilities have brought an end to the sort of loyalty of yesteryear which is epitomised best by Tom Finney.

He was born in Preston, one street away from Deepdale, the stadium at which he played his football for fourteen years. It would have been much longer had the Second World War not brought an end to normal competition. Despite his brilliance, Preston North End won nothing during his time there. He would supplement his £14 per week salary, the maximum under regulations at that time, by working as a plumber. For many years you could ring the phone number of his plumbing business and invariably Tom would answer.

That's how I first got to meet him when he agreed to an interview at his home for *Football Focus*. He seemed genuinely delighted to be asked and was most accommodating about time and place. Before I had met him I had watched only black and white film of him, listened to stories about him and read countless articles, notably in Charles Buchan's *Football Monthly*, that talked of his prowess and often compared his ability with Stan Matthews. It was one of the questions I asked him when we conducted the interview in his modest home. Tom was as complimentary about Stan as Matthews had been about him. They didn't altogether go along with the oft-suggested intense rivalry that the media put forth. Tom had more to his game than Matthews. He was far more versatile and although enjoying the right wing position, which was Stan's domain, Tom was equally at home at inside right or left, centre forward or left winger. He was adept with right or left foot and scored lots of goals. Stan was more of a creator from the right wing. For four of his fourteen seasons at Deepdale he had a strike rate of more than one goal every other game. It took only one month of playing at Preston before England called on him. Seventy-six caps and 30 goals was more proof of Tom Finney's ability. His modesty matched his genius.

He had only positive words to say about the players of his era and those of the modern day. His stories of his time in the Royal Armoured Corps where he was part of Montgomery's Eleventh Army, were amazing, especially the games of football that he played between Army sides and North African opposition.

The perfect gentleman, Tom was interested in comparing his time at Preston with mine at Arsenal. We agreed that loyalty to our respective clubs had sadly become a dying trait.

Such was my excitement at having met Tom that I got carried away in my thanks outside his home. My cameraman had handed the tape of our interview to me to take back to London. I placed the can on top of my car and returned to shake his hand again. Only when I'd travelled several miles did my thoughts return to the tape, which had slid off the roof as I left and was happily retrieved by Tom, who was waiting with a laugh when I duly returned to his residence.

⚽ ⚽ ⚽

Sir Thomas 'Tom' Finney

Born:
5 April 1922, Preston

Position:
Outside right

Clubs as player:
1946–60 Preston North End, 473 games (210 goals)

Internationals:
1946–58 England, 76 caps (30 goals)

Awards:
1954 FWA Footballer of the Year
1957 FWA Footballer of the Year
1961 OBE
1992 CBE
1998 Knighthood

– *Bosman Ruling* –

When a former teammate of mine, George Eastham, challenged the law concerning restraint of trade in 1963 and won, the decision made a huge impact on the game in Britain. Thirty-two years later a Belgian footballer of less fame than Eastham challenged the European Courts, also concerning freedom of movement for workers and also triumphed.

In 1995 Jean-Marc Bosman took the Belgian and European footballing authorities to the European Court of Justice and challenged them on the free movement of workers between member states, arguing that the football regulations on payment of transfer fees stopped EU citizens from having the human right of freedom of movement in employment. Prior to the Bosman case, players were registered with a club and it was this registration which transferred between clubs when a transfer was made. A fee would be demanded for the movement of players. The European Court of Justice ruled in favour of Jean-Marc Bosman, deciding that the existing football transfer rules were in breach of the European Union law on the free movement of workers between member states. As a result of this, 'the European Union demanded that regulations concerning players' transfers and limitations on foreign players be amended almost immediately'.

Jean-Marc Bosman's victory has had a profound effect on any transfer of football players within the EU preventing clubs from demanding transfer fees for out-of-contract players who move from one club to another and removing restrictions on the number of foreigners who can play for a particular club.

The new ruling also means that players are now allowed to discuss and negotiate their own deals with a new employer when their previous contract has expired. This puts top players in a very powerful position with their own clubs – and with potential buyers – when their contracts are nearing an end. Transfer fees that used to be paid directly to the clubs could be reinvested on talented players or on the infrastructure of the clubs. The new rules now mean that top players and their advisors control much of what was previously transfer money.

What it also means is that many other footballers born outside the EU could, by taking advantage of EU naturalisation rules, obtain a passport of a member country. Either having some form of European ancestor or fulfilling long-term residency requirements enables individuals to widen their choice of employment across Europe. The best examples of this policy are the Argentines who obtain Italian or Spanish nationality and many Brazilians who do the same through Portugal.

Jean-Marc Bosnan is something of a hero to many multinational players but not to UEFA who were prohibited by the ruling from imposing any quotas on the number of foreign players. At the time many leagues had in place a system restricting the number of non-nationals and UEFA similarly prohibited teams in the Champions League, Cup Winners' Cup and UEFA Cup from including more than three foreign players in their match-day squads.

Since Bosman, UEFA have continued to look for ways of reversing some of the effects of the ruling and in 2005 52 member federations unanimously approved a rule designed to increase the number of locally trained players. However, several of Europe's big clubs, notably Barcelona and Chelsea made it clear they were not happy with the proposals and even threatened a challenge in the courts.

More recently in 2008 the FIFA president, Sepp Blatter, is pursuing an acceptance of his proposals for a 'six plus five' ruling. This would mean clubs could no longer include, in their team line up, more than five foreign players. The Premier League would suffer if this proposal was adopted as only 34 per cent of current players are 'home-grown'. In countries such as Germany, France, Spain and Italy the percentage is around 60 per cent. It would seem unlikely that Blatter's proposal will be accepted as it goes against European law on employment.

PFA Chief Executive Gordon Taylor describes Blatter's plan as 'tilting at windmills'. However there is an alternative proposal which is backed by the EU and that is for a 'four plus four' rule whereby in any squad of 25 players, at least four players would need to have been trained by a club itself for a period of three years between the ages of fifteen and 21, plus another four players being developed within the same national association, using similar criteria.

Once again there is opposition to this proposal. As an eighteen-year-old, Cristiano Ronaldo signed for Manchester United from Sporting Lisbon for nearly £13 million and Cesc Fabregas joined Arsenal also as a teenager – each of them would qualify under the new proposals as home-grown players.

Jock Stein

The best place to defend is in the other side's penalty box.

Jock Stein

The greatest manager in the history of the game. You tell me a manager anywhere in the world who did something comparable; winning the European Cup with a Glasgow District XI.

Hugh McIlvanney, 1997, *The Football Men*

❂ ❂ ❂

What is it within the Scottish character that creates truly special football managers? Doggedness, vision, enthusiasm, bloody mindedness. Each of the four greatest managers to come out of Scotland had these qualities. Sir Matt Busby, Bill Shankly, Sir Alex Ferguson and Jock Stein. Jock had already achieved success as the first non-Catholic manager of Celtic before he gained immortality by guiding the Bhoys to European Cup glory in 1967, the first British club to lift the trophy. What makes that Celtic team so unique is that all of its members were born within 30 miles of Glasgow.

Jock enjoyed a bet and a drink but neither distracted his attention from the job at hand of winning cups, which he did with his first three clubs. Forty-five days in charge of Leeds United was hardly enough time to add to the 26 trophies he lifted at Dunfermline, Hibernian and Celtic. He left Elland Road when offered the position of Scotland manager in 1978 and it was from that time until his heart attack and tragic death at Ninian Park, Cardiff on 10 September 1985 that his extracurricular activities working as a TV pundit brought us together.

His sheer presence coupled with an extraordinary CV meant that his opinion was always sought first. Often Jock's views were so all-embracing that there was little else to say for the rest of the guests. If they waffled too much he would cut them dead with a sublime aside.

During one of the tournaments when Jock was working for the BBC I asked him and fellow panellists Trevor Brooking and the 1974 World Cup Final referee Jack Taylor if they'd like to come to my Hertfordshire home for lunch. They all accepted and we duly sat around the dining room table as the roast beef was cut and plated. Jack Taylor had already been holding forth about the standard of refereeing we'd seen, asking questions all the time of the rest of us. Scotland's manager politely listened for a few minutes before deciding it was time to concentrate on the food: 'Och Jack man, will ye no stop blabbing. We're all hungry.'

It was not the first or last time Jock Stein expressed himself forcibly to others as well as me. There was an occasion when I had put forward my views about his selection of Alan Rough as Scotland goalkeeper. Alan was a terrific talent but at the time he was only a part-timer at Partick Thistle and having been an amateur myself in a professional game, I laid out what I saw as the dangers of taking Rough to the World Cup finals. I thought he should become a full-time professional first. Jock must have been watching as in an interview with Scottish TV Jock gave me a sharp retort and put me squarely in my place: 'What does Bob Wilson know about it? He's a goalkeeper. Keepers can't see a thing beyond their eighteen-yard box. They're all mad.'

His words received wide coverage on TV and in newspapers and I was duly admonished.

A couple of famous quotes from Jock Stein help sum up the demands he put on his players and the philosophy he held on the way the game should be played:

Celtic jerseys are not for second best. They don't shrink to fit inferior players.

We did it by playing football. Pure, beautiful, inventive football.

(Jock Stein's words after winning the European Cup with Celtic, Lisbon 1967)

The biggest tribute paid to Jock's achievements in Lisbon came from Bill Shankly when he told Stein, 'John, you're immortal now.'

⚽ ⚽ ⚽

John 'Jock' Stein

Born:
5 October 1922, Burnbank, South Lanarkshire
Died:
10 September 1985, Cardiff

Position:
Centre half

Clubs as player:
1942–50 Albion Rovers, 200 games*
1950–51 Llanelli Town
1951–56 Celtic 147, games (2)

Clubs as manager:
1960–1964 Dunfermline Athletic
1964–1965 Hibernian
1965–1978 Celtic
1978 Leeds United

International teams as manager:
1965 Scotland
1978–1985 Scotland

Honours as manager at Dunfermline:
1961 Scottish Cup

Honours as manager at Celtic:
1965 Scottish Cup
1966 Scottish League and League Cup
1967 European Cup, Scottish League, Scottish Cup and League Cup
1968 Scottish League and League Cup
1969 Scottish League, Scottish Cup and League Cup
1970 Scottish League and League Cup
1971 Scottish League and Scottish Cup
1972 Scottish League and Scottish Cup
1973 Scottish League
1974 Scottish League and Scottish Cup
1975 Scottish Cup and League Cup
1977 Scottish League and Scottish Cup

Awards:
1970 CBE

– *Scottish champions* –

1891	Dumbarton & Rangers		1918	Rangers
1892	Dumbarton		1919	Celtic
1893	Celtic		1920	Rangers
1894	Celtic		1921	Rangers
1895	Heart of Midlothian		1922	Celtic
1896	Celtic		1923	Rangers
1897	Heart of Midlothian		1924	Rangers
1898	Celtic		1925	Rangers
1899	Rangers		1926	Celtic
1900	Rangers		1927	Rangers
1901	Rangers		1928	Rangers
1902	Rangers		1929	Rangers
1903	Hibernian		1930	Rangers
1904	Third Lanark		1931	Rangers
1905	Celtic		1932	Motherwell
1906	Celtic		1933	Rangers
1907	Celtic		1934	Rangers
1908	Celtic		1935	Rangers
1909	Celtic		1936	Celtic
1910	Celtic		1937	Rangers
1911	Rangers		1938	Celtic
1912	Rangers		1939	Rangers
1913	Rangers		*Not held from 1940–46*	
1914	Celtic		1947	Rangers
1915	Celtic		1948	Hibernian
1916	Celtic		1949	Rangers
1917	Celtic		1950	Rangers
			1951	Hibernian

1952	Hibernian	1981	Celtic
1953	Rangers	1982	Celtic
1954	Celtic	1983	Dundee United
1955	Aberdeen	1984	Aberdeen
1956	Rangers	1985	Aberdeen
1957	Rangers	1986	Celtic
1958	Heart of Midlothian	1987	Rangers
1959	Rangers	1988	Celtic
1960	Heart of Midlothian	1989	Rangers
1961	Rangers	1990	Rangers
1962	Dundee	1991	Rangers
1963	Rangers	1992	Rangers
1964	Rangers	1993	Rangers
1965	Kilmarnock	1994	Rangers
1966	Celtic	1995	Rangers
1967	Celtic	1996	Rangers
1968	Celtic	1997	Rangers
1969	Celtic	1998	Celtic
1970	Celtic	1999	Rangers
1971	Celtic	2000	Rangers
1972	Celtic	2001	Celtic
1973	Celtic	2002	Celtic
1974	Celtic	2003	Rangers
1975	Rangers	2004	Celtic
1976	Rangers	2005	Rangers
1977	Celtic	2006	Celtic
1978	Rangers	2007	Celtic
1979	Celtic	2008	Celtic
1980	Aberdeen		

Don Revie

An utterly brilliant manager, but knotted with fear.

Gary Sprake, 1980, Leeds goalkeeper

Don Revie was the cleverest of all of us. He walked out before they threw him out.

Sven Goran Eriksson, England manager, 2003

⚽ ⚽ ⚽

A great player with innovative tactical genius and an outstanding manager with Leeds United – how sad it is then that much of what is written about Don Revie is tarnished with harsh judgment and some jealousy.

Rarely has anyone achieved so much and been so criticised in equal proportion. I first took an interest in Don Revie when he was the deep-lying centre forward in a Manchester City FA Cup-winning side of 1956 which contained my hero, goalkeeper Bert Trautmann. Revie's tactical role had evolved from the brilliant Hungarian side who thrashed England at Wembley 6–3 thanks in part to their deep-lying striker Nándor Hidegkuti. Don's footballing brain appreciated the problems such tactics created for opponents and so the 'Revie Plan' was adopted with great reward at Maine Road.

There were only plaudits for Revie the player but despite his brilliance as a manager in turning Leeds United into the major force in English football in the late 60s and early 70s, his methods were clouded by accusations of violent play, gamesmanship, superstition and bribery.

My time in the Arsenal first team goal spanned Leeds' glory years between 1968 and 1974. I claimed the number one jersey at Highbury one week after Leeds had beaten Arsenal in the 1968 League Cup Final. It was a truly horrible spectacle watching from the bench, a game full of bad tackles, bad sportsmanship and an ugly winning goal as Jack Charlton impeded Jim Furnell, and Terry Cooper gratefully accepted the loose ball and volleyed it into the Arsenal net.

It wasn't long before I understood the difficulties my predecessor in goal had faced at Wembley. At every set piece, especially corner kicks, Leeds would put 6' 3" centre half Jack Charlton into a near-post position and then ensure that another of their players, sometimes Paul Madeley or even Peter Lorimer, stood on or close to the opposing keeper's toes. Engaging in conversation with keepers was another distraction that Leeds employed. You simply had to ignore the chat. Judging violent play in that era is difficult. There was little protection offered by referees in the manner of the modern-day approach. Leeds could dish out some 'tasty' tackles with Johnny Giles in particular acquiring an 'evil' tag.

Having said that, Arsenal were no angels; indeed few, if any, of the teams of that era were. So yes, gamesmanship and violent play were part of Leeds' approach. Their superstitions are all hearsay to everyone except their own players, but it did seem that they overdid the beliefs. Many judges feel Don Revie's side would have won far more had their rituals been ignored. Six major trophies lifted is outstanding reward but perhaps the nine runners-up tags explain why such a great footballing team have been judged so harshly.

Leeds were capable of memorable football, passing skills that were beautiful to watch and humiliating to face. Twenty to 30 passes were the norm when Leeds had a stranglehold on a game. They had naturally gifted players who should have won far more. That the Arsenal side of 1970–71 overhauled a twelve-point deficit between February and May on the way to winning the Double is part miracle, part mystery. Don Revie was quick to praise manager Bertie Mee and all the players on the achievement shortly after the end of that season when we met up for BBC TV work. The Leeds manager gave me a huge bear hug saying that he believed that we had 'nicked' it because our two strikers John Radford and Ray Kennedy had outshone and outscored his front men and that I had enjoyed 'one of those crazy seasons goalkeepers can only dream of'. He was passionate about football and the characters it created.

His appointment as England manager seemed a good one but it was a surprise that he was incapable of bringing his Leeds magic to the England national arena. His decision to quit England for monetary gain in the Middle East was questionable but he quite rightly fought and successfully overturned the ten-year suspension the FA imposed upon him for allegedly bringing the game into disrepute.

There were also the numerous claims that Leeds personnel – including Don Revie himself – had tried to bribe opponents but in the often murky world of football the accusations were impossible to prove.

For someone who had contributed so much to the game, had been Footballer of the Year in 1955 and Manager of the Year in 1969, 1970 and 1972, there should be a glittering epitaph. It's sad that has not been the case for Don, but much sadder was his rapid deterioration in health after he was diagnosed with motor neurone disease in 1987. He was bearing his illness stoically when I met him for the last time shortly before his death at the far-too-young age of 61. It was a time to look back rather than forward and his eyes were bright when I recalled the greatness of his Leeds teams.

☻ ☻ ☻

Donald George 'Don' Revie

Born:
10 July 1927, Middlesbrough
Died:
26 May 1989, Edinburgh

Position:
Striker

Clubs as player:
1944–49 Leicester City, 110 games (29 goals)
1949–51 Hull City, 76 games* (12 goals)
1951–56 Manchester City, 177 games (41 goals)
1956–58 Sunderland, 64 games* (15 goals)
1958–62 Leeds United, 84 games (13 goals)

Internationals:
1954–55 England, 6 caps (4 goals)

Clubs as manager:
1961–74 Leeds United
1977–80 United Arab Emirates
1980–83 Al-Nasr
1984 Al-Ahly

International teams as manager:
1974–77 England

Honours as player with Manchester City:
1956 FA Cup

Honours as manager at Leeds United:
1968 League Cup and Inter-Cities Fairs Cup
1969 First Division and FA Charity Shield
1971 UEFA Cup
1972 FA Cup
1974 First Division

Awards:
1955 FWA Footballer of the Year
1969 Manager of the Year
1970 Manager of the Year
1972 Manager of the Year

– *Foreign investors and English clubs* –

Aston Villa – Randy Lerner (US)

Chelsea – Roman Abramovich (Russia)

Derby County – General Sports and Entertainment LLC (US-based company)

Liverpool – Tom Hicks (US) and George Gillett (US)

Manchester City – Abu Dhabi United Group (United Arab Emirates)

Manchester United – the Glazer family (US)

Portsmouth – Milan Mandaric (Serbia) took over the club in 1998 and sold a 50 per cent stake to Alexandre Gaydamak (French) in 2006

Queens Park Rangers – Flavio Briatore (Italy) owns 34 per cent and the family of Lakshmi Mittal (India) owns 20 per cent. Briatore is the boss of the Ferrari F1 team and a further 15 per cent of QPR is owned by Bernie Ecclestone, the head of Formula 1.

West Ham – Bjorgolfur Gudmundsson (Iceland)

⚽ ⚽ ⚽

When Chelsea won back-to-back Premiership titles in 2005 and 2006 you would be hard-pressed to find any dissenting voice among the Blues fans on how that success had been achieved. After all, their previous league title had been won 50 years previously, which is a long wait.

The plain truth is that without the investments into the club made by one of the richest men in the world, Roman Abramovich, it's highly unlikely Chelsea would now be counted among the so-called 'big four' alongside Manchester United, Liverpool and Arsenal. While United and Liverpool have since taken on American investors, only Arsenal continues to strive in the traditional manner, with a board of directors and a group of shareholders. However an American and Russian tycoon recently bought a considerable number of shares in Arsenal. Buying success is nothing particularly new. After all, Blackburn Rovers' league title triumph in 1995 came courtesy of multi-millionaire chairman Jack Walker. Such individuals don't guarantee success, as Sir Jack Hayward's huge investment with Wolves proves, but they sure help.

I am a traditionalist but appreciate fully that football has become big business and that today money talks. My only concern is how the investors buy the British clubs, often borrowing massively to finance the deal. I worry for the immediate future of those great clubs should the owners decide to pull out or lose their enthusiasm. One thing for certain is that, as it exists at present, the main prizes of league championship and Champions League are no longer competed for on a level playing field. Only when every Premiership club has a major investor will we cease to see the three-tier system within the league that exists in 2008. If this is not a worry to the Premiership or FA hierarchy, it should

243

be. If the same four teams continually fight it out for the two top titles the competition will ultimately become a bore, not to the fans of the big four, but to the wider footballing community who are the lifeblood of the game.

Jimmy Hill

If he can find a ground where he scored a league goal, I'll meet him there.

Brian Clough, 1979,
taking up Jimmy Hill's challenge for a debate

It took me sixteen years to realise that football is a passing game and not a dribbling game.

Jimmy Hill, 1974,
former Fulham footballer and TV pundit

⚽ ⚽ ⚽

There have been times when Jimmy Hill has driven me mad, never intentionally, but in an aggravating way. Over the years, as I got to know him, he won my utmost respect, was a valued colleague and became someone I loved. I suspect Jimmy's various wives, acquaintances, close friends and family might say the same. But when you have a personality like his, which is open, honest, infectious and confrontational, there will always be moments of disagreement, alongside a barrel-load of laughs.

The famous Hill chin, often likened to that of comedian Bruce Forsyth, has added to his cult appeal. He has never been afraid to lead with it, put his views on the line, be prepared to take the brickbats full on and then, with a mixture of intensity and humour, leave everyone with whom he came into contact thinking hard about what he had said.

Jimmy Hill deserves a reputation as one of the great innovators in football. He was awarded an OBE but his all-round contribution to the game is more deserving of a knighthood. It is too easily forgotten that, as chairman of the Professional Footballers' Association, he successfully campaigned to have the football league's £20 maximum wage scrapped.

Jimmy Hill continued to think of and implement change wherever he went. At Coventry, as manager, he led the club to Third Division and Second Division championships, he persuaded his chairman, Derek Robbins, to redevelop the Highfield Road ground making it an all-seated stadium, changed the home kit colours to sky blue and penned the club song, which was sung to the tune of the 'Eton Boat Song'. After leaving Coventry in 1967 he moved into the television world, starting as technical advisor to a BBC series called *United*, before becoming head of sport at London Weekend, where he promptly put himself up as a pundit alongside presenters Dickie Davies and Brian Moore.

Jimmy has a huge ego, but why not? It was his idea of a three points for a win system, which the Football Association adopted in 1981, that changed the face of the game. He had boundless energy and undertook roles as managing director and then chairman at Coventry City, a short spell as chairman at Charlton, then chairman of Fulham where he helped his old club avoid bankruptcy and a proposed merger with Queens Park Rangers.

His work for charity has been huge and, with his love of grassroots football, he is life president of the London Football Coaches' Association.

My first contact with him however was at Highbury when famously, he needed some kit to put on, having volunteered to run the line in a First Division game after the referee had pulled a muscle and been replaced by the existing linesman. Jimmy took some stick from the crowd every time he raised his flag. He never seemed to worry about what people thought of him. 'Any publicity is good publicity', he would say. Around the time he waved the flag at Arsenal he had made himself very unpopular with our squad by declaring on TV, with some venom, that our midfield hard man, Peter Storey, should 'realise that if you live by the sword, then you die by the sword'. Peter had received a terrible injury from a reckless challenge in a game at Crystal Palace.

Such strong views characterised his approach to the job and led to deep feelings about him. Once we ran a series of BBC Sport roadshows around the country where we met the fans. At Maine Road, Manchester he turned up late and was booed or heckled throughout the entire evening, but he still made them laugh as well. Laughter was always around the corner if you were in Jim's company. At Goodison Park while covering the match for the BBC, we needed to make our way from the dressing room area to the main camera gantry. I suggested we take the long route outside the ground and away from the fans. Jimmy insisted we walk around the cinder track surrounding the pitch. From the moment he appeared boos rang out and toffees were thrown at him, but his response was typical saying 'I told you they loved me!' followed by a wink and a grin.

Working alongside Jimmy Hill on *Match of the Day* was a lively experience. He rarely did the professional thing of giving a final check to his autocue – a machine which reflects the words about to be spoken, on a screen that surrounds and sits in front of the camera lens. One night, the autocue girl typing out Jimmy's script misread the 'a' in the word 'same' for an 'o'. It made a big difference to Jimmy's closing line but he was too late to correct it when he read: 'That's all for tonight. Hope you enjoyed it. *Match of the Day,* some time next week.' The familiar theme music and closing titles had cut him off by the time he realised his error. 'Oh no, oh dear!' was said in vain.

Another Saturday night all the fire alarms in the studio went off while we were on air. The noise was deafening, various assistants were running hither and thither when Jimmy turned to me and said, 'Bob, what shall we do?' I told him, 'Jim, I think we should get the hell out of here.' Quick as a flash he responded, 'No, no, no, we can't do that. The nation needs us!'

I possess a gold disc that was presented to each of the Arsenal Double squad for their rendition of 'Good Old Arsenal', which made the Top 10 in the charts in the week leading up to the 1971 FA Cup Final. We had been bemused when we learned that Jimmy Hill had written words for our song and even more surprised when Jimmy took time out to tell us all personally that, 'they are great lines and they'll be set to the tune of "Rule Britannia".'

It's a good job he didn't hear our laughter when he left us with copies of the lyrics. The pomp and splendour of 'Rule Britannia' was to encase the following: 'Good old Arsenal, we're proud to say that name. While we sing this song we'll win the game.'

The verse was then repeated three more times deleting Arsenal and inserting 'Bertie' for the second verse, 'Frankie' for the third and 'Charlie' for verse four. Bertie Mee, Frank McLintock and Charlie George had been chosen by Jimmy for their legendary status. Who would have thought that the song would be sung on the terraces nearly 40 years on – only with the names of today's heroes inserted. Surely a testament to Jimmy Hill's foresight and innovative nature.

❂ ❂ ❂

James William Thomas 'Jimmy' Hill

Born:
22 July 1928 Balham, London

Position:
Inside forward/striker

Clubs as player:
1949–53 Brentford, 83 games* (10 goals)
1953–61 Fulham, 276 games* (41 goals)

Clubs as manager:
1961–67 Coventry City

Honours as manager at Coventry City:
1964 Promotion to Division Two
1967 Promotion to Division One

Awards:
1975 OBE

– *Maximum wage* –

For the 1901–02 season a maximum wage of £4 per week was introduced in England by the Football Association. This was double what a skilled tradesman received. At the same meeting they also voted to outlaw match bonuses. The player's wage was only the basic form of remuneration. Benefits and international match fees for the better players needed to be considered alongside other less direct forms of income. To encourage men to play for clubs for some time, players were to be awarded a benefit after five years.

After the First World War, professional footballers received a maximum weekly wage of £10. In 1920 the Football League Management Committee proposed a reduction to £9 per week. The following year it was reduced to £8 for a 37-week playing season and £6 for the 15 weeks of close season.

There was no other change until 1945 when the maximum close-season wage was increased to £7 per week. Two years later a National Arbitration Tribunal was established. It decided that the maximum wage should be raised to £12 in the playing season and £10 in the close season. The minimum wage for players over twenty was set at £7.

The maximum wage was subsequently increased to £14 (1951), £15 (1953), £17 (1957) and £20 (1958). The players made further wage demands in 1960 and when these were backed by a threat to strike on 14 January 1961 the Football League responded by abolishing the maximum wage and increasing the minimum wage to £15.

Players were free to negotiate their terms and Johnny Haynes of Fulham was immediately paid £100 a week – a forerunner of today's high salaries.

Bob Paisley and Joe Fagan

*His great strength was that he knew something about everything ...
He could watch a game, even on TV and forecast that a player was
going to have an injury, and invariably he would be right.*

Kenny Dalglish, 1998, on Bob Paisley
(from *Manager of Millennium* by John Keith)

*Ranting and raving gets you nowhere in football. If you want to be
heard, speak quietly.*

Bob Paisley

*Mind you, I've been here during the bad times too. One year we came
second.*

Bob Paisley

*This is the second time I've beaten the Germans here. The first
time was in 1944. I drove into Rome on a tank when the city was
liberated.*

Bob Paisley, following the 1977 European Cup win
in Rome

❀ ❀ ❀

First Bob and then Joe were the two men given the unenviable
task of following in the footsteps of the legend that was Bill
Shankly. Shanks was almost as famous for his personality and
wonderful quotes as he was for turning around the fortunes
of Liverpool FC. Paisley and Fagan were, in personality, as
different from Bill Shankly as you could possibly imagine.

251

It would be difficult to name two more unassuming people than these. Frankly, with the frenzy of media attention nowadays, you could not see them ever being managers in the current game.

Yet both were winners who had learned their trade and the Liverpool way in the slipstream of Shankly. In his nine years as manager, Bob overtook his predecessor's trophy haul and until Sir Alex Ferguson surpassed his achievements, became the most successful manager in English history. Six League titles, three League Cups, three European Cups ... only the FA Cup eluded him. Joe Fagan's tenure was for only two years but in his first season he won three trophies including Liverpool's fourth European Cup. One year later, on 29 May 1985, just a few hours before Liverpool attempted to retain the trophy he announced his retirement, the ensuing defeat and terrible events of the Heysel Stadium disaster having nothing to do with the decision but impacting upon him in a dreadful way.

Both Bob and Joe were brilliant at their job but uncomfortable in areas it entailed. I became a TV presenter as Bob took over in 1974 and I don't recall one request for an interview being turned down, despite his unease with cameras and questions. Perhaps it was part 'old enemy' respect, although more likely Bob recognised that I was finding a new role and job as difficult to cope with as he was. Regularly I would be invited into Anfield's famous boot room, the small area where opposing managers and coaches would enjoy the special Liverpool hospitality after games. Other clubs have followed the Liverpool idea of a boot room, but few have been as atmospheric and welcoming. It was here that Bob talked about Bill Shankly's ability to deal with the media. He described Shanks as a natural, someone who could always find the perfect quote, one that would satisfy the most demanding of journalists. For Bob, words never came easily. He told me at first he tried to think up some ear-catching phrases before he was interviewed but quickly realised he was cheating both the scribes and himself. He preferred to be considered dull and cautious rather than be vulnerable to a hungry media pack:

> In time maybe, football managers will have to go on a public relations course before they are allowed to run a club. I try to co-operate where I can, but I'm too long in the tooth to change into a tub-thumping extrovert now.

What upset Bob most, and increasingly so, was the accusation that after getting the Liverpool job he gave his great predecessor Bill Shankly the cold shoulder and froze him out of the training ground at Melwood. Bob insisted that was never the case. For a start he never wanted the Liverpool manager's position for himself and after Bill had shocked everyone, including Bob, with his decision to quit, he actually tried to persuade Shankly to stay. It saddened him that their relationship faltered for a short time but he was comfortable that as 'boss' he didn't need any advice from Shanks but wanted to do things his own way. That, he insisted, is exactly what Bill Shankly told his staff when he had arrived at Anfield from Huddersfield.

Perhaps that was the secret of the Liverpool way back then because when Bob called it a day in 1983 after his nineteenth and final managerial prize, Joe Fagan also trusted his own instincts and promptly won a treble of trophies in his first season.

Bob and Joe were so similar in many ways – very knowledgeable, grounded, humble, kind, steeped in the traditions of Liverpool FC and the most unlikely heroes.

⚽ ⚽ ⚽

Robert 'Bob' Paisley

Born:
23 January 1919, Hetton-Le-Hole, County Durham
Died:
14 February 1996, Woolton, Liverpool

Position:
Half back

Clubs as player:
1939–54 Liverpool, 278 games (13 goals)

Honours as player:
1947 First Division

Clubs as manager:
1974–83 Liverpool

Honours as manager:
1975 FA Charity Shield
1976 UEFA Cup and First Division
1977 European Cup, First Division and FA Charity Shield
1978 European Cup, European Super Cup and FA Charity Shield
(shared)
1979 First Division
1980 First Division and FA Charity Shield
1981 European Cup and League Cup
1982 First Division and League Cup
1983 First Division, League Cup and FA Charity Shield

Awards:
1976 Manager of the Year
1977 Manager of the Year
1979 Manager of the Year
1980 Manager of the Year
1982 Manager of the Year
1983 Manager of the Year
1977 OBE

⊛ ⊛ ⊛

Joe Fagan

Born:
March 12 1921, Liverpool
Died:
June 30 2001, Liverpool

Position:
Centre half

Clubs as player:
1947–51 Manchester City, 168 games

Honours as player:
1946–47 Promotion to First Division

Clubs as manager:
1983–85 Liverpool

Honours as manager at Liverpool:
1984 European Cup, First Division and League Cup

– *Referees and respect* –

Without question the respect shown by players towards match officials has deteriorated between my era of playing and before to the current day. Of course all referees and their linesmen, now called referees' assistants, plus the fourth official, have been subjected to a degree of disrespect since football began. Sadly in recent times and almost certainly as a direct result of the amount of money that is at stake in the modern game, officials have been facing disgraceful abuse.

Every time I see an individual player or a group of players chasing referees, turning their backs on them or screaming protestations in their direction, I generally shout 'Send them off!' When the referees fail to take such action it makes me more fearful for their role and, with millions of young eyes watching on, even more upset for the long-term future of football as a true sport.

In my professional career of 525 appearances in an Arsenal jersey, I was never booked or sent off. It's a proud record but I was lucky once. I'm still ashamed of how I set off in pursuit of the referee, Norman Burtenshaw, after he had awarded Leeds United a goal which the Arsenal team thought was offside in 1971. I chased the Great Yarmouth official round the back of the Elland Road goal and back onto the pitch. When I caught up with him he stood his ground, told me to 'bugger off' and 'get on with the game'. Some degree of common sense came back into my head and we got on with the match. Subsequently one of the six camera positions showed Jack Charlton's goal to be onside. I was lucky not to have been given a yellow card. All referees of that era spoke to players in a different manner than they do today.

'Bugger off' was a mild term compared with some of the banter between refs and players. Not only was there explicit language, officials would regularly give as good as they got when challenged. For example 'Ref, you're having an effing nightmare', would usually be met with an equally juicy reply, 'Well Frank, you're not much effing better yourself'.

Rarely, if ever, do I remember a player or group of players continuing to berate the referee and his assistants as they do now. It's one area where a yellow card combined with a sin bin would be of huge value. The yellow card means points accumulating and threat of suspension and the sin bin gives a cooling-off period for the offending person and a temporary advantage to that player's opponents.

If the game is to retain real credibility and provide a good example to the next generation, disrespect must be stamped out. There are numerous examples of disgraceful insolence but I offer two in pursuit of a change of direction.

When referee Andy D'Urso penalised Jaap Stam for fouling Juninho at Old Trafford on 29 January 2000 he was immediately surrounded by a wild, baying, out-of-control mob, which included such great players as Ryan Giggs, Nicky Butt, Gary Neville, David Beckham and skipper Roy Keane. It was another case of footballers going too far and disrespecting the most difficult job of refereeing. All deserved to be sent off. None was, presumably on the basis that the 60,000-plus faithful who had given up so much of their hard-earned cash to attend would have not had full value for money. Had Andy sent the lot off and other refs followed suit with Arsenal, Chelsea, Liverpool and the other clubs' players, the problem of respect for referees would not even be an issue now. Andy D'Urso lost respect that day. So too did Mike Riley in 2008 when he allowed Chelsea's Ashley Cole to turn his back on him for far too long after a shocking tackle on Spurs' Alan Hutton. The Reading manager, Steve Coppell, reflected what all decent folk felt when he said, 'To see the way officials are abused by players on a game-by-game basis, it's no wonder we have problems in society.'

The moment Mike Riley failed to punish Cole correctly he had added hugely to the problem. 'Calm down Ashley. Turn round and face me,' were the words he used. When, initially, that gained a negative response from the England full back, Riley became embroiled in a free for all with the Chelsea captain John Terry, Didier Drogba and eventually Ashley Cole himself. How ironic that the incident occurred in a week when the FA launched a 'Respect for Referees' initiative. Sadly referees can only impose pre-ordained punishments on players. They cannot teach manners.

Change, if ever it comes, will only be possible if the football world's governing body address the problem by a rule change that would permit only a captain of a team and the penalised player to challenge a decision. Surely if they can now prevent referees from reacting to abuse with the 'give as good as you get' attitude of yesteryear, they can impose a solution as simple and effective as this one.

Bobby Robson

It is not the critic who counts; not the man who points out how the strong man stumbles, or where the doer of deeds could have done them better. The credit belongs to the man who is actually in the arena, whose face is marred by dust and sweat and blood, who strives valiantly; who errs and comes short again and again; because there is not effort without error and shortcomings; but who does actually strive to do the deed; who knows the great enthusiasm, the great devotion, who spends himself in a worthy cause, who at the best knows in the end the triumph of high achievement and who at the worst, if he fails, at least he fails while daring greatly. So that his place shall never be with those cold and timid souls who know neither victory nor defeat.

Theodore Roosevelt, President of the United States
Used at the beginning of Bobby Robson's
World Cup Diary 1982–86

⚽ ⚽ ⚽

My first meeting with Bobby Robson was New Year's Day 1966. Fulham versus Arsenal at Craven Cottage. He was an established England international. I was making a rare first-team appearance for Arsenal, three years after joining the club. It was supposed to be my big chance after waiting patiently, following a handful of games as an amateur schoolteacher, for my main rival Jim Furnell to lose form. Ten minutes into the game I dislocated my elbow, but had to stay on the field because in those days there were no substitute keepers. I lasted 90 minutes in agony as Fulham won 1–0 with a Graham Leggatt free kick.

Johnny Haynes, George Cohen and Bobby Robson were all aware of my extreme discomfort and wished me well after the final whistle. Since the playing days our paths have crossed many times, for interview purposes in his various managerial positions. But my abiding memories of him will always return to a chance encounter on the island of Bermuda.

My wife Megs and I were on the island celebrating our 25th wedding anniversary. We were staying in a small chalet close to the beach and the sea. One evening as we were preparing to go off to dine I received a phone call.

'Is that you Bob?' was the question posed by a very familiar voice although I daren't assume it was the then current England manager on the line. When I replied in the affirmative and asked politely who was calling, there was a laugh and then confirmation for me, 'It's Bobby, Bobby Robson.' I then enquired how he knew I was in Bermuda. 'Because I hired my scooter from the same place as you did and they told me you and your wife were here.'

As Bermuda is a small island there is no car hire. You get around by taxi, bus or scooter. Bobby got to the point with two questions. Would we like to play golf and more immediately, could we join them for a barbeque within the hour? Well you don't turn down such a request from the England manager. We promptly cancelled our dinner booking and agreed to meet Bobby at a well-known point at the top of one of the few hills on Bermuda. He would then lead us back to the villa where he, his wife Elsie and two friends were staying. The problem was that he didn't want to be recognised by any paparazzi or media folk. He had just been on the receiving end of some fairly vitriolic publicity from the papers at home.

So Bobby instructed us to keep an eye out for a discreet point on the hill where he would make himself known. Half an hour later, as we neared the spot, we almost fell off our bike. Not only was Bobby standing in the most public of places for one and all to see but he was also wearing a top emblazoned with 'England' and bearing the three huge lions.

So much for being incognito, but it was typical of Bobby in that being in his company has always guaranteed laughter and learning in equal measure. We had a great evening and subsequent rounds of golf provided terrific entertainment. The Robson competitive spirit surfaced as early as the first green. I had drawn him as my partner and he had started with a double bogey. I was left with a tricky six-footer for us to halve the hole. The pressure increased after Bobby had given me one of his looks as I stood over the putt and offered the encouraging words 'Don't miss it!' Strangely I didn't but the mood was set for one of the most daunting eighteen holes I've ever played. The game was halved which Bobby just about accepted!

The prelude to the friendship came from meetings in television studios. My favourite interviewee was Bobby Robson. It was his manner, passion and insights into the game which made him as compulsive as Brian Clough. There was a problem for any presenter like me when Bobby was in full flow. He could often lose track of the original question, so you had to be on your guard, ready to prompt him, especially on the names of players and managers, referees and officials. Pronunciation was another worry for him but viewers generally loved his attempts to pronounce names like Mazzola, Solskjaer, Ljungberg and the like.

Bobby's problem regarding name recognition was not restricted to the studio. Bryan Robson, former England and Manchester United captain will tell you about the time prior to an international game when his manager met him for breakfast and greeted him with, 'Morning Bobby.' 'No Boss. You're Bobby; I'm Bryan!'

Presenting the 1998 World Cup finals for ITV was a highlight of my TV career. We struck lucky when we had exclusive coverage of England's quarter-final tie against Argentina. Alongside me ITV had produced a dream team of guests – two previous England managers; Terry Venables, who came so close to getting England to the final of Euro '96 and Bobby Robson who had gone one better by reaching a World Cup semi-final in Italia 1990, another match that saw England lose on penalties. Brian Moore was in the commentary box, Kevin Keegan alongside him. The game was dramatic from start to finish. Argentina took the lead, Michael Owen equalised with his wonder goal, David Beckham was sent off. Sol Campbell had a goal disallowed. 2–2 after extra-time, England lost 4–3 on penalties. The whole team in front and behind the camera were in top form but Bobby Robson in particular was able to fully transmit the glory and the pain of the occasion better than anyone.

The average audience throughout the entire programme was almost 24 million – it peaked at 26.5 million, the highest number of people ever tuned into one single TV channel. Bobby and all of us shared in an historic moment in the story of television.

At the BBC, *Match of the Day* was one of the programmes I fronted or, for a period, co-hosted with Jimmy Hill. One night, while getting together the news round-up, I took a call from Bobby who was distraught that he had had his car broken into at Birmingham City's St Andrew's Ground. He asked if we could put out an appeal on the programme. He wasn't worried about the clothing that had gone but he was understandably concerned about his 'little black book' that contained all his contact numbers for family, friends, footballers, directors, officials, agents. You name it they were all in that book.

I persuaded Bobby that we should just emphasise the family and close friends importance of the item rather than run the risk of blackmail should we over-elaborate and make a big deal of the details of the rich and famous. It was a difficult appeal. Luck rather than anything else led to Bobby's contact book being found on the street a few days later. Clearly whoever took it failed to realise its value.

Everyone in and outside football shared in the joy of his knighthood in 2002. The honour was for services to sport but it could equally have been for the courage he has shown since his battle with cancer began in 1991. Always thinking of others rather than himself, he phoned me last February not knowing I was on a golf course in Tobago. He instantly recalled our partnership on the fairways and greens of Bermuda. His voice was strong despite his latest daunting prognosis and the prospect of further problems from a scan he'd undergone that day.

The purpose of the call was to ask me to attend a launch of the Sir Bobby Robson Foundation, a new Early Cancer Trials Unit at the Northern Centre for Cancer Care. The Foundation focuses on the early detection and treatment of cancer and the clinical trials of new drugs that hopefully will eventually beat it.

So it was that, together with Jim Rosenthal and Des Lynam, we listened spellbound in March 2008 as Bobby relayed his fifteen-year battle with the disease to the gathered local community and national press corps. Five times Sir Bobby faced his own mortality and each time he came through the other side. Frustrated at the restrictions the illness put upon him, he remained alert, determined and totally enthusiastic about his latest challenge. It was a privilege for all of us to be asked to play a part in such a worthy cause.

I can't end my recollections of Bobby Robson on a serious note. It has to be with a little anecdote from Euro 2000 when we were working together in Holland. One day he arrived in the office in Amsterdam, looking worried and with panic written on his face. He'd lost his new mobile phone. Everyone ventured an idea on how to trace it. The simplest solution was to start by dialling the number and alerting all our ITV offices within the building to listen out for the ringing tone.

Bobby pointed to a mobile on the central desk and asked if he could use it. He then dialled and waited. His face was a picture as he listened intently and then turned to everyone present and said, 'You're not going to believe this, but my mobile's got an engaged tone!'"

One member of our group then said, 'Sure that's not your phone you're using Bobby?' Of course it was, and as laughter broke out over another Bobby Robson faux pas, he just raised his eyebrows, gave a look of embarrassment and promptly exited the room.

❂ ❂ ❂

Sir Robert William 'Bobby' Robson

Born:
18 February 1933, Sacriston, Co. Durham

Position:
Inside forward/midfield

Clubs as player:
1950–56 Fulham, 157 games (69 goals)
1956–62 West Bromwich Albion, 266 games (61 goals)
1962–67 Fulham, 213 games (11 goals)
1967–68 Vancouver Royals

Internationals:
1957–62 England, 20 caps (4 goals)

Clubs as manager:
1968 Fulham
1969–82 Ipswich Town
1990–93 PSV Eindhoven
1993–94 Sporting Lisbon
1994–96 Porto
1996–97 FC Barcelona
1998–99 PSV Eindhoven
1999–2004 Newcastle United

International teams as manager:
1982–90 England

Honours as manager at Ipswich Town:
1978 FA Cup
1981 UEFA Cup

Honours as manager at PSV Eindhoven:
1991 Eredivisie
1992 Eredivisie

Honours as manager at Porto:
1994 Taça de Portugal
1995 Liga de Portugal
1996 Liga de Portugal

Honours as manager at FC Barcelona:
1997 UEFA Cup Winners' Cup and Copa del Rey

Awards:
1990 CBE
2002 Knighthood
2007 BBC Lifetime Achievement Award

– *Match of the Day* –

I have a huge affection for the BBC's flagship football programme *Match of the Day*. Between 1974 and 1994 I enjoyed being part of the show on many occasions as either a co-host with Jimmy Hill, or as presenter.

Match of the Day was launched on BBC 2 on 22 August 1964 when Kenneth Wolstenholme introduced a single match between Liverpool and Arsenal. Ken presented from pitch-side at Anfield and had as a summariser former Arsenal player Wally Barnes. An estimated 20,000 viewers watched the programme and a game which Liverpool won 3–2. Fans that day could gain entrance to the ground for 25p.

MOTD switched channels to BBC 1 as the 1966–67 season began. By August 1970 the programme introduced its now-iconic theme tune, a goal of the month competition and the highlights of two matches. The format has changed very little since then although competition for the rights to show games has meant that there have been several seasons when *MOTD*, as a highlights programme for the league matches, was lost to ITV. In those seasons the BBC retained the *MOTD* title when showing live league, FA Cup or international games. Premiership highlights have been on the BBC from 1992–2001 and back again since 2004. The latest three-year contract between the BBC and the Premier League ensures that *MOTD* will remain on the air until at least 2010. The deal cost the BBC £171.6 million. In 2004 *MOTD 2* was introduced on Sunday evenings showing highlights of that day's action plus a round-up of the previous day.

Gary Lineker is the most recent presenter of *MOTD*, having taken over in 1999 from Desmond Lynam. Previous to Des, between 1973–88, Jimmy Hill was the main presenter with me – for a time – as co-host bringing a latest news round-up to the audience. David Coleman was the second host of *MOTD* when taking over from Kenneth Wolstenholme in 1969. Despite the various battles with ITV to win the rights to show football and the arrival of Sky TV as a big player in the business, the BBC has been able to keep *Match of the Day* on our screens, in one way or another, for 44 years. The programme has become synonymous with Saturday nights. As for the theme tune to *MOTD*, it was written by Leslie Statham of the Welsh Guards. Its real title is 'Drum Majorette'.

Kenny Dalglish

Few great players make the transition into management. The reason is that great players are normally like soloists in an orchestra. That was never Kenny. He was like a conductor who brought others into play. He understood that not everyone was blessed with the greatest skill. He had patience both as a player and a manager.

Bob Paisley, 1991, Liverpool manager

Is he better in mid field or up front? Och, just let him on the park.

Jock Stein

The best player this club has signed this century.

John Smith, 1986, Liverpool chairman

❂ ❂ ❂

Study the list of honours won by Kenny Dalglish in Scotland and England as player and manager and you can only marvel at a remarkably gifted footballing man.

Thirteen league titles; six FA Cups; six League Cups; three European Cups; one European Super Cup; one PFA Player of the Year trophy; twice Football Writers' Footballer of the Year winner; four Manager of the Year awards.

Truly astonishing! Thirty-six major awards (not counting FA Charity Shields), plus 102 international appearances for Scotland.

It is this record number of caps for his country that sort of unites the two of us and earns a smile and laughter when I explain its significance in relation to me. I love to tell people that not only did I play for Scotland but that I was in goal when the great Kenny Dalglish made his full international debut (he had been used as a sub in November 1971) and that Kenny and I went on to win 104 Scottish caps between us! It gets a laugh from the football community who recognise that Kenny received 102 caps while I got two.

It was 1 December when Kenny was selected for his first full game. He played his part in scaring a brilliant Holland team in the Olympic Stadium in Amsterdam. Johan Cruyff captained the emerging Dutch side, which went on to be World Cup runners-up three years later. While Kenny's close control and intelligent runs posed problems for Holland in defence, I was enjoying thwarting all that Rinus Michels' team could throw at us. It was 1–1 with a few minutes remaining. Then Barry Hulshoff's head beat my fists to a near post corner and we lost 2–1. Most of the Scottish squad, including my deputy Bobby Clark and manager Tommy Docherty congratulated me on a great display of goalkeeping. I don't recall Kenny saying anything to me, but I know he was disappointed to be on the losing side on such an important night for him. Only many years later did the truth emerge on how he felt. I bumped into Kenny and Alan Hansen at the Belfry golf course during the Ryder Cup between Europe and the USA. Somehow the conversation turned to that game in Amsterdam and Dalglish recollections came straight to the point: 'Aye, I remember it well Bob. You threw the jerseys' (an expression which basically means a player has made a bad error).

Always with Kenny Dalglish you run the risk of being on the end of a waspish tongue, the words delivered with a glint in his eye and a smile on his face. During my TV career Kenny was a frequent guest on the BBC. Where Bobby

Robson was a challenge to the presenter for his difficulty in remembering names, Kenny's quiet, quick-fire responses, coupled with the Scottish accent, often left me in the dark as to what he had said. It made challenging his arguments awkward and also led to letters from viewers who also found him difficult to follow. His presence though had an equally big impact. There was and is tremendous respect for Kenny and all his achievements. The tragedy of the Hillsborough disaster on 15 April 1989 won him many new admirers. Dalglish was in charge of Liverpool on that dreadful day when Nottingham Forest were the Red's opponents in an FA Cup semi-final. Ninety-six Liverpool supporters died. Kenny and his wife Marina conducted themselves with enormous dignity, leading the Liverpool players to many of the funerals that took place in the dark days that followed.

The Dalglishes continue to understand what is important in life and what isn't. Following Marina's diagnosis with, and subsequent recovery from, breast cancer in 2003, The Marina Dalglish Appeal raised £1.5 million for a centre of Oncology at University Hospital, Aintree which opened in June 2007. They have now set themselves a new and exciting challenge in conjunction with Clatterbridge Centre for Oncology to help build a much-needed Radiotherapy Centre in the Liverpool area, bringing the treatment closer to the patients. It's a hugely worthwhile cause headed by Marina with the help of Kenny – the most successful footballer Scotland has produced.

⚽ ⚽ ⚽

Kenneth Mathieson 'Kenny' Dalglish

Born:
4 March 1951, Glasgow

Position:
Forward

Clubs as player:
1969–77 Celtic, 322 games (167 goals)
1977–90 Liverpool, 515 games (172 goals)

Internationals:
1971–86 Scotland, 102 caps (30 goals)

Clubs as manager:
1985–91 Liverpool
1991–95 Blackburn Rovers
1997–98 Newcastle United
2000 Celtic

Honours as player with Celtic:
1972 Scottish League and Scottish Cup
1973 Scottish League
1974 Scottish League and Scottish Cup
1975 Scottish League Cup and Scottish Cup
1977 Scottish League and Scottish Cup

Honours as player with Liverpool:
1978 European Cup, European Super Cup and FA Charity Shield
(shared)
1979 First Division
1980 First Division and FA Charity Shield
1981 European Cup, League Cup and FA Charity Shield
1982 First Division and League Cup
1983 First Division, League Cup and FA Charity Shield
1984 European Cup, First Division and League Cup

Honours as player-manager at Liverpool:
1986 First Division and FA Cup
1987 FA Charity Shield (shared)
1988 First Division
1989 FA Cup and FA Charity Shield
1990 First Division and FA Charity Shield

Honours as manager at Liverpool:
1991 FA Charity Shield (shared)

Honours as manager at Blackburn Rovers:
1995 Premier League

Honours as manager at Celtic:
2000 Scottish League Cup

Awards:
1979 FWA Player of the Year
1983 FWA Player of the Year
1983 PFA Players Player of the Year
1986 Manager of the Year
1988 Manager of the Year
1990 Manager of the Year
1997 Manager of the Year
2004 MBE

– *The Bhoys* –

Soon after the Celtic FC was founded in 1887, the team acquired the popular moniker of Bold Boys from its fans. It's thought by the club that a postcard from around the end of the 19th century – which referred to the Celtic team as the Bould Bhoys – is the first tangible evidence of this peculiar spelling. Reputedly, the additional 'u' in 'bold' and 'h' in 'boys' was an attempt to indicate the Irish pronunciation of the phrase. The new spelling stuck, but over time it became abbreviated to simply the Bhoys, and the name stands to this day.

Peter Shilton

*I laugh when I recall the amount of players who have come up to
me after a game and said, 'I knew I only had the goalkeeper to beat
Lawrie, but when I looked up and saw it was Peter Shilton my
confidence drained from me!*

Lawrie McMenemy, Southampton manager

*I can remember all the great goalkeepers since the early 50s; Swift,
Trautmann, Yashin, Zoff and Jennings. Of course Banks was a
great goalkeeper as well but it would be hard to say if there was ever
a better keeper than Shilts on a consistent basis over a large number
of years. For me he's still the number one.*

Bobby Robson, England manager

*A good keeper can save you eighteen points a season. That's like
a striker scoring a winning goal every few games. It can mean the
difference between winning a title and missing out. Shilton was a
class act and class acts don't come cheap. In many people's eyes we
were mad to spend a record £270,000 on him. History now tells us
that Shilton was worth twice the price. We weren't mad at all, we
were magic.*

Brian Clough, Nottingham Forest manager

☙ ☙ ☙

'Shilts' is England's most capped footballer of all time. One
hundred and twenty-five caps is testament to his goalkeeping
greatness. His main rival during his England career was Ray
Clemence, who managers Don Revie and Ron Greenwood
considered to be Peter's equal. Ron even had a spell of

alternating the two men, which was wrong in the long-term both for the team spirit and the keeper's confidence. Ray won 61 caps, so it's feasible that the Shilton total could have been nearer 190 caps without his challenger's presence.

Within that record number of appearances for his country Peter Shilton experienced everything football could throw at him – unbelievable saves, occasional moments of misjudgement and, of course, the 'hand of God' and Diego Maradona's infamous goal during the 1986 World Cup.

The dramatic highs and lows inherent in the position make keepers different to outfield players. Some say 'you have to be mad' to be a goalie. I will settle for the word 'different'. Character, personality, courage and presence are the essential ingredients and Shilts' ambition of wanting to be the best made him probably the most dedicated keeper of all time – *Magnificent Obsession* was the title of one of the books written about him. During his playing career he had a plaque near his front door which had inscribed upon it his astrological sign of Virgo. It stated: 'I am a perfectionist, but that's because I pay so much attention to detail. In life I might appear cold but I'm really sincere and always willing to give.'

I first became aware of Peter in May 1966, the year that England won the World Cup, at a time when my three years as a professional goalkeeper at Arsenal had produced only a dozen or so first-team appearances. He was sixteen when he made his debut for his hometown club, Leicester City. City's number one keeper Gordon Banks was about to become a World Cup hero. Within twelve months the young Shilton had issued an ultimatum to his club, 'Banksy or me? Take your pick.' Everyone in the football world was astonished when Leicester decided to let the 28-year-old Banks move to Stoke City. That confidence in himself never left Peter Shilton, at least publicly. He drove himself on in a manner that has rarely been seen in the game. Through thick and thin, success and failure, winning trophies and facing relegations, he never allowed himself to be distracted when it came to goalkeeping.

Playing against him as the opposing keeper was a challenge. His brash youthful approach to his trade could, if you let it, make you edgy. When, for a short time, he wore a white goalkeeping jersey we thought, at Arsenal, he'd got it wrong. A black, blue or green jersey is subdued enough for opponents to be completely confident of your position. Wearing white made it much easier for opponents to assess his position and make the appropriate decision to shoot, chip or hang on to the ball.

Shilts simply kept his belief and it served him well throughout a career in which he played in excess of 1,000 games and won five trophies including two European Cups and a League title. For five of the clubs he represented he made more than 100 appearances, a rarity in keeping with the man.

For a short time during his spell at Southampton, the manager Lawrie McMenemy asked me to do some coaching of his keepers. All, including Peter were respectful, but only Shilts insisted on doing certain activities his way. By then he was in his thirties and decided he knew what was best for him. Peter was not just ambitious; he also had a ruthless streak. He was part loner and, of his own admission, had difficulty living with himself. 'I isolate myself because I want to be my own man. People can see too much of you, get to know you too much. It's just not me. In any case, I can't get close because I'm too involved with myself.'

The two managers who understood him best were Lawrie McMenemy at Southampton and Brian Clough at Nottingham Forest. The build-up to Forest's second European Cup triumph includes a story which illustrates Clough's genius and his use of psychology on his own team and not just the enemy. Ten days before the final against Hamburg the Forest manager took his team away to Majorca so that, after 75 competitive games, they could recharge batteries before one big final match. All the squad enjoyed the sun and the break from training, all that is except his goalkeeper. Without his daily training Peter Shilton was like a bear with a sore head and in Majorca there was little or no grass, just sand and rocks. Shilts kept asking his manager when he was going to be able to train properly. 'When we get to Madrid young man,' was the Clough response, except that when they arrived in Spain the hotel was in the mountains and the Shilton training routine was again thwarted. Cloughie's idea was to keep Peter away from his strenuous workout in the hope that he would react in the appropriate way once he was on a beautiful grassy surface for the last training session and the final itself.

The final of the 25th European Cup took place in the Bernabeu Stadium. At the end of 90 minutes Hamburg's English star Kevin Keegan could only stand and applaud his international colleague Peter Shilton whose goalkeeping had ensured that John Robertson's goal won the day for Forest. On that night there was no better goalkeeper in the world than Peter Shilton, a man possessed with a singular winning streak and passionate beyond distraction. For all his success, Shilts will always be remembered best for his involvement in Diego Maradona's handball goal which Tunisian referee Ali Bin Nasser and his linesman failed to spot. Peter to this day,

fails to understand how the officials could not see that a 5' 6"
Argentine would find it impossible to jump high enough to
head a ball above a 6'-plus keeper's jump. Twenty-two years
on from that incident the governing bodies of the game
worldwide and at home still fail to recognise the value of
instant replays so that a crucial decision ends up being the
correct one.

Harry Hibbs, Frank Swift, Gordon Banks, Pat Jennings and
David Seaman would run Peter Shilton close in any debate
about the greatest British keeper ever, but there would be no
argument about who was the most obsessed by his craft.

✲ ✲ ✲

Peter Leslie Shilton

Born:
18 September 1949, Leicester

Position:
Goalkeeper

Clubs as player:
1966–74 Leicester City, 297 games (1 goal)
1974–77 Stoke City, 110 games*
1977–82 Nottingham Forest, 202 games*
1982–87 Southampton, 242 games
1987–92 Derby County, 203 games
1992–95 Plymouth Argyle, 34 games* (as player-manager)
1995 Bolton Wanderers, 1 game
1996–97 Leyton Orient, 9 games*

Internationals:
1970–90 England, 125 caps

Honours as player with Nottingham Forest:
1978 First Division and League Cup
1979 European Cup and League Cup
1980 European Cup

Awards:
1978 PFA Players' Player of the Year
1986 MBE
1991 OBE

– *The Twelfth Man* –

There is no doubting the effect of the twelfth man. The home World Cup victories of Uruguay (1930), Italy (1934), England (1966), Germany (1974), Argentina (1978) and France (1998) are no coincidence. A study by *The Times* in 2006 found that in the English Premiership, a home team can be expected to score 37.29 per cent more goals than an away team, this of course due in part to the benefit of the twelfth man.

The term originated in Dallas on 2 January 1922, when Texas A&M University were playing defending national champions, Centre College, in the American football Dixie Classic (the forerunner of today's Cotton Bowl). The ferocity of the game and resulting injuries ensured A&M ran out of reserves by the end of the first half. The only eleven remaining fit players were on the pitch. So the coach turned to the stands and from the A&M fans picked out E. King Gill as his possible back-up substitute. Gill agreed so swapped clothes with one of the injured players and stood ready on the touchline throughout the rest of the game. It turned out that there were no further injuries and so Gill was unused. Nevertheless, with his immediate willingness to help under the circumstances, he ensured that he had already written himself into A&M University folklore. He came to be known as the twelfth man.

After his graduation and subsequent departure from the university, all A&M students, in homage to that day in 1922, would remain standing for the duration of each game their team played as a gesture of their loyalty and readiness to play if asked. Over time, the team's loyal fans, and subsequently the university's student body as a whole, also came to be known as the twelfth man.

Over the years, several sports clubs have retired the number 12 shirt so that they can dedicate it to their fans. These have included Bayern Munich, Torino, Boca Juniors, Feyenoord, and Portsmouth – 'Pompey Fans' being listed as player number 12 on the squad roster printed in each home programme.

Pele

Pele is to Brazilian football what Shakespeare is to English literature.

Joao Saldanha, former Brazil coach

Pele had two good feet. Magic in the air. Quick. Powerful. Could beat people with skill. Could outrun people. Only 5' 8" tall yet he seemed a giant of an athlete on the pitch. Perfect balance and impossible vision.

Bobby Moore, England captain

☻ ☻ ☻

The most famous footballer the world has ever known is Pele, living proof that being born into poverty is not a hindrance as long as someone's genes contain a magical mix of athleticism and ambition. His story is inspirational for any generation. He hails from São Paulo, not the prettiest of Brazilian cities. Pele grew up on the outskirts in a place called Bauru. The team where he first showed signs of footballing genius were so poor they couldn't afford any footwear, let alone proper boots. It was ironic that the young Pele would earn some money polishing shoes when his first team were known as 'the shoeless ones'. His dad Dondinho's professional playing career had been cut tragically short by injury, but he was able to teach his young son, known to his family as Dico, the basics of the game, albeit with a ball made of a stocking filled with newspaper and tied by string.

Apart from his dad, Pele's other stroke of good fortune was to have a mentor named Waldemar de Brito. It didn't take the former 1934 Brazilian World Cup player long to appreciate he had on his hands a rare talent. Baquinho Boys team won a local São Paulo league with Pele scoring a staggering 148 goals in 33 appearances.

The rest is, as they say, history. He joined Santos FC at fifteen, played one year in the juniors, made his senior team debut at sixteen and won the first of his historic three World Cup winners' medals at the ripe old age of seventeen years and 249 days. Little wonder the emotions overcame him at the conclusion of the final against Sweden in 1958 in which he scored two of Brazil's five goals. Pele fainted, recovered and cried throughout the medal ceremony and celebrations. I watched that final and marvelled that someone who was only one year and seven days older than me could capture the attention of the entire football world.

As Pele's career progressed and his international fame made him a megastar, I always hoped I might one day get to meet him. That wish has been granted on several occasions but the first was undoubtedly the most bizarre.

Football Focus, a programme I presented for the BBC, was granted an interview with the Brazilian. It took place at London's Savoy Hotel. After finding Pele's suite where the interview was to take place, I paced up and down waiting for our film crew to arrive. A hotel cleaning lady saw me adjacent to the door of the suite and, picking up a pad and pen from her trolley, came to me poised for an autograph request and said, 'Excuse me love, are you Pele?' I was about to disappoint her when Pele opened the door of his suite, leaving one embarrassed cleaner and one highly amused reporter!

Pele signed his autograph. His public relations are immaculate, always have been and always will be. He also has great respect for fellow pros with Bobby Moore and Gordon Banks his favourite Englishmen. No one will ever forget Bobby and Pele exchanging shirts at the end of Brazil's 1–0 victory over England in the 1970 World Cup finals. It is an iconic photo, representing everything that is best about the sport Pele dubbed 'the beautiful game'.

Banksy's place in Pele's heart comes from a save that I still believe is technically the greatest I have ever seen. There have been miraculous reflex stops by every keeper who ever pulled on the number one jersey but the amount of distance Gordon had to make up on that day in Guadalajara plus the dive and instinctive reaction of his hand that kept the ball out of the net turning it up and over the crossbar was miraculous, sensational, breathtaking. Pele's celebratory shout of 'Goal!' told its own story and Bobby Moore's applause and Alan Mullery's touching of Banks' hair encapsulated the moment.

An interview I conducted between Pele and Banks remains special for me. After it was concluded I got Pele to sign a book I had written in 1970 shortly after the save was made called *The Art of Goalkeeping*. On the chapter entitled 'The Greatest Save – A Salmon's Leap', which analyses the confrontation between them, I have Gordon Banks' signature and alongside it Pele's. What makes it different – indeed a rarity – is that the Brazilian signed it 'Edson Pele', his full name of course being Edson Arantes do Nascimento.

Quite rightly FIFA officials decided to make Pele the Footballer of the Century alongside the people's choice, who was Diego Maradona. Truly great footballers both, but with a differing view on setting an example for all those who followed in their footsteps and dare I suggest it – handprints!

☻ ☻ ☻

Edson Arantes do Nascimento, 'Pele'

Born:
23 October 1940, Tres Corações, Brazil

Position:
Forward

Clubs as player:
1956–74 Santos 1,120 games (1,087 goals)
1975–77 New York Cosmos, 107 games (64 goals)

Internationals:
1957–71 Brazil, 92 caps (77 goals)

Honours as player with Santos:
1958 Campeonato Paulista (elite football league in São Paolo, Brazil)
1959 Torneio Rio-São Paulo
1960 Campeonato Paulista
1961 Campeonato Paulista and Taça Brasil
1962 Campeonato Paulista, Copa Libertadores, Intercontinental Cup
and Taça Brasil
1963 Torneio Rio-São Paulo, Copa Libertadores, Intercontinental
Cup and Taça Brasil
1964 Campeonato Paulista, Torneio Rio-São Paulo and Taça Brasil
1965 Campeonato Paulista and Taça Brasil
1967 Campeonato Paulista
1968 Campeonato Paulista and Torneio Roberto Gomes Pedosa
1969 Campeonato Paulista
1973 Campeonato Paulista

Honours as player with New York Cosmos:
1977 NASL

Honours as player with Brazil:
1958 World Cup
1962 World Cup
1970 World Cup

Awards:
1973 South American Footballer of the Year
1999 International Olympic Committee Athlete of the Century
2000 FIFA Footballer of the Century
2005 BBC Sports Personality of the Year Lifetime Achievement Award
1998 KBE Honorary knighthood

– *Soccer* –

The Football Association was formed in London in 1863 from a meeting of eleven clubs and schools to establish the laws of the game. One of the rules distinctly prohibited the carrying of the ball, and the sport required a name to distinguish it from rugby football, so Association Football was chosen. But on the whole, people found this long-winded and abbreviated it to socca. It was then adapted to socker, before soccer was finally settled on by the end of the nineteenth century. It is thought to have evolved with public school and university students, most notably from Oxford, thanks to their propensity to shorten words and then add '-er'. Rugby was also afforded a similar treatment at the time, becoming rugger.

I'm glad to say it's rarely used in this country any more, as I prefer the more self-explanatory 'football'. Soccer was, however, also adopted by the US, and they still use the name as a way of differentiating the sport from both rugby and, more importantly for them, the sport of American football.

Kevin Keegan

The only thing I fear is missing an open goal in front of the Kop. I'd die if that happened. My eyes water when they sing 'You'll Never Walk Alone'. I've actually been crying while playing.

Kevin Keegan, 1974, Liverpool

Some parts of the job I did very well, but not the key part of getting players to win football matches.

Kevin Keegan, 2000, on his resignation as England manager

❀ ❀ ❀

On the day that I walked out at the old Wembley Stadium to help Arsenal win the FA Cup and secure only the second Double of the last century, our opponents Liverpool had a brand-new signing sitting in the stands watching on. His name was Kevin Keegan and manager Bill Shankly had bought him from Scunthorpe for £33,000 (paying him £50 a week basic salary). Few thought then that the small young striker would go on to such fame and fortune. A glittering career at Anfield, further success in Germany with Hamburg, 63 caps for England, twice European Footballer of the Year – this was the player Shanks would lovingly describe as 'exploding all over the park'.

When his playing career came to an end management beckoned, a natural progression for such an infectious, enthusiastic but highly impulsive character. Kevin is one of my favourite people. I like individuals who are bright, smiley and up-front. He wears his heart on his sleeve and is generous with his time and his money. His main duty is always to his wife Jean and their two girls.

Although our playing careers overlapped briefly, it was in my role as TV presenter and latterly, through my work with the Willow Foundation, that I got to know the real qualities of 'Special K'. As an interviewee for any of the football programmes I fronted over 28 years, he was sharp, lively, informative and never dull. Always watchable, often provocative and funny – 'I don't think there is anybody bigger, or smaller than Maradona,' he once quipped.

There was and is a great humility within Kevin. Despite his fame he is still able to recognise that the greatest gift a celebrity can give back is their time.

In the build-up to the European Cup Final the BBC sent me to Hamburg to try and capture a sense of what it was like for an Englishman living and playing on foreign soil. Despite a media schedule that would have frightened off the majority of footballers, Kevin would not be hurried as he led us into the Hamburg stadium. His popularity with the German fans was obvious and our interview time overran simply because he insisted on responding to every request for a signature.

Sitting close to the action with our film crew while he played re-emphasised the ability that Bill Shankly had once recognised and described so accurately and vividly. Kevin's style of play did see him 'explode' in all areas of the field. His competitive nature is often overlooked but for me his punch-up with Leeds' Billy Bremner in the FA Charity Shield at Wembley underlined his passion and determination to stand his corner. He regretted it quickly as he and the fiery little Scot ripped their shirts off after being sent off in disgrace.

There are many examples of his impulsive nature, with the rant at Sir Alex Ferguson and Manchester United when United and Keegan's Newcastle were fighting it out for the Premiership title perhaps the most memorable. Kevin was unhappy with Fergie's suggestion that Newcastle would blow their chances. The strain imposed on managers at the top level was never better emphasised than in his outburst and that famous 'I'd love it if we beat them' moment caught during a TV interview. Walking away from the England manager's job after seeing his team lose 1–0 to Germany in the last game at the old Wembley was equally dramatic. No thought of lucrative pay-offs from the FA in his mind, just an instinctive feel that it was time to go, time to move on.

As for the infectious personality, well I can sum that up best by telling you about an auction held for our charity the Willow Foundation at Brocket Hall in Hertfordshire. Kevin and Jean had already generously provided us with the considerable sponsorship money that enabled our annual golf day to take place. At the auction after dinner he then offered a day to be spent in his own box with his family as a package to watch the team he managed at that time, Manchester City. Rarely, if ever, have I seen anyone capture a room as Kevin did, carrying his chair as fast as he could from one bidding table to another amid great hilarity as the price for the item rose and rose. Sweat pouring, smile ever-wider he then stopped proceedings and asked if the final two bidders would pay similar sums as long as he provided a second day. In one moment he doubled the income, kept both parties happy and left one and all with a lasting memory.

The little man returned to the game 'big time' at Newcastle United in January 2008, his third coming at a club with amazing fans. Once again there proved to be disappointments and frustrations along the way. With Kevin Keegan there is never likely to be a dull moment. He will always be his own man. Kevin encapulates comedian Charlie Chaplin's famous saying, 'A day without a smile is a day wasted'. Shanks will be pleased to know KK is still 'exploding all over the place'.

⚽ ⚽ ⚽

Joseph Kevin Keegan

Born:
14 February 1951, Doncaster

Position:
Forward/striker

Clubs as player:
1968–71 Scunthorpe United, 141 games (22 goals)
1971–77 Liverpool 321, games (100 goals)
1977–80 Hamburger SV, 90 games (32 goals)
1980–82 Southampton, 80 games (42 goals)
1982–84 Newcastle United, 85 games (49 goals)

Internationals:
1972–82 England, 63 caps (21 goals)

Clubs as manager:
1992–97 Newcastle United
1998–99 Fulham
2001–05 Manchester City
2008 to date Newcastle United

International teams as manager:
1999–2000 England

Honours as player with Liverpool:
1973 UEFA Cup and First Division
1974 FA Cup
1975 FA Charity Shield
1976 UEFA Cup and First Division
1977 European Cup, First Division and FA Charity Shield

Honours as player with Hamburger SV:
1979 Bundesliga

Honours as player with Newcastle:
1984 Promotion to First Division

Honours as manager at Newcastle United:
1993 Division One

Honours as manager at Fulham:
1999 Division Two

Honours as manager at Manchester City:
2002 Division One

Awards:
1976 FWA Footballer of the Year
1978 European Player of the Year
1979 European Player of the Year
1982 PFA Players' Player of the Year
1992 OBE

– *Richest football clubs* –

Club	Revenue £ millions (2008)
Real Madrid	236.2
Manchester United	212.1
FC Barcelona	195.3
Chelsea	190.5
Arsenal	177.6
AC Milan	153.0
Bayern Munich	150.3
Liverpool	133.9
Inter Milan	131.3
AS Roma	106.1
Tottenham	103.1
Juventus	97.7
Lyon	94.6
Newcastle United	87.1
Hamburger SV	81.0
Schalke 04	76.9
Celtic	75.2
Valencia	72.4
Marseille	66.6
Werder Bremen	65.5

Bobby Gould

Aye, Bobby Gould, he couldn't trap a bag of cement. The ball was a constant source of embarrassment to the boy.

Bill Shankly, Liverpool manager

The Crazy Gang have beaten the Culture Club.

John Motson, BBC commentator, 1988 FA Cup Final

Being in football management is like being in a mental asylum.

Bobby Gould, 1997, when Welsh international manager

⚽ ⚽ ⚽

The wonderful thing about the game of football is that it caters for all sorts; tall, small, heavy, lightweight, the naturally gifted and those who, with sheer endeavour, work like mad to become professional players. Bobby Gould falls into the latter category. During his two-and-a-half years at Arsenal he was my best pal and roommate. I think we recognised in each other a passion for football despite a lack of God-given talent. I finished up playing and working for just one club throughout my professional career. Bob was on the books of nine clubs as a player and managed or was assistant manager to another eleven, not counting his four-year tenure in charge of the Welsh national side.

He is an unlikely entry in these pages but he is not here simply because of our continuing friendship. It is because his one major honour, in an ongoing football career that has now reached 45 years, produced what I believe to be the greatest upset in FA Cup history. Even now the 1988 result is still a case of bewilderment. Liverpool (league champions) 0, Wimbledon (the 'Crazy Gang') 1.

The story behind that day and the tactics employed are as amusing as they were effective. Perhaps Bobby Gould and Wimbledon were made for each other. The Crazy Gang, as they were named for their wild antics on and off the field, had risen to prominence under the guidance of Dave 'Harry' Bassett. Like Bobby, Dave had not been the most gifted of players and he too knew that a match could be won in many different ways and with many differing styles of play. Set pieces and long passes deep into enemy territory were the basic ploy of Wimbledon. The football world at large hated it and its effectiveness. Bobby Gould's first masterstroke was to employ Don Howe as his number two. Eighty-four percent of Wimbledon's goals came from set pieces. Gould and Howe decided to go with the flow tactically and also with the traditional noisy dressing room and unusual travel traditions.

They got to Wembley in 1988 by beating Luton Town at White Hart Lane in the semi-final. Everything in the build-up to the kick-off was normal for the Wimbledon team, including players' travel. Those players who lived north of the River Thames drove themselves to Tottenham, the rest plus the kit man travelled in a small club minibus driven by the manager. En route two motorcycle policemen waited on London Bridge to escort the team coach for the remainder of the journey. When the minibus arrived and Bobby told the outriders that this was the Wimbledon bus the police responded with expletives that finished with the word 'off' and 'You can't be serious. This is an FA Cup semi-final.' At White Hart Lane the minibus was then refused entrance to the official car park because it was not a normal team coach. Another expletive preceded 'You can't come in'.

Eventually they were permitted entry. The usual noisy preparations in the tunnel prior to entering the field of play included shouting and banging of floor and walls. Decorum was not part of the Crazy Gang style. In Bobby's words, 'Imagine the worst school in the country, breaking every rule and then multiply it by two or three. That was us. But every day was a fun day as well.' Luton were beaten 2–1 setting up a final of Wimbledon against mighty Liverpool, managed then by Kenny Dalglish, his sights set on a League Championship and FA Cup Double.

Plotting Liverpool's downfall began 24 hours before kick-off; they decided to train in the afternoon at 3 pm, the same time as kick-off the following day. In discussion, Bobby and Don decided that there had to be a major tactical change if Wimbledon were to have any chance of subduing Liverpool's attacking capabilities and especially John Barnes whose form was at a peak at that time.

So they switched two players, moving Alan Cork from outside right to outside left with Dennis Wise told emphatically that whenever Wimbledon lost the ball he must go and stand right in front of John Barnes. The tactical switch was then practised diligently and training concluded for the outfield players. Only keeper Dave Beasant stayed out, asking Cork and Wise to simulate Liverpool striker John Aldridge's method of penalty taking. It involved an initial run up towards the ball, a check in his stride and almost a stop and then normally, a shot to the keeper's left. For three-quarters of an hour the three men played out what was to become a significant moment the following day.

The eve of the FA Cup Final found the Wimbledon players away from their hotel and in a pub, Bobby replicating a Brian Clough idea and giving the players a hundred pounds spending money towards the 'half-pint' of beer each. Team spirit was crucial to the Crazy Gang and it was needed the next day following some of the worst vilification possible directed at Wimbledon for their style of play by the majority of the media.

I was so shocked reading the morning's opinions and decided to ring Bobby at the team hotel. In wishing him luck I expressed my anger at the vehement views of the scribes. The gist of the writing suggested a Wimbledon victory would be the 'worst possible thing for British football'. Bobby's reaction was equally strong: 'Willow, I feel like ringing Kenny Dalglish and telling him they can have the Cup. The game's a waste of time. We may as well play them at cricket.'

How ironic that Wimbledon's winner came from a free kick that they practised daily in 1988 and that which, twenty years on in 2008, is now copied by most top teams. Dennis Wise delivered the curling cross, Lawrie Sanchez the killer finish. Liverpool were stunned but still had time to come back. It would have been easier for them had Vinnie Jones received a red card for a brutal tackle on Steve McMahon; he would certainly have been sent off nowadays.

A quarter of an hour before halftime, Don Howe ordered the Wimbledon kit man, Joe Dillon, to go to the dressing room and soak eleven towels in cold water and ice. The halftime talk was delivered to eleven players buried beneath their cold towels. In the second half Dave Beasant's rehearsal of John Aldridge's penalty kicks paid dividends with a great save diving to his left. Bobby got carried away and ran up and down the line. 'Sit down, there's still 24 minutes to go,' Don told him. At the final whistle Bobby and Don embraced and while the manager celebrated with his team, the coach made straight to the dressing room refusing any accolade.

As Wimbledon made their way around the Wembley pitch, Bobby Gould took the Cup from his players at one point and held it up to the television studio where I stood looking down on him. Ten days later following a celebration of the win in his home town of Portishead near Bristol, the two of us could be found late at night washing and drying dishes with the FA Cup sitting on the sink beside us.

Bobby Gould deserved his moment of glory. He never failed to believe in himself as a player or manager. 'I knew I could always score goals, so if I wasn't wanted at a club I moved on to where I was wanted.' You need great attitude and resilience to have a career like Bobby Gould's, a man whose motto has always been, 'get more from less'.

⚽ ⚽ ⚽

Robert Anthony 'Bobby' Gould

Born:
12 June 1946, Coventry

Position:
Striker

Clubs as player:
1963–68 Coventry City, 84 games (42 goals)
1968–70 Arsenal, 73 games (22 goals)
1970–71 Wolverhampton Wanderers, 40 games* (18 goals)
1971–72 West Bromwich Albion, 52 games* (18 goals)
1972–73 Bristol City, 35 games* (15 goals)
1973–75 West Ham United, 53 games (19 goals)
1975–77 Wolverhampton Wanderers, 34 games* (13 goals)
1977–78 Bristol Rovers, 36 games* (12 goals)
1978–79 Hereford United, 45 games* (13 goals)

Clubs as manager:
1981–83 Bristol Rovers
1983–84 Coventry
1985–87 Bristol Rovers
1987–90 Wimbledon
1991–92 West Bromwich Albion
1992–93 Coventry City
2000–01 Cardiff City
2002–03 Cheltenham Town

International teams as manager:
1995–99 Wales

Honours as manager at Wimbledon:
1988 FA Cup

– *Trotters* –

In 1874, a team was formed at Christ Church Sunday school in Bolton. They played their games on the local recreation ground and used the school as their headquarters. They wore red-and-white quartered shirts and became known as the Reds. In time the vicar decided he didn't like the church's buildings being used as a meeting point for the football team without his presence and so put a stop to it.

On 28 August 1877, the team got together at the nearby Gladstone Hotel. Having now severed all ties with the Sunday school and consequently homeless, they agreed to call themselves the Bolton Wanderers. Although early in their wandering days, it was certainly a prophetic choice as they didn't settle at a permanent home for another eighteen years.

During that time, one of their pitches was next door to a working piggery. In reference to the name of pigs' feet and the frequent necessity for the players to trot through the slurry of the pigpens in order to retrieve the ball, they acquired the nickname, Trotters.

Alex Ferguson

I don't think the salaries can ever be good for the game. You think to yourself, 'How has it come to this?'

Alex Ferguson, 2004, on signing Rio Ferdinand

In the early days we named him 'The Hair Dryer' because he would come right up to your face and scream at you.

Gary Pallister, 1997, Manchester United defender

This is the toughest, meanest and most cussed competitor I've met in the whole of my football life. To be any use to him, you have to win.

Steve Bruce, 2000, former Manchester United captain

I have never seen anyone work so hard. I never remember arriving at the training ground before Sir Alex, and he was last to leave every day.

Carlos Queiroz, 2003,
Manchester United assistant manager

✪ ✪ ✪

Just 61 days separate Alex Ferguson's date of birth and mine. I was born on 30 October 1941; he was born on 31 December. There is a confrontational side to his nature, and there is to mine. He likes to win. So do I. We are both Scots. Therein end the similarities.

It's fair to say that the earliest of our meetings was not too friendly. He was already manager of Manchester United, taking over from Ron Atkinson in November 1986. Almost three years into the job at Old Trafford, he was still seeking the same sort of success he had enjoyed in Scotland with Aberdeen. Some disgruntled United fans had displayed a banner which read, 'Three years of excuses and it's still crap. Ta ra Fergie.' Journalists were jumping on the bandwagon with articles clearly suggesting that his time at United was up. Two decades later he stands alone as the most successful manager in the history of English football.

A former Arsenal teammate, Liam Brady, had been my guest on *Football Focus* on the day preceding Manchester United's game at Arsenal. Liam was very accurate in his views on the side Alex was putting together, complimenting him on building a stronger defence, even though it meant United were less attractive in attack. That was the mistake it seems, because the following day, at Highbury before a game, the United manager made his feelings on the matter very clear, not to Liam, but to me.

I was waiting outside the United dressing room with Alex's book about his days at Aberdeen in hand. When he appeared I asked if he'd sign it for me. Facing the Ferguson wrath close to is not enjoyable. Alex lambasted me for the previous day's interview and included Liam, questioning what he had even won in the game. It would have been easy to make matters worse by mentioning the Brady 1979 FA Cup triumph and his Serie A glory in Italy. Instead I chose to walk away and then, a few days later, sit down and write a letter expressing my regrets at the confrontation, but explaining that Liam's comments were complimentary, not derogatory.

Alex wrote back but his letter only backed up his initial views. Only later, at a charity dinner he was hosting with his friend Gordon Ramsay, did he tell me how, at the time he was penning his reply, the former United Secretary

Les Olive, had told him of my connection as a kid with United and how I so nearly became a Busby Babe. It didn't make any difference to Alex or the response I received from him. Quite simply, Sir Alex Ferguson is a winner. Strong-willed, a disciplinarian, not someone you want to cross.

There is, happily, another side to his personality and nature. It is one of huge compassion for people who are facing troubled times, especially sadness. When I joined ITV as their principal presenter of football in 1994, my daughter Anna was almost five months into her remarkable journey living with one of the rarest cancers known to man. The journey took almost five years in total, the most enriching five years of my life. Anna's attitude to her life-threatening illness kept us all together as a family. Her knowledge as a nurse had taught her that the evil that is cancer tries to destroy not just the patient, but all who love that person. A few outsiders had an extraordinary gift in understanding the turmoil that we were undergoing. Alex Ferguson was one of those individuals. He was aware of the publicity that had surrounded Anna's fight for life.

At the time, Manchester United were the biggest audience attraction of ITV's then-exclusive coverage of the Champions League games. Alex would meet up with our commentator Brian Moore, reporter Gary Newbon and myself and give us his team line-up, subs and injury worries, trusting that we would keep it secret until just before kick-off. At the end of our briefings over a cup of tea, he would send Brian and Gary away and take me on one side to ask the latest news of Anna's health. He was brilliant, absolutely outstanding, listening intently, always positive in his approach, never failing to ask how my wife Megs, Anna's husband Mitchell and our family were coping. Finding time for me, just four hours before managing a United team in their latest challenge says a lot about his humanity. I needed help. Alex gave it to me. I will forever be grateful. So too will Megs for the way in which he phoned us, sensitively a few days after Anna had succumbed to her illness on 1 December 1998. After a brief chat with me he talked to my wife helping her at a time when the enormity of her loss was at its height.

Since those sad days he has both encouraged and helped us build Anna's charity, the Willow Foundation. So many requests for special days relate to Manchester United, tickets for games, meet and greets with Sir Alex and his players. He has ensured that all our needs and those of the recipients are met.

The football world and those who represent it often attract less than desirable headlines. Good-news stories don't sell newspapers, but people should get to know about acts of kindness and generosity. They make a massive difference to the quality of time and quality of life of people whose ability to smile is challenged every day. Sir Alex Ferguson is someone who has the ability to make a difference, whether it is on the field of play or off it.

⚽ ⚽ ⚽

Sir Alexander Chapman 'Alex' Ferguson

Born:
31 December 1941, Glasgow

Position:
Striker

Clubs as player:
1957–60 Queen's Park, 33 games (15 goals)
1960–64 St Johnstone, 47 games (23 goals)
1964–67 Dunfermline Athletic, 136 games (89 goals)
1967–69 Rangers, 68 games (36 goals)
1969–73 Falkirk, 124 games (49 goals)
1973–74 Ayr United, 24 games (10 goals)

Clubs as manager:
1974 East Stirlingshire
1974–78 St Mirren
1978–86 Aberdeen
1986 to date Manchester United

International teams as manager:
1985–86 Scotland

Honours as manager at St Mirren:
1977 Scottish League

Honours as manager at Aberdeen:
1980 Scottish League
1982 Scottish Cup
1983 UEFA Cup Winners' Cup and Scottish Cup
1984 UEFA Super Cup, Scottish League and Scottish Cup
1985 Scottish League
1986 Scottish Cup and League Cup

Honours as manager at Manchester United:
1990 FA Cup and FA Charity Shield (shared)
1991 UEFA Cup Winners' Cup and UEFA Super Cup
1992 League Cup
1993 Premier League and FA Charity Shield
1994 Premier League, FA Cup and FA Charity Shield
1996 Premier League, FA Cup and FA Charity Shield
1997 Premier League and FA Charity Shield
1999 UEFA Champions League, Intercontinental Cup,
Premier League and FA Cup
2000 Premier League
2001 Premier League
2003 Premier League and FA Community Shield
2004 FA Cup
2006 League Cup
2007 Premier League and FA Community Shield
2008 UEFA Champions League, Premier League and
FA Community Shield

Awards:
1984 OBE
1994 Premier League Manager of the Year
1996 Premier League Manager of the Year
1997 Premier League Manager of the Year
1999 Premier League Manager of the Year, League Managers'
Manager of the Year and UEFA Champions League Manager
of the Year
1999 Knighthood
2000 Premier League Manager of the Year
2001 BBC Sports Personality of the Year Lifetime
Achievement Award
2003 Premier League Manager of the Year
2007 Premier League Manager of the Year
2008 Premier League Manager of the Year and League Managers'
Manager of the Year

– *Champions League* –

The tournament originally began in 1955 as a competition for just the winners of the national football leagues throughout Europe. A French sports journalist and editor of the sports paper *L'Equipe* called Gabriel Hanot suggested the idea and although its official title was the European Champions Clubs' Cup it was known simply as the European Cup.

The format was simple and a true reflection of the best teams from the competing countries. A two-legged knockout format saw the teams play two matches, home and away, with the team with the overall highest score going through to the next round.

Entry was restricted to the champions of the national leagues, plus the current holder of the European Cup, and it continued like this until 1992. For the 1992–93 season there was a widely-criticised enlargement of the tournament. The criticism was directed at the eligibility of not just domestic champions but also the best-performing runners-up as based on UEFA's coefficient ranking list. In other words, UEFA decided that a team finishing second in Serie A in Italy or La Liga in Spain were more deserving of an automatic place in the renamed UEFA Champions League than a team finishing first in the Polish championship or the San Marino league. Those deserving champions from the so-called weaker leagues were made to take part in an extra round of qualification for a new batch of group stages.

The number of places in the competition now depends on a nation's standing in the UEFA table. Associations ranked 1–3 get four places; those ranked 4–6 receive three places; 7–15 have two positions and 16 or lower get one place.

An association's ranking also determines the stage at which the clubs enter the competition. Dress it up as much as they like, but the Champions League cannot be disguised by UEFA in any way and nowadays it is purely about money, sponsorship and TV audiences.

Today football has become such a worldwide product that a group of multinational corporations sponsor the Champions League. Currently the tournament has a maximum of eight sponsors who receive prime advertising boards around the pitch, as well as logo placement at all pre- and post-match interviews. Worse for the loyal fans of the clubs involved, the sponsors also receive large numbers of tickets.

The competition naturally attracts massive audiences on television, not just in Europe but worldwide. In my time at ITV as presenter of football we had exclusive Champions League rights in the UK and audiences regularly topped 10 million, with a 19 million audience registered for Manchester United's historic win against Bayern Munich in the 1999 final.

The games are now broadcast to more than 70 countries, in 40 different languages. Considering that a 'huge' game can attract a global audience of 200 million, it is easy to understand how certain clubs have become richer and why players are demanding extortionate salaries.

However, despite the actions of UEFA, in the end the competition does pit together the very best club teams from across the continent. To win it is a massive challenge and any player or manager who has done so will treasure their victor's medal forever. Whatever view is taken as to the competition's current merits, therefore, it is appropriate that the winners of the new Champions League format and the original European Cup receive their rightful place in the history of the game.

Graham Taylor

Possession and patience are myths. It's anathema to people in the game to say this, but goals come from mistakes, not from possession.

Graham Taylor, 1982

I used to like turnips. Now my wife refuses to serve them.

Graham Taylor, 1995

I can live with a newspaper putting a turnip on my head, except that it encourages people to treat me like shit.

Graham Taylor, 1998

⚽ ⚽ ⚽

Never in the history of England international football has any manager received the vilification of that directed at Graham Taylor. Not even Don Revie's desertion of his England post for greater monetary reward equalled the headlines which berated Graham during his three-year tenure as manager of his country. As well as being described as a 'turnip' and a 'Spanish onion', other headlines directed at the England team during Taylor's reign included 'Swedes 2, Turnips 1', 'Norse Manure' and 'Yanks 2, Planks 0'.

Graham Taylor's achievements in club management are terrific and were easily good enough to warrant the FA's decision to appoint him as Bobby Robson's successor as England boss after Italia '90. At 27, the youngest person to become an FA Coach and the youngest manager in the league when he was 28, he led Lincoln City to the Fourth

Division title in 1976, breaking the most wins, fewest defeats and most points records in the process. In his time at Watford between 1977 and 1987, he led the small Hertfordshire club from the Fourth Division to the First in five years. An FA Cup Final appearance against Everton came in 1984. In 1987 another appearance in an FA Cup semi-final preceded his move to Aston Villa, who had just been relegated from the First Division. Graham brought Villa back immediately and almost took the league title to Villa Park.

From the moment he donned an England tracksuit, the media homed in on his lack of playing experience at the top level, the fact that the only trophies and success came mainly with lower division teams and – possibly with some justification – his belief in 'long ball' tactics and exploitation of any set piece situations whether it be free kick, corner kick or throw in.

As the son of a Lincolnshire journalist, Graham has always tried to be approachable for the press corps, understanding the demands of newspapers and television. However his good nature backfired when he allowed a Channel 4 documentary to follow England's 1994 World Cup qualifying campaign. 'Do I not like that' was an utterance that became a catchphrase, but worse was the bad language within the film that simply undermined his position and authority.

I have known Graham Taylor since he was eighteen and playing for Lincolnshire Grammar Schools. Whenever we meet we tend to recall our teenage rivalry and a game in 1960 at Saltergate, home of Chesterfield FC, when I faced him as opposing keeper in the Derbyshire Grammar Schools XI. Forty-eight years on I still have huge respect for him and his achievements, especially at Watford where he not only took Elton John's club to new heights on the field, but led the English football world into innovative strategies that embraced the local community. Watford was one of the many clubs I helped in developing specialised coaching for goalkeepers. Graham understood the whys and wherefores of my initiative. One of his young keepers who immediately caught my eye as full of potential was David James. Bertie Mee made the initial approach to me on behalf of Graham, who had recognised the organisational skills and experience that my old manager still had to offer as his assistant, after Arsenal had dispensed with Bertie's services. It was an enjoyable experience at Vicarage Road, not least because the Christmas parties meant live entertainment in the shape of Elton John himself.

It didn't surprise me that Graham Taylor – with all his success at smaller clubs – would ultimately look to manage one of the recognised 'big boys' and I was happy to inform an Arsenal director that the Watford manager would be approachable prior to their appointment of George Graham.

The one occasion when Graham Taylor and I did not see eye to eye came well into his time as England boss. I was surprised that he was continually overlooking one of my Arsenal keepers as England's number one. David Seaman had established himself brilliantly at the top level of club football, but Graham seemed set on Chris Woods. Of course, I had no right to put the Arsenal keeper's case, despite my being his coach. But I shared Seaman's frustration and phoned Graham Taylor. Quite rightly he told me where to go and even now I am amazed, if not amused, that I spoke to the England manager in such a forthright manner.

Another Taylor phone call is unforgettable for me, not that he was aware of my discomfort throughout it, and not as a result of it. It was London Marathon day and in my role as BBC interviewer I had completed around seven to eight miles while chatting on the run to 50 or 60 competitors. Back home I was relaxing on the settee with a cup of tea when the England manager phoned. As I stretched to lift the receiver both legs went into cramp. Not wanting to interrupt Graham's flow I simply listened, clamping my hand over the mouth piece so he couldn't hear my agonised cries, while my wife did her best to push my toes up towards my knees to try and relieve the pain. Any conversation I had with Graham came with a strange staccato delivery and made little sense.

It's fair to say that, despite England losing just one game in Taylor's first 23 in charge and their qualification and quarter-final place in Euro '92, his failure to lead England to the 1994 World Cup finals was unacceptable to his FA employers and the watching fans. Management of your country is the greatest achievement for anyone in football, but World Cup success or failure will ultimately decide your fate.

Graham Taylor left the national job on 24 November 1993. To his credit he didn't let the harsh judgement of the media destroy him. Returning to club football he took Wolves to the Division One playoffs in his first season before returning to Watford for four and a half years where his team won the Second Division championship in his first season. A year later Graham Taylor's Watford won the Division One playoff final against Bolton and with it promotion to the Premier League, albeit for one season only.

Graham Taylor was far from a 'turnip' throughout his managerial career – more a 'rocket man'. Sad for him then that the one time that his craft failed to reach orbit it was carrying the hopes of the English nation with it.

⚽ ⚽ ⚽

Graham Taylor

Born:
15 September 1944, Worksop

Position:
Full back

Clubs as player:
1962–68 Grimsby Town, 189 games* (2 goals)
1968–72 Lincoln City, 150 games* (1 goal)

Clubs as manager:
1972–77 Lincoln City
1977–87 Watford
1987–90 Aston Villa
1994–95 Wolverhampton Wanderers
1996 Watford
1997–2001 Watford
2002–03 Aston Villa

International teams as manager:
1990–93 England

Honours as manager at Lincoln City:
1976 Promotion to Third Division

Honours as manager at Watford:
1978 Promotion to Third Division
1979 Promotion to Second Division
1982 Promotion to First Division
1998 Promotion to First Division
1999 Promotion to Premier League

Honours as manager at Aston Villa:
1988 Promotion to First Division

Awards:
2002 OBE

– *Coaching qualifications* –

The one good aspect of my belated route to a permanent place in the Arsenal first team was that I was able to continue to use the teaching qualifications I'd acquired at Loughborough and apply them to the FA's preliminary coaching badge and then the full badge qualifications.

These days the climb to the top ladder of coaching in this country is demanding and more complex. The attributes essential for good coaching are exactly the same as those required for teacher's training: knowledge, organisation, personality, patience, sensitivity, adaptability, courage and a great love and enthusiasm for the subject. It is not essential to have been a very good player but it can help, especially when practical demonstrations are valuable to the learning process. At this moment these are the stages of coaching qualification:

FA Level 1 Certificate in Coaching Football

This is the first step on the formal coaching ladder. It embraces both theory and practice. The certificate permits the holder to coach at grassroots level with teams in the age group six to sixteen. Anyone can take the course which usually requires three sessions and eight hours to complete. There is also a compulsory training in emergency first aid and child protection. There is real value in the award which, apart from being the start of the UEFA coaching road, carries over into other areas of the game like refereeing or lining and sports therapy. This qualification is ideal for someone with little or no experience of coaching and wants to help young people develop the basics of the sport.

FA Level 2

Once again this involves a practical course and class-based theory of the game. There are no big demands or pre-requisites for taking this award although it is helpful to have taken the Level 1 certificate and to have had a reasonable amount of coaching experience. To be successful, a candidate would be asked to deliver two carefully planned sessions and, within an organised six-a-side match, show their technical awareness in front of external assessors.

UEFA 'B' Licence

This is quite a step up and is best described as a refinement of skills and techniques which are then applied to both children's groups and adults. Small-sided games are developed to eight-a-side and the requisites include the learning and teaching of positional play, individual skills of a more complex nature, phases of play involving attack and defence. It would take around 120 hours to complete the 'B' Licence course which is assessed eventually through two formal coaching sessions.

UEFA 'A' Licence

Simply an extension of the 'B' Licence but becoming more complex by consolidating the technical, tactical, mental and physical development of footballers.

UEFA Pro Licence

This is designed for Europe's elite coaches and UEFA's guidelines recommend that any individual should experience an extra year's work above and beyond the 'A' licence before undertaking it. It is the ultimate qualification and would take some 240 hours before completion. Within the requirements a coach would have to show that he could plan and evaluate a key player's performance and explain how to be a winner in a key fixture.

When I read the requirements now explicit in the different levels of coaching I have to smile, thinking back to the likes of Matt Busby, Bill Shankly, Jock Stein, Joe Mercer and the rest of those glorious coaches and managers of yesteryear. I wonder what words of wisdom they would impart about the modern way.

Lawrie McMenemy

Lawrie believed in characters and he had his share at The Dell. He had footballers, mimics, know-alls and whimsies who added up to a collection of talented players. I admired the way Lawrie McMenemy ran the club.

Alan Ball, former Southampton player

His greatest strength as a manager was his ability to handle problem players. In a game where players sneer at managers – 'How many caps did you win?' – he faced a grave disadvantage because he was one of the few managers who had never played a single league game, let alone an international game. But he overcame that by force of character and earned the respect of players of international reputation like Alan Ball, Mick Channon and Peter Osgood.

Brian Scovell, former *Daily Mail* journalist

☙ ☙ ☙

The closest I ever came to going into football management was in 1978. The World Cup in Argentina was the major event that year. I had only left the game as a player four years previously. Work at the BBC was challenging but frustrating. I was getting more job satisfaction from developing the specialist coaching of goalkeepers than I was in the sports department at the Beeb. I felt at that time I was continually being overlooked in areas where I had real expertise and knowledge.

One of the bright spots of my TV work was working alongside Lawrie McMenemy, the 6' 5" ex-guardsman who had taken Southampton to FA Cup glory at the expense of Manchester United in 1976. I had already made trips to the Saints training ground to undertake some goalkeeping coaching for which Lawrie would reward me with a case of wine, rather than the unseemly method of normal payment! Lawrie understood better than most the frustrations and anxieties I was expressing, and especially my concern about jumping into TV in 1974 rather than maximising my teaching and coaching skills as a manager.

Lawrie actually believed I was a natural on the coaching front and was prepared to teach me the intricacies of management first-hand. He offered me a position at Southampton as his assistant manager. My wife Megs and I went down to the old ground, The Dell, and in the company of Lawrie and later his wife Anne, we touched on my role to the point where he would accept my moving on once I had followed his guidance. Lawrie had a hands-on approach at his club, with an input into all areas and activities at Southampton.

I faced a big decision and was on the point of accepting his offer when Lawrie was suddenly offered the manager's job at Leeds United. I thought he'd accept it and had he done so I would probably have gone with him. In phone conversations the two of us covered all possibilities, but he was the one with the bigger quandary. He loved Southampton and the fame it had brought him and it was providing a powerful tug at his heart strings, one he decided to follow.

As he turned Leeds down, my personal problems also affected my thoughts. Megs miscarried and together we came to the conclusion that football management could wait a while longer. I decided to write to Lawrie with my decision. He understood but clearly believed it was a matter of time before I left television. His letter of reply touched on the 'anxiety' Megs had shown on her face at the prospect of a return to professional football.

It was the closest I ever came to management, although a former Arsenal coach of mine, Bobby Campbell, sounded me out for a similar role at Fulham. Nothing came of that either and neither did a misguided enquiry I made to my old club Arsenal when they were looking for a new manager prior to George Graham's arrival and success at Highbury.

☺ ☺ ☺

Lawrie McMenemy

Born:
28 July 1936, Gateshead

Clubs as player:
1959–61 Gateshead

Clubs as manager:
1968–71 Doncaster Rovers
1971–73 Grimsby Town
1973–85 Southampton
1985–87 Sunderland

International teams as manager:
1998–99 Northern Ireland

Honours as manager at Southampton:
1976 FA Cup

Awards:
2006 MBE

– *Football and the use of technology* –

I will always love the basic idea of football as a sport, its simplicity and beauty, but I have grown to hate cheating, diving and the abuse of referees and their assistants. It all became too apparent during the World Cup finals in France in 1998. By then the game's greatest tournament had become a multi-million pound extravaganza, with massive sponsorship deals allied to the spiralling costs of television companies covering the event. As many as 25 cameras followed each match, exposing warts and all.

France '98 was a great tournament, won by the hosts, but spoiled by the upsurge in the diving and dramatics of virtually every competing nation. FIFA, football's governing body, recognised the problem and announced that they would look at ways to reduce, if not eliminate the practice. Ten years on they have done nothing to help resolve the issue, and recently decided against the use of technology even to solve the simplest of problems, which is whether the ball has crossed the goal line or not. It's now 42 years since Geoff Hurst's 'goal that wasn't' helped England to become world champions for the one and only time in 1966.

Football in 2008 is quicker, probably more skilful and played with an ever-changing ball that is lighter by the year and designed to move in the air and create more goals. The treatment of referees by players has never been worse at the top level and it is time that officials received proper respect as well as help in making the correct decisions. One referee and his two assistants can no longer hope to call correctly on a multitude of incidents played out at a pace that is frankly beyond them, however fit they may be.

Other sports, notably tennis, cricket and rugby have all reacted to changing times in their arenas by using technology to aid umpires and referees in making the correct call, which in turn helps earn them greater respect.

Hawkeye at Wimbledon enables a player to challenge an umpire's or line judge's decision on what they consider to be three wrong calls in any one set. In cricket a run-out is now confirmed or otherwise in similar manner. But it is rugby which is showing FIFA, UEFA, the FA and all other footballing bodies just what can be achieved by sensible use of TV replays and more.

Ninety-nine percent of disputed tries at the top level of rugby are now called correctly. The use of replays can lead to lengthy bans for offending players involved in 'ungentlemanly conduct'. A red card remains the ultimate punishment as in football, but a sin-bin sensibly allows less serious incidents to be punished by a cooling-off period for the guilty party. Being wired for sound is another brave initiative by rugby and its referees. Their explanation on decisions and the response of the captains and the punished is instant and improves professional conduct.

One explanation of why TV technology is not used in football is that it would take too long and break up the flow of a game. At this moment the arguments and questioning of decisions often lead to a free-for-all between officials and opposing players lasting several minutes. Today's technology means that incidents can be replayed in less than two seconds and in most cases, a correct decision would be apparent within 30 seconds maximum. Goalkeepers and outfield players purposefully waste 30 seconds during games right now, but generally escape punishment. Football is a multi-billion-pound business at the top end. It should be imperative that the officials nowadays are given as much help as is possible to come up with the right decision.

In my opinion there is only one way to stamp out cheating and diving, shirt-pulling and underhand behaviour, and that is by the retrospective use of technology. I would employ teams of former professional players and referees to study matches in the early days after they had been played. The punishment for any one of the aforesaid crimes would range from a two- or three-point deduction, which would accumulate to a maximum six points. An instant ban ranging from three games to three months would be punishment for serious misconduct.

Disputed goal-line decisions could be decided by technology and if there was any doubt it would be no goal. A team could perhaps be allowed a maximum of three calls and the use of technology in order to decide disputed offside goals and debatable penalty decisions. Where there was any doubt, the referee's initial decision would stand.

I would also advocate an extra assistant on the pitch to cover areas that remain difficult for the referee: corner kicks and free kicks. I have no doubt that one day the use of technology in deciding right and wrong will be embraced in all team games. Sadly I don't think I will be around by the time football's governing bodies contain enough individuals with the courage to implement the necessary changes.

John Burridge

You may well be asking the question 'John who?' A few fans will have an idea that he was a goalkeeper. Old professional players will have a laugh and tell you he was eccentric. Members of the 'Goalkeeper's Union' are also likely to smile, and with amusement also comes respect for a keeper who loved what he did, never wanted to stop and reportedly went to any lengths to ensure he could still understand the complexities of a ball even when he was 45 years of age.

His nickname was 'Budgie' and his professional career began at Workington in the 1970–71 season. Almost 30 years later John was still in goal having played for 26 different clubs and accumulating 771 league games in the English and Scottish divisions. Towards the end of his career, many non-league clubs invited him to play or rescue them from an injury crisis. I've included him in these pages because I loved his passion and enthusiasm, his total obsession with the art of goalkeeping.

He was an extraordinary character and I have no doubt that he will still be lecturing anyone who will listen about how goalkeeping has changed, how difficult the new balls and rules have made it, and how the 'old boys' were better technically between the sticks than the new crop.

I have no reason to disbelieve stories about Budgie that say a lot about him and come from reputable sources – former keepers who kept in touch. They involve his dedication and relate to a phone call one of my old charges made to John's home. Intense discussion ensued between the two, only broken by a regular ba-boom sound down the phone line.

After ten minutes or more the caller asked John what the constant noise was. Budgie told him it was the sound of the ball rebounding off his lounge floor and walls as he threw and caught it throughout the conversation, with the phone hooked between his shoulders and ear. Imagine his poor wife's plight. Even worse for her was that John would take a ball to bed with him, so as to ensure his familiarity with it was that much more acute.

For all the dedication, his playing honours added up to one Anglo-Italian Cup winners' medal with Blackpool, a League Cup winners' medal with Aston Villa and a Skol Cup triumph with Hibernian. Not much return for this extraordinary journeyman of a goalkeeper, but considering that he holds the record of having played for fifteen Football League teams, which no one else has done, and the accolade of being the oldest player ever to appear in the Premier League at 43 years 4 months and 26 days, you can only admire the man.

His intensity in conversation could be quite frightening. Laughter didn't come easily to him but he was one lucky man. He loved his job and his life as a goalkeeper.

⚽ ⚽ ⚽

Jonathan 'John' Burridge

Born:
3 December 1951, Workington

Position:
Goalkeeper

Clubs as player:
1970–97 15 football league clubs, (771 games*) and
11 Non-League Clubs

Honours as player with Blackpool:
1971 Anglo-Italian Cup

Honours as player with Aston Villa:
1977 League Cup

Honours as player with Hibernian:
1991 Skol Cup

– *Football and education* –

'Sorry son, football's not a proper job. I've said "no" to Matt Busby. Joining Manchester United will have to wait.'

With such words my dad told me that my dream of becoming a footballer was effectively over. I was fifteen years of age, a member of the England under-15 schoolboys XI and wanted by the Busby Babes' boss. My international teammate Nobby Stiles signed, while I went back to school to study and complete my O- and A-level examinations.

Whose dad made the right decision, Nobby's or mine? Nobby joined his local club and within nine years was a Manchester United hero and England World Cup-winner. As he gained legendary status on that sunny summer's day in 1966, I was back chasing the dream but still a year and a half away from establishing myself in the Arsenal team. Today Nobby still enjoys a role on the after dinner speaking circuit having experienced coaching and management after his playing days. I also speak at many events in aid of the Willow Foundation, having fulfilled the original dream of being a half-decent player with another of the great clubs, spent 28 years as a TV sports presenter, and a similar period developing the coaching of goalkeepers in the UK.

I know that it is unlikely that I would have been able to fulfil these roles without having continued my education at Chesterfield Grammar School and subsequent study to be a physical education teacher at Loughborough College. I think it highly unlikely that I would be writing this book, one of several, without the aid of a ghost writer.

Then again the old unanswered and unanswerable questions come back to haunt me. If I'd signed for United in 1957 would I have been a better goalkeeper, won more trophies, played more international football and attended World Cups as a member of the squad?

With hindsight it is easy to give advice. I think my dad was right, even though it was a decision which temporarily broke my heart. There are thousands of aspiring young players around the country every year and only a relative handful ever make it to the top. I am continually asked for advice by parents facing a similar dilemma for their sons. The odds remain the same now as they did 51 years ago, even if the monetary rewards do not. Nowadays, success can result in huge wealth and a bank balance at the end of a career that will sustain them for life.

What I advise is a slight compromise. Sign when there is an initial opportunity to sign because, as I found, missing an apprenticeship as a player is risking almost everything, but ensure that additional education is guaranteed alongside those early days and years. At most major clubs academic subjects and IT skills are taught alongside football. Almost as much time is spent in a classroom as on a pitch. British players would benefit if they were made to learn another language alongside the other subjects. Watching numerous new foreign players arrive at the Arsenal training centre with only a smattering of English and then be transformed within a matter of weeks is amazing – Thierry Henry, Patrick Vieira and Cesc Fàbregas are all examples. We are in a multi-cultural society, freedom of trade is part of our life and yet in England we remain too insular by far. If things don't turn out in the pursuit of a football career, it's great to be well-prepared when tackling a 'proper job'.

Osvaldo Ardiles

I will never return to play in England, even if they gave me all the money in the world.

Ossie Ardiles, June 1982, Spurs and Argentine
midfielder during the Falklands conflict

I can't wait to get back. Every night I go to bed dreaming of Wembley.

Ossie Ardiles, December 1982

⚽ ⚽ ⚽

The fame that Ossie Ardiles acquired in England did not simply revolve around his World Cup-winner's glory of 1978, the FA Cup triumphs of 1981 and '82 or Spurs' UEFA Cup success in 1984. Unusually for a footballer, he had also furthered his education and sought a guaranteed income by training as a lawyer. Surprisingly, perhaps, he is also remembered for his singing, or to be precise, one solo line within the FA Cup Final recording of 'Spurs are on their Way to Wembley'. The whole squad sang together with typical disharmony until Ossie was left with the definitive line: 'In dee Cup for Tottingham.'

Inadvertently the Argentine accent of the little man from Bell Ville produced a catchphrase the like of which Bruce Forsyth would have been proud. That clipped accent of his endeared him to one and all, regardless of any national prejudice.

Ardiles is a delightful man, bright, respectful, caring and intelligent. As a World Cup-winner he was guaranteed cult status long before he visited the recording studios. It's worth noting that the three medals acquired at Spurs did not signify the end of his footballing achievements. As Swindon Town manager he won promotion to the top division for the first time in the club's history, only for it to be cruelly snatched away ten days later when the Football League demoted the club for irregularities in payments to players. In 1993 as West Bromwich Albion boss, he secured promotion for the Baggies and during his time in Japan, five trophies were won.

My friendship with Ossie blossomed after a couple of interviews that I conducted with him in his Broxbourne home, close to Spurs' old training ground. A one-to-one chat for a football magazine gave me a clear insight into his presence and dignity. Then a *Football Focus* interview revealed his love for Spurs and the country that provided his living. That love was tested in the extreme with the outbreak of the Falklands War in 1982.

The World Cup finals were held in Spain that summer and the war came to an end just three weeks before Argentina, the reigning champions, were knocked out by Brazil 3–1 in Barcelona. My role for BBC TV Sport during that tournament was as England reporter.

Argentina's demise was a big story but the problem lay in having to make meaningful contact with the players of a country which was coming to terms with defeat at war and at play. They were hurting badly. At an editorial meeting I found myself suggesting I try the mobile phone number that Ossie Ardiles had given me on one of my visits to his home.

With a private plane at the BBC's disposal there was no problem getting quickly from Madrid to Barcelona should he answer. I was encouraged to give Ossie's mobile a call. To everyone's surprise, notably my own, the familiar Ardiles voice came on the line. Despite his deflation at losing to Brazil, Ossie instantly understood that there could be real value from an interview, both for himself and for his country. Whatever the rights and wrongs of the Falklands conflict, the little Argentine agreed to speak.

There were strict instructions on how my two-man crew and I would set up on the roof of the Argentine team hotel. Only I was to wait in the hotel lobby, which was supposedly barred to all Brits. He told me to refrain from speaking English. Security was incredibly tight when I arrived but Ossie came out, shook hands and briefly discussed the game and the contents of our interview. Other members of the beaten Argentine side passed us by, a young Maradona included. With daylight fading fast we quickly set up on the hotel roof and the interview proceeded. Ossie was frank, revealing and emotional as he talked of his distress at the war and the bitter relations that had developed between his homeland and his adopted country. His cousin, first lieutenant José Ardiles was a victim of the war while flying in the Argentine Air Force.

The interview exceeded all expectations and was guaranteed huge appeal and impact throughout the UK. After thanking him profusely we rushed the tape to our Barcelona studio for instant transmission by satellite and promptly boarded our aircraft. A severe thunderstorm could not dampen our spirits on the flight back to Madrid. The most revealing aspect of our scoop was the promise that Ossie made to try and return to play in England in due course. For most of the 1982–83 season he played his football in France for Paris St Germain, and then he was back with Spurs, chasing more honours in the shape of the 1984 UEFA Cup.

Since that interview in 1982, Ossie has remained the same friendly, dapper, proud man. Whether bumping into him and his wife in Spain where he now spends a lot of his time, or at some of the charity golf days that we both frequent, time spent in his company is rewarding.

His life has been full of drama, containing both the highs and lows of the game of football and the politics that create tensions between nations. Argentina should be very proud of him. As far as British football fans are concerned he will simply be remembered as the skilful little midfielder who played so beautifully for a team called 'Tottingham'.

☺ ☺ ☺

Osvaldo Cesar 'Ossie' Ardiles

Born:
3 August 1952, Bell Ville, Argentina

Position:
Midfield

Clubs as player:
1973 Instituto, 14 games (3 goals)
1974 Belgrano, 16 games (2 goals)
1975–78 Huracan, 113 games (11 goals)
1978–88 Tottenham Hotspur, 311 games (25 goals)
1982–83 Paris St Germain (loan), 14 games (1 goal)
1988 Blackburn Rovers, 5 games*
1988–89 Queens Park Rangers, 8 games*

Clubs as player-manager:
1989–91 Swindon Town, 2 games*

Internationals:
1973–82 Argentina, 63 caps (8 goals)

Clubs as manager:
1989–91 Swindon Town
1991–92 Newcastle United
1992–93 West Bromwich Albion
1993–94 Tottenham Hotspur
1995 Chivas de Guadalajara
1996–98 Shimizu S-Pulse
1999 Croatia Zagreb
2000–01 Yokohama F Marinos
2001 Al-Ittihad
2002–03 Racing Club
2003–05 Tokyo Verdy
2006 Beitar Jerusalem
2007 Huracan
2008 Cerro Portero

Honours as player with Tottenham Hotspur:
1981 FA Cup
1982 FA Cup
1984 UEFA Cup

Honours as player with Argentina:
1978 World Cup

Honours as manager at Swindon Town:
1990 Promotion to First Division (cancelled and relegated for
financial irregularities)

Honours as manager at West Bromwich Albion:
1993 Promotion to First Division

Honours as manager at Shimizu S-Pulse:
1996 Nabisco Cup

Honours as manager at Tokyo Verdy:
1969 2005 Emperor's Cup

Awards:
1998 J League Manager of Year

– *Winter breaks* –

How and why do all of the major European leagues, except those in England and Scotland, have winter or mid-season breaks? In all, 30 out of 48 UEFA countries include a break in their domestic seasons.

I think most players and fans in the UK would accept and enjoy such a break but it is highly unlikely to get a nod of approval from the FA, Premier League or Football League hierarchy. They will point to the current fixture congestion problems which are created by an overload of fixtures caused by too many competitions: leagues, Champions League, UEFA Cup, FA Cup, League Cup and play-offs, as well as international commitments.

The truth, as so often in the modern game, revolves around its finances and the need for clubs to have an ongoing turnover throughout a competitive season. Our current campaign began on 16 August 2008 and will finish on 24 May 2009 (not including pre-season games and post-season tours). The more successful clubs will play between 60 and 65 competitive matches, plus another six to ten friendlies. It adds up to quantity, not always quality, and arguably to the detriment of our international teams and their progress in major tournaments.

Bruce Grobbelaar

I have been a gypsy all my life. I don't think I will ever change. I will always be Jungle Man on the field if not off. We are not just professional footballers but professional entertainers and if football is to ever regain its stature after the events of Bradford, Brussels and Hillsborough, it needs all the help it can get.

Bruce Grobbelaar

He makes the odd mistake but that is due to the tremendous amount of work he does for his defenders and he is often blamed for their errors. There is however, a wild untamed streak in him and that will never change because it is an essential part of his character.

Bob Paisley, Liverpool Manager

⚽ ⚽ ⚽

The range of Bruce's goalkeeping was spectacular. So too were the saves and errors. There were many who laughed at him. Goalkeepers come and go, some good, some great; a few remembered, many forgotten. Most keepers are much the same. Bruce Grobbelaar, 'Jungle Man', was different.

His great service to the art of keeping goal was a daring style and approach that made every other number one of his era question whether they could do more for their team in keeping a ball out of the net. It is sad that the many medals and trophies that should surround his fame and contribution are still buried under accusations of match fixing. Along with fellow keeper Hans Segers and striker John Fashanu, he was charged with attempting to fix a number of Premiership games so that a Far East gambling syndicate could win vast sums of money by betting on the results. Their trial received huge publicity following the *Sun* newspaper's incredible sting operation involving Bruce and a bitter former business partner of his named Chris Vincent. Grobbelaar faced an additional charge in relation to, allegedly, accepting a sum of money from Vincent, which had been supplied by the *Sun*.

Some time after the story broke, sports lawyer Mel Goldberg, who was representing Hans Segers, and David Hewitt, who was building a defence for Bruce, approached me. They asked me if I was prepared to be called as an 'expert' witness in the trial of the two keepers. They explained that my experience and reputation as a goalkeeper and goalkeeping coach could help clarify whether either or both men had deliberately let in 'bad' goals. The key legal words that I had to bear in mind should I choose to help were 'beyond reasonable doubt'.

Without initially committing myself to supporting the two men, I agreed to review carefully the five key matches, which were central to the accusations against Bruce Grobbelaar and the eighteen games pertaining to Hans Segers. These were the 23 games which the prosecution were alleging the keepers had fixed.

I faced a tricky balancing act. I respected both men from the times we had met. I knew Hans more than Bruce as he was a regular guest at the goalkeeping school I had set up in 1983 in an effort to provide specialist coaching for young keepers. Hans never asked for payment for his visits, but inspired youngsters with his demonstrations and words of advice. Previously I had only met Bruce at matches and during interviews. Over many hours and days I studied and collated every incident involving the two men. I had made it clear that should I find anything untoward I would abort any help offered.

I studied the evidence innumerable times and was happy, eventually, to go into the witness box on behalf of both goalkeepers. In my opinion if they were guilty of any impropriety it was not evident in the charges that had been made against them.

Going into the witness box during the two trials at Winchester was an ordeal. Court three, where the trial was held, was the same court room where a year or so earlier the Rosemary West 'House of Horror' trial had been held and where she had been sentenced to ten life terms for mass murder. Bruce and Hans expressed how grateful they were but the strain on their faces and on their families was apparent.

It took two trials, in January and August 1997, for the two men to be found 'not guilty' but it wasn't the end of the matter. Bruce, typifying his often rash and daring style of goalkeeping, decided to bring a libel action against the *Sun*. It was a bad move. Once again I was asked to take the witness box. Court fouteen of the High Court in London was the venue this time; the legendary QC George Carman was representing the *Sun*. His intention was to discredit Bruce Grobbelaar with an intimidating approach, mocking the goals that the Liverpool keeper had let in. He sought an explanation of how a 'great' keeper could make such slips. My own citing of examples of other goalkeepers' 'nightmare' moments, like Ray Clemence allowing a mishit Kenny Dalgish shot to go through his legs in an England vs. Scotland international, did little to appease Carman. Bruce, however, won the case and was awarded £85,000 damages, only for the *Sun* to lodge an appeal and have three High Court judges overturn the verdict. Ultimately Bruce Grobbelaar reversed that judgement as well, but the token £1 damages he received represented a hollow victory that had bankrupted him.

In the time I was able to talk to Bruce about football and his career, and not legal issues, I was left with a more commendable and lasting impression of him, in particular his description of the two horrific tragedies in which Liverpool FC were involved – Heysel and Hillsborough.

After the disaster in Europe, a chain of errors leading up to the FA Cup semi-final between Liverpool and Nottingham Forest led to 96 people losing their lives. It could have been more had Bruce Grobbelaar not reacted to desperate cries behind him on the terraces soon after kick-off. One fan in particular was screaming to him, 'Bruce, they're killing us.' The goalkeeper could see the crush that was developing behind locked gates. It was his pleas to the police that led to a gate being opened for fans to pour back through to safety. The actions of Grobbelaar and the police saved many lives.

On a much happier and lighter note I had talked with Bruce about his antics during the penalty shootout at the 1984 European Cup Final. Roma were leading the shootout when Italy's World Cup hero, Bruno Conti, stepped up to try and beat Bruce. Memorably the goalkeeper crossed his arms, then put his hands on his knees and did a good interpretation of a 'Black Bottom' dance routine. It was intended as mock fear and it worked: Conti missed. More was to follow when Graziani arrived for Roma three penalties later. This time Bruce bit the back of the netting, half laughing, half growling like a caged lion. Graziani, in turn crossed himself, before Grobbelaar went into a hilarious limp body, wobbly knees act. Everyone laughed, both those in the crowd and those watching on television. It put Graziani off his stride. The ball missed the goal and Alan Kennedy's penalty won the European Cup for Liverpool for the third time.

Bruce refused to claim all the credit when asked why and how he had settled on such antics. He heaped praise on manager Joe Fagan who had, prior to the start of the shootout, come up to his keeper, put an arm around him and said, 'Son, if we lose, it won't be your fault. You've had a great game … but Bruce, make sure you try to put them off.'

⚽ ⚽ ⚽

Bruce David Grobbelaar

Born:
6 October 1957 Durban, South Africa

Position:
Goalkeeper

Clubs as player:
1979–81 Vancouver White Caps, 24 games
1979–80 Crewe Alexandra, 24 games*
1980–94 Liverpool, 628 games
1993 Stoke City (on loan), 4 games
1994–96 Southampton, 40 games
1996–97 Plymouth Argyle, 41 games
1997–98 Oldham Athletic, 4 games*
1998 Bury, 1 game
1998 Lincoln City, 2 games*

Internationals:
1975–98 Rhodesia/Zimbabwe, 21 caps

Honours as player with Liverpool:
1982 First Division and League Cup
1983 First Division, League Cup and
FA Charity Shield
1984 European Cup, First Division and League Cup
1986 First Division and FA Cup
1987 FA Charity Shield (shared)
1988 First Division
1989 FA Cup and FA Charity Shield
1990 First Division and FA Charity Shield
1992 FA Cup

– *Women's football* –

The More Beautiful Game.

> The billboard slogans for the 2005 Women's European
> Championship Finals in England

Women's football is a game that should only be played by consenting adults in private.

> Brian Glanville, 1990, journalist

✪ ✪ ✪

The path and history of women's football reminds me in part of the women's suffragette movement. That inspirational cause came to a head during the First World War when working-class women – frustrated by their social and economic status, but taking on traditional male roles because of the shortage of able-bodied men – challenged Parliament and ultimately won equal rights in 1928. The fight for the acceptance of women playing football may not have been quite so dramatic, with no Emily Davison figure throwing herself in front of the monarch's horse and dying for the cause, but it has been a longer campaign and, to a degree, remains in place to this day.

Vic Akers has been coach to the Arsenal Ladies team for 21 years. He started the team and under his inspirational leadership the club have won the Women's Premier League ten times, the League Cup nine times and the FA Cup nine times. Two seasons ago they made history by becoming the first British team to lift the European Cup. Last season the Arsenal Ladies team surpassed even Arsene Wenger's 'Invincibles' team record with one of the greatest winning streaks in sport: played 51, won 51.

Vic is better placed than most to talk about the fight for acceptance of women's football:

> We are not looking for total equality. We just want our own game to be recognised in a proper manner. We are not competing against men and never have been. The biggest factor and difficulty remains chauvinism, a male ignorance of a woman's ability to play good, entertaining football. That remains, although over the last five years there has at least been some progress at club and international level. The last two women's FA Cup finals have attracted crowds in excess of 20,000 and national teams have got anything from 8–10,000 spectators and up to 28,000.

This degree of optimism comes from an individual for whom women's football means a great deal, and it is a cause worth fighting for. The worry is that the fight began as early as the game of football is known. There is clear evidence that an ancient version of the game (Tsu Chu) existed during the Han Dynasty 25–220 CE and was played by women. The earliest realistic dates given for any game resembling football are 5000 BCE.

The game of Association Football, as we have come to know it, involving women's matches, took place in France in the twelfth century and there's evidence of women playing in Scotland in the 1790s. However the first recorded women's match in the UK was in 1892 and took place in Glasgow, with one in England following suit three years later. As with all worthwhile causes, the women's game produced an activist and pioneer. Nettie Honeyball simply placed an advert in a newspaper and asked for 30 young women interested in joining the British Ladies' Football Club. With the help of a Tottenham Hotspur player, J.W. Julian, coaching sessions took place twice a week in a park by the old Alexandra Park racecourse in Hornsey. Honeyball's explanation for creating a team was to the point, touched on feminism and pre-empted the Suffragette movement:

> I founded it with the fixed resolve of proving to the world that women are not the 'ornamental and useless' creatures men have pictured. I confess my convictions on all matters where the sexes are so widely divided are all on the side of emancipation and I look forward to the time when ladies may sit in Parliament and have a voice in the direction of affairs, especially those which concern them most.

Vigorous opposition to the women's game was led by the majority of the press. The *Daily Sketch* reported that 'the first few minutes were sufficient to show that football by women, if the British Ladies' be taken as a criterion, is totally out of the question. A footballer requires speed, judgement, skill and pluck. Not one of those qualities was apparent. For the most part, the ladies wandered aimlessly over the field at an ungraceful jog-trot. North London beat South London 7–1.'

The *British Medical Journal* went much further in its condemnation: 'We can in no way sanction the reckless exposure to violence, of organs which the common experience of women had led them in every way to protect.'

The kit worn by the women attracted comment as well:

The orthodox jerseys were made the basis of the attire but it was seen that a great deal had been left to the coquetry and taste of the wearers. In many instances they were made loose after the manner of blouses and were relieved at the edges by a little white embroidering. Some sleeves, too, were extremely wide, being evidently made after a decidedly fashion-plate pattern. There was the same variety in the make of the knickers. This would seem to be a personal matter for the ladies themselves. Several of them probably more advanced in reformed dress ideas than their sisters, wore the lower garments in the ordinary football fashion.

The next significant movement in the development of women's football came during the First World War. The necessary employment of women to help industry and the war effort, with so many men absent in the forces, led to a preciously limited popularity of the game. During lunch and tea breaks, ladies kicked a ball around and then formed teams who competed and helped raise money for war charities. The Tyne Wear and Tees Alfred Wood Munitions Cup Competition, known as 'The Munitionettes Cup', was won by Blyth Spartans in 1917 and the ladies of Palmer's Shipyard in Jarrow in 1918. The greatest impetus though came from women working at a munitions factory in Preston called Dick, Kerr and Company. They boldly took on men's teams as well as facing other women's sides. Their first serious fundraiser in 1917 attracted a crowd of 10,000 and raised £600 for the wounded military. The Dick, Kerr teams, wearing black and white striped shirts, won 4–0.

The arguments about football being too physical raged on but by 1920 the popularity of Dick, Kerr Ladies led to a match at Everton watched by 53,000, with a further 10,000 unable to gain access to the ground. That same year, the Dick, Kerr side went 'international' with a game in Paris against a French ladies' team.

Just as the women's game was becoming popular, the Football Association in London stepped in and banned it from all football league grounds on the basis that 'the game is quite unsuitable for females and ought not to be encouraged'. The Scottish FA then did the same.

However, tell a good woman that she cannot do something and the response will generally generate a furore. Such was the case in 1921 as the FA's ban was ignored. They couldn't play under the FA's jurisdiction, nor on top grounds but there was no law against women playing football. The Dick, Kerr Ladies, who had played 67 matches in 1921 while still working full time, continued to spread the word and accepted invites to the USA and Canada.

The FA was unhappy that women then formed the English Ladies FA in 1921, playing their matches on rugby grounds or park spaces ... anywhere not affiliated to the Football Association. Although publicity for the women's game was restricted by the male governing body, a fact which slowed its growth, women's football continued to have a dedicated following of players and supporters.

It was clearly an uphill struggle for the ladies but in 1937 'A Championship of Great Britain and the World' saw Dick, Kerr Ladies meet Edinburgh Ladies. Not until 1969 did the male-dominated FA see a degree of commonsense when, as a direct result of the increased interest in football generated by England's 1966 World Cup triumph, the English Women's FA was formed. The first and only secretary of this organisation was Linda Whitehead. She remained in the position until

1993, at which time the same Football Association who had originally banned the women's game, now took control of it, establishing a Women's Football Committee.

Linda was promptly made redundant but has remained 'in love with the game' and following spells at Millwall Ladies and Fulham, now works alongside Vic Akers at the hugely successful Arsenal Ladies. During her years as secretary at the Women's FA there was a lot more recognition of the needs of the ladies' game. One sad aspect was the disbandment in 1969 of the ground breaking Dick, Kerr team, but the part they played in fighting their corner will never be forgotten. Nor their playing record: 838 games during 48 years with 758 wins, 56 draws, 24 defeats and 3,500 goals scored.

Between 1969 and 1993 the following events helped push the women's game forward. In 1971 the FA lifted its ban on women playing on football league grounds and that year the inaugural WFA Cup Final saw Southampton beat Stewarton and Thistle at Crystal Palace National Sports Centre. The following season, in 1972, the first official international took place between England and Scotland. In 1983 the FA invited the WFA to affiliate with them on the same basis as county FAs, and in 1991 the WFA launched a National League with 24 clubs in two divisions plus a League Cup.

The First Women's World Cup took place, also in 1991, although England failed to qualify. Apart from centralising the women's game in 1993, the WFA National Cup Competition was also brought under the control of the FA, becoming the FA Challenge Cup with 137 teams competing.

In 1994 the FA became responsible for the organisation and administration of Women's National League and League Cup Competition with the name changing to the FA Women's Premier League consisting of three divisions of ten teams.

1995 saw the second Women's World Cup held in Sweden and won by Norway. England did qualify but went out in the quarter-finals. In 1997 the FA launched its 'Talent Development Plans for Girls' and Women's Football', and in 1998 twenty centres of excellence for girls were established.

The third Women's World Cup took place in 1999 and saw the USA win while England again failed to qualify. In 2002 a significant moment for women's football came with the declaration that it was now officially the top sport played by women and girls in England. The fourth Women's World Cup in 2003 was retained by the USA, although England were absent once more. The States' star player was Mia Hamm, who retired shortly afterwards following fourteen years representing her country and scoring more goals (158) in internationals than any other player, male or female, in the history of the game.

The 2005 UEFA Championship was staged in England and won by Germany, and that was followed in 2006 by the FA's Women's Premier League being reorganised into two Divisions – North and South – each of twelve teams, below which were four Combination Leagues – North, South East, South West and Midland – also of twelve teams apiece.

Significantly, England did qualify for the 2007 Women's World Cup in China, but the USA knocked them out in the quarter-finals and Germany won the tournament. This was the season that the Arsenal Ladies achieved an unprecedented quadruple by winning three domestic trophies and the UEFA Cup, Europe's top competition. In the latest season, 2008, Vic Akers' Arsenal Ladies side won the Premiership for the fifth consecutive season, their tenth title in sixteen years.

So women's football has come a long way from the early tentative steps taken by Nettie Honeyball and the Dick, Kerr

Ladies team, but what should be the next step forward? Vic Akers and Linda Whitehead have clear visions of the way ahead. Vic believes that:

> We have still to improve the product. The skills of the girls and the physical side have advanced hugely. Although there is a healthy respect between the international and club games, there needs to be more input from the FA into the grassroots level. There is a thought that playing women's football between March and August as a summer league could work. Sky TV would possibly broadcast it on Thursday evenings. Let's try it and test it. Money will be the key issue as always.

Linda is less enthusiastic about the possibilities of the summer game for women but agrees that 'the FA have a big part to play with the input at existing club and grassroots level. £120,000 is a drop in the ocean for the FA but if twelve teams could apply for a £10,000 grant it would enable them to gain enough players to field a first and reserve side or good physio back-up.'

In talking to people like Linda and Vic you begin to fully appreciate the full story of women's football, its appeal and its problems. Vic Akers has never set to gain from his role which is unpaid and, until recently, unheralded. For him it's 'always been a pleasure' and it would be fitting for his dedication to women's football to be recognised publicly. The 2008–09 season could be his last and the women's game is in his debt.

The next big step forward for women's football should be to make it professional. A brief attempt in England by one club failed, and although the USA is currently proposing such a move we shouldn't hold our breath about it happening in the UK. The suffragettes achieved their aims. Women and football are still seeking a greater degree of respect and recognition alongside the man's game.

Gary Lineker

Football is a simple game. 22 men chase a ball for 90 minutes and at the end, the Germans win.

Gary Lineker

It's not deliberate. I don't think anyone would contrive an image as sickly sweet as mine.

Gary Lineker

☉ ☉ ☉

Different generations of footballers, different lifestyles and yet Gary Lineker and I have several things in common. We both love golf, although he has a single figure handicap; neither of us was booked or sent off in our entire professional playing days, something which is quite rare; he succeeded me as the presenter of BBC's *Football Focus* programme; both of us faced the ordeal that presents itself when one of your children is diagnosed with cancer and oh, I guess we both like crisps.

Gary was a terrific goalscorer, a great striker but strangely his brilliance is not reflected in team honours won with England or with his five clubs – Leicester City, Everton, Barcelona, Spurs and Nagoya Grampus Eight. Two hundred and eighty-three goals scored in 567 appearances is magnificent, but in return one Copa del Rey and a UEFA Cup Winners' Cup with Barça and one FA Cup with Spurs – three trophies – is disappointing.

Similarly with England, he had an amazing strike rate – 48 goals in 80 appearances – but no tournament triumph. Not that it stopped him gaining immense popularity. Some of his performances in an England shirt were breathtaking. As top scorer in the 1986 World Cup tournament he was presented with the Golden Boot Award, the only England player ever to achieve that distinction.

In the 1990 World Cup finals in Italy, four Lineker goals helped England to the semi-finals, only for West Germany to triumph in the penalty shootout. During that fateful game Gary showed his experience and understanding in a very public manner. The TV cameras picked up his very visual gesture, which made manager Bobby Robson aware that Paul Gascoigne was in tears following a booking which would have ruled him out of the final, had England made it.

National hero status has sat easily upon Gary Lineker's shoulders. He has a presence and an intelligence which has led to a fine career in the media. It is in this TV arena, not football that I may just have had some small influence upon him and what he wanted to do once he retired as a player. For nearly two seasons when he was contracted to the Japanese team Grampus Eight, he was a regular guest alongside me in the *Football Focus* studio. The fact that I had by then enjoyed more than eighteen years working for the BBC in that and other presenting roles must have had an impact upon him. It would have been interesting to see what the hierarchy at the Beeb would have done had I not been headhunted by ITV Sport at the same time as Gary retired as a player in 1994 before moving into a presenter's chair.

He certainly would have learned a lesson or two from me on how not to present. On one occasion the words 'passed a late fitness test' came out from my mouth as 'pissed a late fatness test'! Such are the perils of live TV. The Lineker presenting style is, I believe, quite close to the Lynam method, with Gary always using a little whimsy in a similar vein to the great Des.

Huge commercial opportunities have come his way, notably the Walkers Crisps campaign which he has fronted since 1995. He is a very wealthy man but knows only too well from first-hand experience that money is secondary to the health of yourself and those you love.

Gary's eldest son George was diagnosed with a rare form of leukaemia as a baby in the early 90s. With great medical assistance, George fought his cancer and won. Today he is a healthy teenager. My daughter Anna fought her rare malignant schwannoma type of cancer as well. She definitely won her fight with the evil disease but ultimately was not as lucky as George.

Our children's respective battles with a life-threatening illness mean there will always be a common bond between Gary and me. I support his charity golf days which raise much needed funds for the ongoing treatment of Leukaemia. He supports my charity's cause in return – two lucky footballers who understand better than most what is really important in life and what isn't.

⚽ ⚽ ⚽

Gary Winston Lineker

Born:
30 November 1960, Leicester

Position:
Striker

Clubs as player:
1978–85 Leicester City, 216 games (103 goals)
1985–86 Everton, 52 games (38 goals)
1986–89 FC Barcelona, 138 games (53 goals)
1989–92 Tottenham Hotspur, 138 games (80 goals)
1992–94 Nagoya Grampus Eight, 23 (9 goals)

Internationals:
1984–92 England, 80 caps (48)

Honours as player with Leicester City:
1980 Promotion to Division One
1983 Promotion to Division One

Honours as player with FC Barcelona:
1988 Copa del Rey
1989 UEFA Cup Winners' Cup

Honours as player with Tottenham Hotspur:
1991 FA Cup

Awards:
1986 FIFA World Cup Golden Boot, PFA Player of the Year and
FWA Footballer of the Year
1992 FWA Footballer of the Year
1992 OBE

– *Penalty shootouts* –

I hate penalty shootouts as a means of settling any game, final or tournament. I would prefer a replay (or replays) so that a result doesn't come down to Lady Luck. What upsets me most is that it is usually goalkeepers who become instant heroes with a save (or saves).

It is strange perhaps that, as a goalkeeper, I feel so strongly on this issue, but the reason is that in penalty shootouts the keepers decide the outcome with a mixture of skill and usually breaking of the rules. I maintain that the majority of times that a goalie guesses correctly and saves, he has his feet at least one yard, if not more, off his goal line. This contravenes 'Law 14: The Penalty Kick', which states quite clearly that the defending goalkeeper 'remains on his goal line, facing the kicker, between the goalposts, until the ball has been kicked'.

So a keeper can jump around as much as he likes on the line, but not move off it until the ball is on its way. Referees and assistants have ignored this clause for years. In the last yard or metre before a penalty taker strikes the ball, all goalies venture off their line in an attempt to cut down or narrow the size of the goal – and you can't blame the keeper for taking advantage.

Either the laws are there to be upheld or we may as well not have any. I have discussed this with countless officials and have yet to get an explanation of why the rule continues to be ignored.

⚽ ⚽ ⚽

Significant shootouts

1970: First penalty shootout in England in a professional match

Semi-final of Watney Cup Hull City vs. Manchester United

George Best first player to score

Denis Law first player to miss

1976: Euro '76 Final – first major international tournament to be decided by penalties

With the score at 2–2 after extra-time, Czechoslovakia beat West Germany 5–3 in the shootout

Uli Hoeneß is the only player to miss for West Germany

Antonin Panenka scores the winning kick

1994: First FIFA World Cup Final decided on penalties

With the match between Brazil and Italy locked at 0–0 after extra-time, Brazil hold their nerve to win the shootout 3–2

Marcio Santos misses Brazil's first penalty

Franco Baresi, Daniele Massaro and Roberto Baggio all miss for Italy

2005: First FA Cup Final decided on penalties

After a goalless game, Arsenal beat Manchester United 5–4 on penalties

Paul Scholes misses early on for United

Patrick Vieira scores the decisive spot-kick

England vs. Germany:

Success rate in penalty shootouts at World Cups:
Germany 100 per cent (4 out of 4)
England 0 per cent (0 out of 3)

1990 World Cup semi-final

England	*Germany*
Lineker scores (1–0)	Brehme scores (1–1)
Beardsley scores (2–1)	Matthaus scores (2–2)
Platt scores (3–2)	Riedle scores (3–3)
Pierce misses (3–3)	Thon scores (3–4)
Waddle misses (3–4)	

1996 European Championship

England	*Germany*
Shearer scores (1–0)	Hassler scores (1–1)
Platt scores (2–1)	Strunz scores (2–2)
Pearce scores (3–2)	Reuter scores (3–3)
Gascoigne scores (4–3)	Ziege scores (4–4)
Sheringham scores (5–4)	Kuntz scores (5–5)
Southgate misses (5–5)	Moller scores (5–6)

Glenn Hoddle

His control was superb and he had perfect body balance. His skill in both feet was uncanny. I couldn't understand why he hadn't been appreciated in England. Perhaps he was a star in the wrong period, years ahead of his time.

Arsene Wenger

If Hoddle had been French he would have won 150 caps.

Michael Platini

I hear Glenn Hoddle has found God. That must have been one hell of a pass.

Jasper Carrott, comedian

❂ ❂ ❂

Glenn Hoddle was one of, if not the most, naturally gifted club players of his generation but never fully appreciated by a country that preferred huff and puff in their footballers. He then became one of the most tactically astute managers England had ever appointed but was discarded prematurely.

Popularity with the public can be a brittle thing as ability and personality seem to be necessary qualifications, allied to the knack of being articulate. Glenn found it difficult to explain the real reason why the nation's favourite player, Paul Gascoigne, was excluded from a World Cup squad, and caused offence while trying to convey strongly-held views on religion.

Glenn is not an extrovert. He is down to earth, loves football, enjoys a joke but can appear solemn and serious. Frankly religion and football are uncomfortable bedfellows so, at the start, Glenn Hoddle's strong belief in God was bound to suffer in the face of a cynical media. When the press got to know that England players were visiting Eileen Drewery in the hope that her healing powers would improve long-term injuries, many decided he was a crank. I believe that no player was ever forced to go to see Eileen and several will tell you the visits were beneficial. Some will testify to her amazing powers of healing and a few will ridicule her as a joke. I got to know Eileen during my daughter Anna's time with cancer. Anna herself reached a stage in her illness where she was prepared to consult with anyone who just might be able to relieve her pain. She found her visits to Eileen extremely beneficial in creating a feeling of calmness and peace that in turn helped to soothe her mind.

As for Glenn Hoddle's reasons for not picking Gascoigne for the England squad that went to France for the 1998 World Cup finals, he was surely correct. The problems Gazza was creating on a daily basis in the lead-up to the choice of the final squad were witnessed by everyone covering the England preparation. His wild antics and behaviour were fuelled by excessive drink, a habit that should never be tolerated in any player representing his country. Everyone in the squad was aware of the problem that the manager faced: Gazza was a great talent, amusing company, but under the influence of drink had a tendency towards violent behaviour. Glenn Hoddle would have been kidding himself had he decided to select Gascoigne. He could have made it easy for himself by going public at the time on Gazza's reaction to his exclusion. It is to Glenn's credit that he chose to remain private on the player's behaviour. Only later would he reveal how Paul initially shook his manager's hand in acceptance, only to turn violent within seconds, smashing a lamp in the process. The omission of a player who could add a different dimension to any England team became a lead story in the national news.

Gazza had his supporters in figures such as Chris Waddle and Chris Evans, close friends of his whose words only fuelled the debate and made life even more uncomfortable for Glenn. His decision was brave and correct. England were unlucky to lose to Argentina on penalties in France '98, and that after a great Michael Owen goal, a fine headed goal by Sol Campbell that was disallowed, and the David Beckham dismissal. In the days that followed England's elimination, Glenn Hoddle took up a role for the rest of the tournament as an ITV analyst. There was never any self-pity, only disappointment.

It's a shame that a playing and management career, in which Glenn Hoddle achieved so much, still centres on Gazza, Eileen Drewery and what he insists were misinterpreted words that were credited to him in which he suggested that disabled people were punished for sins in a previous life. Those who knew about his commitment to charitable causes, including organisations that help the disabled, see a different person to the one vilified and sacked by the Football Association. I prefer to recall a player of sublime balance, great control and unrivalled ability when passing a football.

⚽ ⚽ ⚽

Glenn Hoddle

Born:
27 October 1957, Hayes, Middlesex

Position:
Attacking midfielder

Clubs as player:
1975–87 Tottenham Hotspur, 490 games (110 goals)
1987–91 AS Monaco, 87 games (30 goals)
1991–93 Swindon Town, 75 games (3 goals)
1993–95 Chelsea, 38 games (1 goal)

Internationals:
1979–88 England, 53 caps (8 goals)

Clubs as player-manager:
1991–93 Swindon Town
1993–95 Chelsea

Clubs as manager:
1996 Chelsea
2000–01 Southampton
2001–03 Tottenham Hotspur
2004–06 Wolverhampton Wanderers

International teams as manager:
1996–99 England

Honours as player with Tottenham Hotspur:
1978 Promotion to First Division
1981 FA Cup and FA Charity Shield
1982 FA Cup
1984 UEFA Cup

Honours as player with AS Monaco:
1988 Ligue 1

– *The academy system* –

However justifiable the claims made by the Premier League about the worldwide appeal of their product, they need to heed the ongoing question posed by most football fans: 'But where is the next generation of England international players coming from?'

Between them, the Premier League and the Football Association will point to what's known as the academy system. Now ten years old, it has still to be accepted by many coaches involved with youth development as producing the excellence and top-class individuals for the England national side for which it was designed.

To learn more about the system I turned to Neil Banfield, now reserve team coach for Arsenal, but who has spent seventeen years involved with youth development, first with Charlton and then his current club. To suggest that Neil is less than enthusiastic about the success of the academy system is an understatement. He immediately homed in on a couple of anomalies – the fact that the real aim of producing world-class footballers has simply not happened and that the idea of keeping players confined to their local area has not exactly been thought out properly. Youngsters with potential have to be within an hour's drive of an academy, which leaves a club like Everton with a problem as 45 per cent of their catchment area is in the sea!

Neil's experience is that the best players like Wayne Rooney would have developed naturally, regardless of the system now in place. To fulfil academy status, a club must have a team in each of the designated age groups. In the opinion of the Arsenal coach:

The system is being diluted, a case of having quantity not quality with seven or eight players in each age group not being good enough. The system at present is developing teams not individuals, which it was primarily set up to do. The quality of your overall group dictates the level of your coaching. If it's a poor group you may need more than one coach. What is really needed is to put the best with the best, not place restrictions by age groups. There are too many kids in the system. It needs a real shake up. We need to be concentrating on coaching the very best talent, someone like sixteen-year-old Jack Wilshere at Arsenal. I see a player like him and I get really excited at his potential. In Arsene Wenger's words, 'the game talks to Jack'. Why is it that countries like Holland and Croatia, with relatively small numbers of players, continue to produce outstanding individuals and we don't? It's about the time spent with the very best, the time we have with our players. Currently we have a couple of days with our twelve-, thirteen- and fourteen-year-olds. Take Cesc Fabregas at a similar age in Spain. He was coached five times a week and that is the case, in the main, on the continent. Time spent educating the outstanding young talent, that's the answer. It may well be we need not only a total shake-up to the system, but a new breed of coaches as well, perhaps led by a foreigner. In my opinion it is no surprise that Bobby Robson was the most successful England manager in recent history. After Ipswich Town and England, he decided to go abroad to Holland, then Portugal and finally Spain. He had the guts and the foresight to go and work and see how it's done in

Europe and complete his coaching and managerial education.

Neil Banfield is not alone in his views about the value and lack of success of the academy system as it exists in 2008. There is an air of frustration within so many fine coaches who are desperately striving to develop great players but who, at this moment, are unable to convince the FA and Premier League that the radical shake-up is required. In essence the best solutions are usually simple, and in Neil Banfield's opinion, 'We need to put the best with the best. They need to be stretched.'

David Beckham

After training he'd always be practising, practising, practising, but his life changed when he met his wife. She's in pop and David got another image. He's developed this 'fashion thing'. I saw his transition to a different person.

Sir Alex Ferguson, 2003

There is nothing more important than the state of David Beckham's foot.

Tony Blair, 2002

Beckham can't kick with his left foot. He can't head a ball, can't tackle and doesn't score many goals. Apart from that, he's alright.

George Best, 2000

⚽ ⚽ ⚽

My meetings with David Beckham, the latest of which came at the Arsenal training ground in January 2008, have been few and far between. As always, he had a ready smile and a handshake. He was receiving a massage as part of his time spent maintaining his fitness prior to rejoining LA Galaxy for pre-season training. David was enjoying his time as a guest of Arsene Wenger who, in turn, felt that Beckham's experience would be of value to his talented young team. The Arsenal squad were suitably impressed by David's personality and the opportunity to get to know better the richest British footballer in the history of the game.

The Beckhams' wealth is well documented, Victoria's life as a Spice Girl creating one of the biggest celebrity lifestyles that the world has ever witnessed. Two aspects of David Beckham's continued rise intrigue me: the fact that a brilliant footballer, but by no means one of the greatest of all time, could amass such fame and fortune in such a relatively short period of time; and the near-impossible task Becks faces in trying to live a normal life, remain grounded and stay in touch with the real world.

Make no mistake; his skills on a football field have contributed to the success of his clubs in Manchester and Madrid. The 'honours won' list is impressive. His entry into that unique 100-cap club has also added to his legacy and ensured a comfortable lifestyle for the rest of his days. But it is his fame beyond football which makes him a megastar. Chiselled good looks, plus the sporting gifts, plus a celebrity wife have created the most marketable of commodities. Fashion, hair, cosmetics, fitness and health are just a small part of the Beckham brand. In 2007 David and Victoria Beckham reportedly received in excess of $13 million to launch their fragrance line alone.

A few years ago, as a Real Madrid player, he was the highest-paid sportsman in the world with an annual salary of around €6.5 million and advertising deals worth more than double that in a total given as €22.4million. Of course these figures are all guesswork but give or take the odd million or two they are a pretty accurate reflection of the astonishing world that David now lives in. His American adventure and Hollywood lifestyle remain front-page news.

It is to his credit that he still retains a shy, almost modest persona. You would think such a thing impossible but it is fact. He knows how lucky he has been, how lucky he is and where he came from, the son of a kitchen fitter and a hairdresser.

The demands on his time and the threats to his security demand a large and vigilant team around him, one that protects as well as advises the family. Admittedly it is very difficult to make personal contact, unlike with players of my generation. If we didn't exactly travel on public transport with fans on the way to matches, we did walk in and out of grounds freely and openly, pens at the ready for the obligatory autographs. Times have changed. A David Beckham signature can be worth a lot of money on eBay. As a retired footballer I still receive numerous requests for my signature each week. Multiply what I am asked to sign by a thousand and you might get some idea of the problems facing today's stars. Whenever there is a deserving cause, a request for worthwhile charitable work, there will be a positive response from David Beckham. The Willow Foundation has reason to be grateful to him on more than one occasion and one of the most poignant requests emphasises the impact that someone like David can have on a seriously ill young person and their family.

Our charity received a request from a dad whose son wanted to meet David Beckham. When we got in touch, the England captain agreed to fulfil the wish at an international training session. Sadly the young man was not well enough to leave his bed and it was decided that a phone message would have to suffice. During the conversation, which lasted more than ten minutes, the recipient discussed his condition and how he spent some time, illness permitting, on a Playstation. David duly offered to send the latest game, which arrived a day or so later. At the end of the conversation the young man asked if it was possible to have a signed David Beckham shirt. In due course that arrived as well and the combined effect of the two presents and the chat ensured that the last days of a young man's life contained smiles as well as lovely memories for his family.

Such understanding and consideration is the means by which David Beckham remains as approachable as he does, a perfect ambassador and one who is guaranteed to give back to the game that created his fame.

☺ ☺ ☺

David Robert Joseph Beckham

Born:
2 May 1975, Leytonstone

Position:
Midfield

Clubs as player:
1993–2003 Manchester United, 394 games (81 goals)
1995 Preston North End (on loan), 5 games (2 goals)
2003–07 Real Madrid, 153 games (19 goals)
2007 to date LA Galaxy

Internationals:
1996 to date England, 101 caps (17 goals)

Honours as player with Manchester United:
1993 FA Charity Shield
1994 FA Charity Shield
1996 Premier League, FA Cup and FA Charity Shield
1997 Premier League and FA Charity Shield
1999 UEFA Champions League, Premier League, FA Cup and
Intercontinental Cup
2000 Premier League
2001 Premier League
2003 Premier League

Honours as player with Real Madrid:
2003 Supercopa de Espana
2007 La Liga

Awards:
1997 PFA Young Player of the Year
1999 UEFA Club Player of the Year
2001 BBC Sports Personality of the Year
2003 OBE

– Cards –

The concept of red and yellow cards for helping to officiate football matches was invented by English former referee and then chairman of the FIFA international referee committee, Kenneth George Aston. He was going about his business in the FIFA offices one day when a call came in from the 1966 World Cup tournament manager, querying whether Bobby and Jack Charlton had been cautioned in the England–Argentina match the previous day, in which the referee spoke only German. It turned out he'd just received a call from the Charlton brothers asking him to check – as the first they knew of their booking was from reading the Sunday papers over breakfast.

Aston thought little more about it, but, while driving home, he encountered four sets of traffic lights, all green as he approached but all halting his progress as they quickly changed to yellow and then red. At the fourth set of lights, the idea came to Aston that this was a way of overcoming the language barrier in international matches. The cards were first used in the World Cup finals in Mexico in 1970, and due to their immediate success were soon used in leagues all over the world – even when language differences were not an issue.

David Seaman

I've told him to cut off his ponytail. It makes him less aerodynamic!

Arsene Wenger, 2002

A great ability of Seaman's, one I lacked, was his knack of calming people down ... the big smile and the arm round the shoulders providing a steadying influence on his teammates.

Peter Schmeichel, 2004

❖ ❖ ❖

I was David Seaman's coach during his entire career at Arsenal between 1990 and 2003, having previously helped him for a short time at QPR. During our time together I watched him pick up nine major trophies, finish as a runner-up on seven more occasions, take his England caps tally to 75 and receive an MBE following Euro '96 when tournament sponsors Philips named him Player of the Tournament. However such is the goalkeeper's lot, whereby weird goals are remembered as much as outstanding saves, that many observers recall a speculative Nayim shot and an even more fluky strike by Ronaldinho when talking about 'The Goalie'.

Neither did it help his cause to be ridiculed over growing a ponytail. Ask David in Catherine Tate manner whether he is 'bovvered' and you'll get a big chuckle and an even bigger smile. Together with Pat Jennings, he has the greatest presence of any goalkeeper I have watched, an inbuilt calm that has allowed him to accept the plaudits and brickbats inherent in the position he chose with dignity.

Our friendship has exceeded a simple coach-player relationship. At work we developed an almost telepathic understanding. At play we shared many happy moments and occasionally a downer. I was best man at his wedding to Debbie. He was a rock for me as I struggled to come to terms with losing a daughter to cancer.

I first met David when former Arsenal coach and manager Don Howe asked me to find a day free to coach the goalkeepers at QPR. Initially David gave me the impression of being his own man, single minded, even bloody minded, a proud Yorkshireman intent on reaching the top of his tree. This attitude allied to a remarkable physique – 6' 4½", 15st 3lbs – gave him a huge advantage over many of his peers. He was a natural for sport in general, excelling at cricket, tennis, golf and, most important to him, fishing. I played a part in his move from Loftus Road to Highbury by confirming to Arsenal manager George Graham that he had chosen the best available.

What that meant was a rare consistency matched at the time perhaps by only Peter Schmeichel of Manchester United. On the training field David always demanded self-perfection. Any error of judgment or handling saw him react with genuine anger at himself. Any stupendous save and you might elicit a deep chuckle and a sheepish grin. He loved his job and appreciated the lifestyle it afforded him. His teammates liked him immensely and gained strength from his calm. As his coach and mentor I was aware that he needed to be challenged constantly. I would set him targets. When it came to 'crunch' games and cup finals I usually crept into the dressing room before he arrived, whether it was Highbury or Wembley, and left him a message and a keepsake as a harbinger of luck.

Before one of his four FA Cup Final wins I placed a pair of my old green cotton goalkeeping gloves on his bench. They were all that was available in my day, cost five shillings and sixpence and were useless compared to the highly technical goalkeepers' gloves of the modern era. The accompanying message was to the point, 'If I could play well in these, there can be no excuses for you today.' Before his very first FA Cup Final in 1993 I wrote down the names of previous Arsenal Cup-winning keepers: '1930 Preedy; 1936 A. Wilson; 1950 Swindin; 1971 R. Wilson; 1979 Jennings; 1993 Seaman'.

Nine photos exist showing us together at the moment of triumph, a League Championship win, FA Cup, League Cup and European glory, but there are no recorded moments of when it went wrong. When Nayim won the Cup Winners' Cup for Real Zaragosa in extra-time with a 45-yard shot there were dressing room tears, unusual in itself for David Seaman. Similarly Ronaldinho's free kick goal in the World Cup quarter-final against Brazil also led to a tearful England keeper. Those were the moments I was most useful, the occasions when I could get on his wavelength of despair and talk him through the agony. His starting position for both Nayim and Ronaldinho's goals was one that the majority of keepers would have adopted. Part of the goalie's expertise is in playing percentages when it comes to leaving his goal untended in order to support his defence. His recovery from the misery was always remarkable, accepting of criticism, ready to display his talent and enjoy the next challenge. His save from Paul Peschisolido in the Arsenal vs. Sheffield United FA Cup semi-final in 2003 was comparable with Gordon Banks' stop from Pele in 1970. Peter Schmeichel recognised it when he stated, 'That was one of the best saves I've seen, one of the greatest ever.'

Having an intimate insight into David's glittering career has been a privilege, acting as his best man in 1998 was as challenging. There is almost a 32-year age difference between us, but it mattered little to him when he approached me on the training ground one day and said before a training session, 'By the way, I need you to put a date in your diary 'cos you're going to be best man at my wedding.' It was a lovely way for him to express his gratitude to me for the work we undertook together.

Money is of secondary importance to health and David recognised this as he shared our family's journey with Anna during five sad, yet enriching, years in her fight with cancer. He and Debbie became friendly with our daughter and her husband Mitchell. They played a part in organising with Megs and the BBC the *This Is Your Life* programme which was sprung on me on 2 November 1998 at the Arsenal training ground. As I went out to coach David and the other keepers he told me that there would 'probably be another film crew around' that day. It was nothing new. He was the England keeper, a household name, famous throughout the UK. Sure enough, a BBC TV crew were in position as we began the session. It was interrupted by the entire Arsenal squad running unusually in a group towards our goalkeeping area. They stopped in front of a puzzled looking coach and from the middle of the pack there emerged my lovely Breakfast TV work friend, Jill Dando and Michael Aspel, who held in his grasp the famous red book. When I initially declined to go ahead with the programme because Anna's health was so poor, David helped persuade me that she was behind the surprise. Later that day he was the second guest to appear from behind the *This Is Your Life* screen. He remains a patron of the Willow Foundation set up in Anna's memory a few months after that extraordinary day.

Unlike me he is not a fanatical follower of the game. Only rarely does he go to watch a match live. His personality is such that he has remained a well-known celebrity and his sporting prowess has led him to ice dancing fame. I would like him to give back to the game of football some of the priceless knowledge he acquired during his 22-year career. So would he, and the specialist goalkeeping badges that he requires are now in place.

Since 1966 the England international team has enjoyed three world-class goalkeepers and not one of them has been asked by the Football Association to help restore some sense of pride in a position which was once dominated by England and the likes of Gordon Banks, Peter Shilton and David Seaman.

☙ ☙ ☙

David Andrew Seaman

Born:
19 September 1963, Rotherham

Position:
Goalkeeper

Clubs as player:
1982–84 Peterborough United, 106 games
1984–86 Birmingham City, 75 games*
1986–90 Queens Park Rangers, 149 games
1990–2003 Arsenal, 563 games
2003–04 Manchester City, 26 games

Internationals:
1988–2002 England, 75 caps

Honours as player with Arsenal:
1991 First Division
1993 FA Cup and League Cup
1994 UEFA Cup Winners' Cup
1998 Premier League and FA Cup
2002 Premier League and FA Cup
2003 FA Cup

Awards:
1997 MBE

– *Transfer spending* –

British clubs can sign players between the end of the season and 31 August. The only other window lasts throughout January. The following list shows, apart from 2004, the continuing rise in transfer payments made by British clubs, a trend that surely cannot continue at this rate:

2003	£230 million
2004	£215 million
2005	£235 million
2006	£282 million
2007	£375 million

Paul Gascoigne

George Best without brains.

Stan Seymour, 1988, Newcastle United chairman

I've got the full set of problems. It's not just the booze, it's the panic attacks, bipolar disorder, the purging – it's everything I have to deal with every day. For me to be alive proves there is a God.

Paul Gascoigne, 2005

He wears a number 10 jersey. I thought it was his position but it turns out to be his IQ.

George Best

Tyneside's very own Renaissance man. A man capable of breaking both leg and wind at the same time.

Jimmy Greaves

Gazza reminds me of Marilyn Monroe. She wasn't the greatest actress in the world but she was a star and you didn't mind if she was late.

Michael Caine

✪ ✪ ✪

Everyone who has got to know and spend time with 'Gazza' will have a story to tell. At best it will recall his footballing ability, a rare talent the like of which should be nurtured, polished and cherished. At worst the tales will border on the lurid; unseemly stories touching on a demented soul, often alone confronting his demons.

'Daft as a brush' was Bobby Robson's description of a lad who was, arguably, the best player on view in the 1990 World Cup. England, with Robson in charge, came within a missed penalty of making the final in that tournament. Had they done so, Gazza would not have been eligible, booked famously in the semi-final against Germany. Distraught for all to see, his tears captured the hearts of a nation.

It is an iconic image even now, eighteen years later. So too is the photo taken three or four years earlier which sees Paul expressing a shout of surprise and pain as Wimbledon 'hard man' Vinnie Jones reaches backwards and grabs the brash, young, talented Newcastle lad's 'goolies'.

In the following week after this incident I met Paul Gascoigne for the first time. He was the subject of a *Football Focus* profile having burst on to the senior stage and caught the eye of the footballing world with his running ability, exquisite touch of a ball and eye for a telling pass at Newcastle United. Paul has always recalled the interview as his first 'big' moment in the public eye. Access to him was out of the ordinary. Most footballers are happy to make themselves available for publicity purposes but for a limited time only. On that day Paul met us after training at 1.30 pm and was still with us as we shot the closing sequence with the sun setting dramatically on a lake where we sat in a rowing boat, talking about one of his favourite hobbies, fishing. Few pros have been so cooperative.

Within that chat we discussed the expectation of many great judges who had given a view on his potential. One was Jackie Milburn, the legendary 'Wor Jackie' whose feats in a Magpies shirt included three FA Cup triumphs and 238 goals in 492 games. Today the St James' Park West Stand is named after Jackie and two statues of him exist locally, one adorning his birthplace at Ashington and the other close to Newcastle's ground. In an interview that day, the old hero was effusive in his praise of the emerging kid, actually suggesting that Paul could become the 'greatest' footballer England had ever seen. He had watched Gazza's progress carefully from youth days to his breakthrough into the first team. Jackie's only concerns were related to Paul's choice of friends and his hyperactivity. At that stage there were no worries about booze and drugs.

We now know the truth, a long litany of abuse by Gazza of alcohol and worse has taken him to the brink of suicide and extreme mental depression. The wonderful naturally friendly and funny side of this enormous talent has provided unforgettable memories for those who have seen it. Colleagues like David Seaman could tell you a million entertaining tales of Paul's times in the England camp. Less amusing would be the stories of an out-of-control player who needed a protective arm around him for the majority of the day. During the 2002 World Cup finals, Paul was one of ITV's panel of experts. It was a huge gamble by the ITV hierarchy and it was one that did not work because he was constantly under the influence of drink.

The saddest aspect of Gazza's career is that it will be remembered for its genius and madness in equal proportion. We can all visualise his wonder goal against Scotland in Euro '96, but in the same moment came the infamous 'dentist's chair' and the mimicking of an alcohol induced celebration with his England teammates. That was at Wembley and so too was his breathtaking free kick for Spurs that beat his fishing pal David Seaman in the Arsenal goal and took Spurs to the

'91 FA Cup Final. Totally hyped up in the early stages of the final against Nottingham Forest he tackled wildly and a self-inflicted injury left him seriously hurt and hospital-bound.

My wish for Gascoigne is for him to find peace with himself to recognise, even now, that people still love him for his footballing talent and natural humour. Gazza has always been so well-intentioned but ultimately reckless. The late Jackie Milburn would be sad that Paul Gascoigne did not become the 'greatest English footballer ever', but he did add a rider to his prediction during that interview, 'If only ...'

⚽ ⚽ ⚽

Paul John Gascoigne

Born:
27 May 1967, Dunston

Position:
Midfield

Clubs as player:
1985–88 Newcastle United, 104 games (25 goals)
1988–92 Tottenham Hotspur, 112 games (33 goals)
1992–95 Lazio, 47 games (6 goals)
1995–98 Rangers, 104 games (39 goals)
1998–2000 Middlesbrough, 48 games (4 goals)
2000–2002 Everton, 38 games (1 goal)
2002 Burnley, 6 games
2003 Gansu Tianma, 4 games (2 goals)
2004 Boston United, 5 games

Internationals:
1988–98 England, 57 caps (10 goals)

Honours as player with Tottenham Hotspur:
1991 FA Cup

Honours as player with Rangers:
1996 Scottish League and Scottish Cup
1997 Scottish League and League Cup

Awards:
1988 PFA Young Player of the year
1990 BBC Sports Personality of the Year
1996 Scottish Players' and Writers' Player of the Year

– *The Old Firm* –

The rivalry between Celtic and Rangers is one of the oldest and most ferocious in world football, going back to when they first met at Celtic Park in 1888, watched by around 2,000 fans. Today, this collective term for these two Glaswegian clubs is used principally as a short nickname – for instance, when they meet in a local derby. However, when it was first used early in the twentieth century, it was intended as a more scathing implication that the two clubs were in charge of Scottish football at that time, and ran it without consideration of other clubs. The term was chosen to signify the lucrative aspect of their frequent meetings, and the belief that the two clubs colluded to ensure their own profit and consequent domination, at the expense of the other Scottish clubs.

Whether this is true or not, no two teams across the world have dominated their national championship like Celtic and Rangers. As of 2008, between them they have won 92 of the 113 Scottish titles available since 1890.

Although I never knew him, a great uncle of mine – Sir John Ure Primrose – was chairman of Rangers at the turn of the twentieth century, and in 1902 he officially opened Hampden Park.

376

Ian Wright

On his first day at Palace he told me he wanted to play for England, a bold statement for someone who had just walked in off a building site.

Steve Coppell, 1993, Crystal Palace manager

He has put me on grilled fish, grilled broccoli, grilled everything. Yuk!

Ian Wright on the Arsene Wenger diet

⚽ ⚽ ⚽

'Wrighty's' route into professional football followed a similar pattern to my own. He was a late starter, just three months short of his 22nd birthday when he joined Crystal Palace, after pursuing a full-time job as a plasterer. His late teens were strewn with minor offences and involvement with petty crime. He even spent five days in Chelmsford Prison, an experience that impacted upon him in the best possible way for his future behaviour.

Football and his brilliance at scoring goals saved Ian Wright. Without it he may well have hit the headlines for the wrong reasons. He has a personality which is best described as kaleidoscopic – at one moment the funniest and most entertaining of people, the next moody and angry, wearing his heart on his sleeve for all to see.

In a football dressing room he was usually the loudest and most vocal. Such a character is a vital ingredient in creating team spirit. Often his colleagues would tell him he was mad, almost always he made them laugh. But a player doesn't win respect on personality alone; they need to be accepted for an ability to play. Wrighty had already won over Crystal Palace fans by the time he arrived at Arsenal in September 1991. Together with his pal Mark Bright they created a deadly goalscoring duo and it was largely their goals which elevated Palace to the top flight in 1989. In the 1990 FA Cup Final against Manchester United he was used only as a substitute because of injury but came off the bench to equalise for Palace minutes after his arrival, forcing extra-time, during which he put his team ahead. The game ended 3–3, and Palace lost the replay 1–0, but he had made an impact and his 117 goals in 253 starts in all Palace teams over six seasons led him to Arsenal.

At the time, in 1991, the £2.5 million fee was a club-record but what followed in the next seven years will never be forgotten by any fan of the Gunners. Quite small for a main striker, Ian possessed greased-lightning reactions in the penalty area, knew exactly where he was in relation to the goalposts and what was required to beat an opposing goalie. The bigger and better the custodian, the greater challenge it was for the striker, with Peter Schmeichel of Manchester United a main target for Wrighty's wrath.

Ian went on to be the club's top scorer for six seasons in a row and played a major part in the club's many successes up to and including the 1998 Double, although injury curtailed his appearances. He loved great talents and was tactile enough to let them know it – Vieira, Bergkamp and co. were often hugged by their teammate. Thirty-one England appearances seems a small return for such a prolific striker as, in turn, Graham Taylor, Terry Venables and Glenn Hoddle all used Ian Wright spasmodically.

When he broke Cliff Bastin's Arsenal goalscoring record on 13 September 1997, he celebrated as you would expect – extravagantly. Few people anticipated it would be a record that, in turn, stood for a relatively short time, with Thierry Henry surpassing it in October 2005. There was little doubt about what Ian Wright would do when his career eventually petered out at West Ham, Nottingham Forest, Celtic and Burnley. In an age when celebrity seems to have pre-eminence in media circles, Wrighty was a natural. Never afraid to act the fool, never short of a word or two, funny and with a huge smile, he was soon invading our TV screens on programmes like *Friday Night's All Wright*, *What Kids Really Think About*, *They Think It's All Over* and *Gladiators*. TV ads and radio work were also part of the Wright package.

He has maximised the natural talents he has been given and helped the black community when racism was a bigger issue than it is now. He shows respect when he feels it is due and still calls me 'Mr Wilson'. He is also lucky and knows that people like his old manager George Graham could guide him when he was in the wrong and get him to channel all that energy in the right direction. Ian recalls a shocking punch-up involving Spurs' player David Howells in the biography *Mr Wright*:

George Graham slaughtered me and told me that I was a disgrace to myself and a disgrace to Arsenal and that he wouldn't put up with another incident like the Howells affair. But he also told me that it was the fire in my belly that made me such an effective player and that I should never lose that, just learn to control it.

❁ ❁ ❁

Ian Edward Wright

Born:
3 November 1963, Woolwich

Position:
Striker

Clubs as player:
1985–91 Crystal Palace, 277 games (117 goals)
1991–98 Arsenal, 288 games (185 goals)
1998–99 West Ham United, 26 games (9 goals)
1999 Nottingham Forest (loan), 10 games* (5 goals)
1999–2000 Celtic, 10 games (3 goals)
2000 Burnley, 15 games* (4 goals)

Internationals:
1991–98 England, 31 caps (9)

Honours as player with Crystal Palace:
1989 Promotion to First Division

Honours as player with Arsenal:
1993 FA Cup and League Cup
1994 UEFA Cup Winners' Cup
1998 Premier League and FA Cup

Awards:
2002 MBE

– *Falling leaves* –

In my playing era, footballs were made of thick heavy leather, which got even heavier when it rained. They went from A to B in a straight line and that was it. At the 1970 World Cup, a combination of Mexico's thin air and the unique ability of Brazil's legendary Garrincha to hit across the ball produced the first dramatic swerve I had ever seen. However, these days, the modern football is much lighter and if hit hard enough moves around in the air erratically enough to give the keeper a real headache. One swerve and it's a banana, two and it's a falling leaf, mimicking the path of a leaf buffeted by the air. Probably the most famous example of this came at the Tournoi de France in 1997, when another Brazilian, Roberto Carlos, blasted a 37-yard free kick wide of the French wall. Although it seemed to be easily heading out for a goal kick, it took a devastating left swerve at the last minute and ricocheted off the inside of the post into the net. The French goalkeeper at the time, Fabien Barthez, hadn't even moved.

Ruud Gullit

A goalkeeper is a goalkeeper because he can't play football.

Ruud Gullit, 1997

Ruud loved conflict. He enjoyed being at loggerheads with certain players. And he was just so arrogant. His ego was as big as Amsterdam and he didn't even try to disguise it.

Rob Lee, 2000, Newcastle United midfielder

⚽ ⚽ ⚽

Study the goalscoring record of Ruud Gullit at his eight clubs and for Holland and then consider the honours won and marvel and applaud this richly talented son of Amsterdam. The basis of his greatness lay in his self-belief and technical ability. The majority of truly outstanding footballers have a bearing that exudes arrogance. Ruud was arrogant but also had a good sense of humour. The challenge for a football presenter was to get him to show it, to smile and if you were successful, get him to laugh. Des Lynam could often do that and built a lively relationship after Ruud's appealing description of beautiful play as 'sexy football'. I never got much more out of the Dutchman than a smile. More often he exuded an intensity that also appealed to many viewers because it contained a highly critical edge and he was never scared to upset the managers, coaches or players of whom he was asked to give an opinion.

Ruud often lacked humility and his various contretemps throughout his playing career and in his managerial life back this view. A bust-up he had at Newcastle with local hero Alan Shearer and captain Robert Lee is an example of how he could aggravate fans and players alike.

I was less than enamoured when, as a guest of ITV, he became openly critical of aspects of its coverage during France '98 and at Euro 2000, which was held in his homeland. Of course, there was a compulsive appeal about Ruud's style for the watching viewer. His knowledge of the game and personal achievements gave him huge credibility.

I enjoyed it most when he was the lone guest on any programme and our most memorable moment together, no doubt, amused those viewers who find analysis and chat a total switch-off. During the World Cup Finals of France '98 we were in Marseilles where the infamous Mistral winds can play havoc with a live outside broadcast. At halftime the two of us were analysing the first 45 minutes' action. Suddenly we were under siege as a huge swarm of insects swept in on a Mistral current, travelled into our presentation position straight into our eyes, mouths and clothes. It takes quite a lot to stop Ruud Gullit when he is in full flow giving his view. That day proved the exception. I even got a laugh from him as together we warded off the invasion with our hands and arms, and led quickly to an earlier-than-anticipated commercial break.

It was in conversation with one of Ruud's first managers that his greatness was brought home to me. Barry Hughes – a real character and a bald-headed Englishman who had played for West Bromwich Albion – took a young Gullit under his wing at HFC Haarlem. At sixteen he became the youngest player in the history of the Dutch first division. Barry was under no illusions about the ability that Ruud Gullit possessed. He proudly told anyone who would listen that the youngster's power and mobility allowed him to play in any outfield position in a team in the same way that Duncan Edwards had played for Manchester United. A 'total footballer'. His record backs Hughes' judgement.

⚽ ⚽ ⚽

Ruud Gullit

Born:
1 September 1962, Amsterdam, Netherlands

Position:
Midfield/striker

Clubs as player:
1979–82 HFC Haarlem, 91 games (32 goals)
1982–85 Feyenoord, 103 games (41 goals)
1985–87 PSV Eindhoven, 75 games (53 goals)
1987–93 AC Milan, 157 games (52 goals)
1993–94 Sampdoria 41 games (19 goals)
1994 AC Milan, 11 games (3 goals)
1994–95 Sampdoria, 22 games (9 goals)
1995–98 Chelsea, 40 games (7 goals)

Internationals:
1981–93 Netherlands, 66 caps (17 goals)

Clubs as player-manager:
1996–98 Chelsea

Clubs as manager:
1998–99 Newcastle United
2004–05 Feyenoord
2007 to date Los Angeles Galaxy

Honours as player with HFC Haarlem:
1981 Eerste Divisie

Honours as player with Feyenoord:
1984 Eredivisie and KNVB Cup

Honours as player with PSV Eindhoven:
1986 Eredivisie
1987 Eredivisie

Honours as player with AC Milan:
1988 Serie A
1989 UEFA Cup, European Super Cup and Inter-Continental Cup
1990 UEFA Cup, European Super Cup and Inter-Continental Cup
1992 Serie A and Italian Super Cup
1993 Serie A
1994 Italian Super Cup

Honours as player with Sampdoria:
1993 Lotto Cup
1994 Italian Cup

Honours as player with the Netherlands:
1988 European Championship

Honours as player-manager at Chelsea:
1997 FA Cup

Awards:
1984 Dutch Footballer of the Year
1986 Dutch Footballer of the Year
1987 Dutch Sportsman of the Year and FIFA World player of the Year
1989 FIFA World Player of the Year

– The local derby –

Although this term is most commonly used for football, it can be applied to any sport. It's thought to have originated with a tradition started in the Elizabethan era in the town of Ashbourne in Derbyshire, a few miles from where I was born in Chesterfield. Each year, on Shrove Tuesday and Ash Wednesday, the people of the town board up shop windows and take to the streets to play the largest football match in the world. Although it is called the Ashbourne Royal Shrovetide Football Match, a fairly brutal game of rugby with fewer rules and a round ball might be a more accurate description. One team is made up of those born on the north side of the Henmore River, otherwise known as the Up'ards, and the other of those born on the south side – the Down'ards. The game kicks off at 2 pm and is then played until 10 pm on a pitch three miles long. As if that wasn't enough, much of it is played out in the cold waters of the Henmore, including the two goals, which were originally the wheels at the two local mills.

In my twelve years at Arsenal, there were rarely more important, competitive or violent encounters than our local derbies with Spurs, our North London rivals. Victory for one or the other was hugely important for both players and, of course, the fans, in what is always referred to as the North London derby.

Arsene Wenger

*He can explode, especially at half time, if we've been playing badly
and making mistakes. But it's more like a father getting angry with
his sons.*

Emmanuel Petit, 1998

*I like to read books or talk to my wife or daughter, for an hour or so.
But to have a whole day without thinking about football – that is
impossible.*

Arsene Wenger, 2003

*Arsene's a miracle worker. He's revolutionised the club. He's turned
players into world-class stars. Since he has been here, we have seen
football from another planet.*

David Dein, former vice-chairman of Arsenal

Passion has to be part of the game. It is the character of the nation.
You say England, I say passion
You say Germany, I say determination
You say French, I say subtlety
You say Spain, I say pride.

Arsene Wenger, *Arsenal Opus*

⚽ ⚽ ⚽

On 2 October 1996, I was preparing to work with the Arsenal
goalkeepers, when my old teammate Pat Rice walked into the
coaching staff dressing room with a tall, studious, bespectacled
Frenchman. It was my first meeting with Arsene Wenger and

his first full day in charge of Arsenal FC. His face bore a worried expression. The previous day when he had been unveiled by the club as the new manager he had finished up having to defend himself on the steps of Highbury in front of a media circus who were following up lurid accusations, originating on the internet, about his personal life. It was a dreadful beginning and I wouldn't have blamed Arsene if he had caught the next plane back to France and Monaco where he had made his name, or even Japan where his most recent job had been with Nagoya Grampus Eight.

Having faced that ordeal with courage, Arsene's first view of the training ground used by one of the finest British football clubs was another shock for him. Shaking his head in surprise as he looked around the modest facilities which the club rented from the University College of London, he said quizzically 'This is Arsenal?'

That moment signalled the beginning of a French revolution which has totally transformed the old club on the field and off it, an era in which Arsene Wenger has become the greatest manager in Arsenal's illustrious history. That title doesn't just reflect the record number of trophies won compared to any previous manager. It challenges and surpasses even Herbert Chapman's visionary approach to making Arsenal a special club.

Under Arsene's guidance, Arsenal's board of directors have found the finance to set new standards and sanction a state-of-the-art training ground and magnificent new 60,000-seat stadium. The innovative and scientific approach to training methods, dietary matters and the like introduced by Wenger have been copied by all the leading British clubs. Then there is his belief in how teams should play. He demands that his teams provide value for money, spectacle and entertainment worth the sacrifices that so many fans make to support their team by buying tickets costing anything between £40 and £90. Arsene remembers his youth in Strasbourg when he would save up to go and watch his local team only to come away frustrated at poor entertainment and left thinking he had wasted his money.

In almost twelve years Wenger's teams have won the Premier League three times, been runners-up five times, won the FA Cup four times and been runners-up once. They have also finished as runners-up in the League Cup and Champions League. They may not have won as many trophies as the demanding Frenchman would have wished but they have consistently been among the most entertaining to watch. Arsene will not sacrifice his principles and his philosophy should be admired rather than be subjected, as it often is, to scorn. Talent alone is the prime factor in a Wenger team. He inherited a famous back five: Seaman, Dixon, Winterburn, Adams and Bould. They were already ageing when he arrived but he recognised a group of winners who, if they accepted his stretch routines and dietary demands, could extend their careers. He gave a second chance to Tony Adams and Paul Merson, one a recovering alcoholic, the other a gambling addict.

Normally Arsene would start to question a player's capabilities once they reach their thirties. Contracts of one year duration are the norm offered at this age. He believes that is when injuries become more prolific and difficult to heal as opposed to when a player is in his teens or twenties. What he always looks for in a player is power, pace, youth and, as a priority, great technique. He was concerned, even shocked, by the lack of such technique in the vast majority of British footballers. In developing the Arsenal Academy he believed it would take a decade to produce home grown talent. At this moment seven or eight promising English players are on the verge of breaking through into the higher echelons of the game at Arsenal or elsewhere. Those, like David Bentley and Steve Sidwell, who grow impatient, are reluctantly allowed to leave.

A typical day in Arsene's life would start at 6.30 am with him exercising at home prior to leaving for work. He arrives at the training centre at around 9 am. After changing into training kit he tries to catch up on reading the sports sections of the various foreign newspapers. Generally though, he would have to succumb to the constant ringtone of his mobile, switching effortlessly from speaking English to French, German to Spanish, Italian to Japanese.

Training begins at 11 am. He snatches lunch at 2 pm and returns to his office where he deals with all sorts of administrative issues before leaving. He's usually the last to depart for home at 6.30 pm. He doesn't generally go to watch other live matches, choosing instead to have an intimate knowledge of the televised games that might be available to him during the evening.

On one occasion during his early days at Arsenal, I arrived at his home to pick him up to attend a London Football Coaches' Association question-and-answer session. I was a little early, went inside and expressed surprise that there appeared to be no TV in the lounge. Arsene smiled and proceeded to lower a huge screen from one wall which received its picture from an overhead projector. There is a long-standing joke that Arsene only knows three places in London: his home, the training ground, and the Emirates Stadium.

390

He is a workaholic, a man of discipline and one who honours his word. Arsene Wenger hates to lose, but as the old saying goes, 'Show me a good manager who doesn't hate losing and I'll show you a loser'. He tries to come to terms with the fact that football is only a game but in his words, 'You get sucked in and you always feel you can do more. The people who suffer are those you live with.'

With a degree in engineering and economics, Arsene is well placed to give his views on the use of technology in the game. He believes it's time to use technology to assist the four officials who currently have little or no chance of getting every crucial decision correct. He argues:

> Surely all the hard work which goes into scoring goals deserves to receive the correct decision. When there is doubt or a mistake by officials they will gain more respect when turning to an instant replay and coming up with 'the truth'. You need justice to be done. Billions of people are watching and using technology would ultimately give the referees and their assistants more credit and respect. Cheating should not be rewarded as it is now. FIFA talk about people to act as referees on a goal line decision. Why use two or three individuals when one machine can do the job?

Sometimes Arsene can spend many hours studying visual images of his side's movement in defence or attack. He agrees it is an obsession but he likes to go to the root of the problem. 'My job is to win for Arsenal.'

He is equally forthright in his opinion on how clubs should manage their finances. Gate receipts, sponsorship and television money are the three areas that underpin any club's revenue and he feels that turning to wealthy investors is treading a dangerous path and could lead to bankruptcy or an overly autocratic approach.

Predicting the future is something that sits easily on Arsene's shoulders. When he forecast that his team had the capability of going through an entire league season unbeaten, opposing managers, fans and the media poured scorn upon him. Arsenal promptly won the 2003–04 Premiership title without a single defeat, the first top flight team to achieve this feat since 1888–89 when the old Invincibles, Preston North End, played a dozen or so games less. An historic 49 games unbeaten was the final tally for Wenger's side. The magnitude of that achievement has still not been truly recognised.

While his daily existence revolves around football, Arsene has an intellectual interest in life in general. Once on a pre-season tour in Austria, when the players had retired for their evening meal, the Arsenal coaching and medical staff sat on a table with the manager, and silence descended. As the elder statesman, I would tend to offer up a subject for which I would ask Arsene to give his view. I asked him, somewhat mischievously, why mistresses were accepted in France and not in Britain. Arsene gave a glancing smile and then began not a three-sentence answer, but a fifteen-minute lecture that touched on French royalty and government officials and the different attitudes between French and British society. He is very well-read and always receptive to any discussion that reveals changes in everyday life, or challenges involving the human spirit.

If we have ever failed to see eye-to-eye it has ironically been over goalkeepers and the coaching of them. I know he disliked my involving the likes of David Seaman and John

Lukic in my sessions as thoroughly as I did. All my keepers would take turns in goal or in acting as a server for the specialist exercises I had designed. I regularly complained to Arsene that I didn't have the keepers for long enough before they joined the rest of the squad. He constantly worried about all of his players over-training.

In my life in the beautiful game I have been lucky to meet and get to know some great personalities and characters, outstandingly gifted players, wonderful coaches and managers. Very rarely have I been fortunate enough to have regular contact with an original thinker. Arsene Wenger is such a man – the greatest manager in the history of Arsenal. He is charismatic, fun and above all else intelligent. In his time in England his methods and approach to the game of football have made every top club and every leading manager review their strategies. Only when he is gone will all those who love the game appreciate his full genius.

⚽ ⚽ ⚽

Arsene Wenger

Born:
22 October 1949 Strasbourg, France

Position:
Defender

Clubs as player:
1973–75 FC Mulhouse, 39 games (7 goals)
1975–78 ASPV Strasbourg, 80 games (20 goals)
1978–81 RC Strasbourg, 11 games

Clubs as manager:
1984–87 AS Nancy
1987–94 AS Monaco
1994–96 Nagoya Grampus Eight
1996 to date Arsenal

Honours as player with RC Strasbourg:
1979 Ligue 1

Honours as manager at AS Monaco:
1988 Ligue 1
1991 Coupe de France

Honours as manager at Nagoya Grampus Eight:
1996 Emperor's Cup
1996 J-League Super Cup

Honours as manager at Arsenal:
1998 Premier League, FA Cup and FA Charity Shield
1999 FA Charity Shield
2002 Premier League, FA Cup and FA Charity Shield
2003 FA Cup
2004 Premier League and FA Community Shield
2005 FA Cup

Awards:
1988 French Manager of the Year
1995 J-League Manager of the Year
1998 FA Premier League Manager of the Year
2000 Onze d'Or Coach of the Year
2002 FA Premier League Manager of the Year,
Onze d'Or Coach of the Year, LMA Manager of the Year and
BBC Sports Personality of the Year Coach Award
2002 Légion d'Honneur
2003 Onze d'Or Coach of the Year and OBE
2004 FA Premier League Manager of the Year, Onze d'Or Coach
of the Year, LMA Manager of the Year and BBC Sports Personality of
the Year Coach

– *The Invincibles* –

In the history of English Football only two teams have remained unbeaten for an entire league season. Although there are huge differences in how Preston North End and Arsenal managed this feat, it remains a remarkable achievement and one which I doubt will ever be seen again. One hundred and five years elapsed between Preston's unbeaten season and Arsenal's, and although there are a few examples of clubs losing just one match in a season, the fact is they lost.

Preston set the standard in the inaugural league season and also went on to win the FA Cup without conceding a goal, an extraordinary Double. Out of the five clubs to have completed the league and FA Cup Double on one or more occasion, they are the only ones to have done so unbeaten. Preston's complete record on the way to the league title reads: played 22, won 18, drawn 4 and defeated 0.

The first thing that strikes you about Arsenal's unbeaten league season is the number of games played, not far off twice as many as Preston had in 1888–89. Arsenal played a total of 38 matches, winning 26, drawing 12 and suffering no defeats. It was a wonderful experience to witness Arsenal's 2003–04 season at such close quarters, to hear the banter within the training ground and to watch the dramas of players fighting to recover from injury and achieve full fitness in time to play.

The season also provided manager Arsene Wenger with the perfect riposte to all the critics, media, managers and fans after he had predicted the possibility of an unbeaten season by his team some twelve months earlier.

Such football achievements are made up of great talent and teamwork, a true guiding hand and one hell of a lot of good fortune. Arsenal accepted the luck whenever and wherever it presented itself. At Highbury, five games into a new season they were trailing Portsmouth 1–0 when Robert Pires tumbled dramatically under a slight challenge from Dejan Stefanovic and won a penalty, which enabled Arsenal to draw 1–1, thanks to a twice-taken strike from Thierry Henry.

Equally fortunate was an escape against old enemies Manchester United, a week later on 21 September. The games at Old Trafford are rarely beautiful and little vendettas have accumulated over many years between the two great clubs. When Ruud Van Nistelrooy clashed overdramatically with Patrick Vieira, resulting in the Arsenal captain's dismissal, the Arsenal team were incensed. To make matters worse Van Nistelrooy had a chance to end any Arsenal unbeaten opportunity, in their sixth game of the season, by scoring a disputed injury-time penalty. The Dutchman smashed his spot kick against the bar and was subjected to an unacceptable, if understandable, buffeting from four Arsenal players – all of whom were fined and suspended after pleading guilty to improper conduct.

That game was a defining moment in Arsenal's unbeaten season and the togetherness that grew out of the battle played a major part in what was to follow. Fate decreed that the title could be won on 25 April 2004 at White Hart Lane, home of the local North London enemy, Spurs. A 2–2 draw, in which Tottenham came back from a two goal deficit, was enough to see the Gunners crowned as champions with four league games still to go. Two wins and two draws left them unbeaten in all 38 games, a run which finally ended up spanning a record-breaking 49 league matches, which had started during the 2002–03 season and ended at Manchester United in the 2004–05 season.

The background to Arsenal's achievement suggests that it was a more difficult task than the one completed by Preston in the first ever league season. In 2003–04 the Arsenal side were threatened on three sides by the spending prowess of Manchester United, Liverpool and the $200 million that Chelsea had extracted from Roman Abramovich's deep pockets.

It doesn't matter to either Arsenal or Preston whose achievement was the greater. All that matters is that they remain the only two clubs in English football history to have proved to be 'Invincibles'.

Tony Blair

*Policemen, useless! They have two on the door at 10 Downing Street
and the prime minister still gets out.*

Bill Shankly

⚽ ⚽ ⚽

The former British prime minister never played professional
football, but like so many people he enjoyed the game
and supported a team. It was Newcastle United and their
appearance in the 1998 FA Cup Final that brought us
together.

The Magpies' opponents on that sunny day at Wembley
were an Arsenal team heading for the second of three league
championships and FA Cup Doubles in the club's history. As
the presenter of ITV's coverage of the final I was expected
to come up with some bright ideas on items and interviews
in the build up to kick-off. I suggested an interview with the
PM and received a fairly apprehensive response from my
colleagues. Contacts are all-important in the TV business so I
phoned Alastair Campbell with whom I'd previously worked
at BBC's *Breakfast* news and who now worked as Tony Blair's
director of communications and strategy. Alistair was a keen
Burnley fan and whenever he came into the BBC to discuss
the day's newspapers on the *Breakfast* show, we would have a
cup of tea together and talk football.

So with little real optimism, I called him at his Downing
Street office and asked if an interview with Mr Blair was
feasible. To my astonishment I received a very positive

response. Alastair never missed a trick when it came to putting the PM in touch with the people. After all, he helped coin the 'People's Princess' phrase after Princess Diana's death, delivered with such poignancy by Tony Blair on that dreadful Sunday morning in August 1997.

Within an hour of my asking, a time and day was arranged for me to go to 10 Downing Street. Alastair met me, guided me through the Cabinet Room to the garden area at the rear of the prime minister's residence. He then sat with me and asked what sort of drift my interview would take. Satisfied that I was on safe ground, he then added a question for me to put to the PM. 'Ask him what his favourite Newcastle XI ever would be,' Alastair instructed. I was surprised Mr Blair knew enough about the history of Newcastle United to select the greatest eleven St James' Park had ever seen. Alastair told me the PM probably wouldn't have that immediately in his grasp, but if I could wait ten minutes to start the interview, he and Tony would work it out, put a team together and, as the prime minister had a photographic memory, he would probably get it right first time.

Ten minutes later Tony Blair walked into the garden with a beaming smile and friendly welcome. He sat down, his time precious, and I began the interview about the forthcoming final, which he obviously hoped Newcastle would win. When it came to asking him to name his favourite Newcastle XI of all time, he never faltered, reeling off great names like Jackie Milburn, Alan Shearer and Paul Gascoigne and produced a good piece of TV in take one. With a laugh and a shrug he was gone.

Tony Blair's ability to produce words and names given very little preparation was, whether in sport or foreign affairs, very impressive. I may not have always agreed with his politics but for the rest of my days I will appreciate the letter of condolence he sent to Megs and me following our daughter Anna's death on 1 December 1998 and the Christmas cards he continued to then send us until he left office in 2007.

I was able to thank him personally when he took part in the unveiling of the Bobby Moore statue at the new Wembley and when he spoke with such knowledge and clarity about England's greatest captain, my thoughts returned to our interview in the walled garden at Downing Street.

⚽ ⚽ ⚽

Anthony Charles Lynton 'Tony' Blair

Born:
6 May 1953, Edinburgh

Achievements:
1983–2007 Member of Parliament for Sedgefield
1994–97 Leader of the Opposition
1997–2007 Prime minister of the United Kingdom

– *The Magpies* –

When Newcastle United began playing at St James' Park in 1892 they wore red shirts and over those, jerseys of red and white stripes. To avoid confusion with neighbouring Sunderland, they needed to change their strip. At a club board meeting on 2 August 1894: 'It was agreed that the Club's colours should be changed from red shirts and white knickers to black and white shirts (two-inch stripe) and dark knickers.' At no point in those official minutes does it state why they selected black and white. Here are a few theories that have emerged over the years.

During the English Civil War, the Earl of Newcastle raised an army of volunteers on Tyneside to fight for the king. He assembled what would become the cream of the royalist infantry in the North. They wore black pants and hats, with black leather boots, belts and pouches and were known as the Newcastle Whitecoats, because of their coats of undyed wool. Over the following two years the Whitecoats, or Newcastle's Lambs as they were sometimes otherwise known, fought valiantly, securing much of the North. However, with the Scottish invasion of England in January 1644, Newcastle was faced with a war on two fronts and the Battle of Marston Moor six months later would prove too much. A combination of the Scottish Army in the North and a further three Parliamentarian armies attacking from the South saw Newcastle well and truly beaten. The Whitecoats ultimately fought to their deaths and it's perhaps for this heroic last stand that Newcastle's very own regiment and their signature black-and-white uniforms were honoured by Newcastle FC, exactly 250 years later.

Another theory is based on the close proximity of the city's Blackfriars monastery to St James' Park, and one of its 19th-century inhabitants, Dutchman Father Dalmatius Houtman. He was an ardent supporter of the team, spending much of his time at the ground. Some think that the club, inspired by the traditional black and white of his habit, adopted the colour scheme as their own.

Club folklore also talks of a pair of magpies that made their nest in the old Victorian Stand at St James' Park towards the end of the 19th century. The team became so attached to them, and the supposed luck that a pair of magpies brings, that they insisted upon adopting the colours of the birds as their own.

However the decision was ultimately reached, this basic colour design of the home kit has remained resolutely unchanged since 1894, although the sock colour has occasionally changed from black to white over the years – notably during the Ruud Gullit era, who believed white was lucky. Either way, the black and white of their strip has seen them dubbed the Magpies.

Tony Adams

When he was sent to prison he whispered to me, 'I have done wrong and I'm going to take my punishment. I don't want to appeal.' That's Tony. If you're in a battle on a pitch, he's the first bloke you'd want on your side.

David O'Leary, 1995, Arsenal colleague

Tony, I cannot believe how you achieved everything you have with the way you abused your body and mind. You have played to only 70 per cent of your capacity.

Arsene Wenger in conversation with Tony Adams

Privately, in all honesty, criticism hurt like hell and the only way I knew how to deal with that pain was to get drunk and get on with the next game. Drink and football, my two saviours. I just thought, 'Well, we're going to win the League and show them.' I was more sensitive about those things than my tough-guy image would indicate, but if I had thought about it too much, I might have gone under.

Tony Adams, *Addicted*

❀ ❀ ❀

'Mr Arsenal' is a nickname that indicates the club's most loyal of players. Tony Adams earned the title for spending his entire playing career of 22 years in a Gunners' shirt. I saw him arrive as a schoolboy in 1980 and watched him leave in the summer of 2002. After making his debut for the club in 1983 he went on to accumulate 667 appearances.

It is perhaps fitting that his first game against Sunderland took place on Guy Fawkes Day, 5 November, because there followed a career as explosive as any in the club's history. The acceptable side was the four league titles, three FA Cups, two League Cups and one Cup Winners' Cup in which he captained Arsenal. The youngest Gunners' captain at 21, he was still wearing the arm band fourteen years later as the leader of the famous Arsenal back four.

Within that period of time this extraordinary man let himself and his club down as he battled against alcoholism, a path that ultimately led him towards great respect but at some cost. In December 1990 he was jailed for four months after a drink-driving crash near Southend. The impact of his absence and missing everyday training at Arsenal proved difficult for the whole club. After serving half of the sentence he was released but the demons were not banished.

Throughout the majority of this first period of his career at Highbury, only his closest pals were aware there was any sort of problem. He trained as hard as anyone, was inspirationally vocal on match days and played with a commitment and enthusiasm that singles out winners from losers. Captaincy affords different approaches. Bobby Moore led by example and was relatively quiet. Tony Adams was visual, in your face, waving and thumping fists and telling it as he saw it, regardless of the reputation of his teammates. At times the deep-throated shouts of the boy from Essex could be heard throughout the entire length of the corridor that separated home and away teams at Highbury.

With England selection and increasing success in winning trophies, the Adams leadership impacted on visiting sides, especially on their less-experienced players. He never changed the style, even after Arsene Wenger's arrival and introduction of a new approach. The critical moment for Tony came in September 1996 when the training ground was buzzing with rumours of an impending press conference that was to be held. By now everyone connected with the club and a majority of the public knew he had a drink problem. It was a brave and correct decision to go public and to talk about the treatment he would undergo. We knew, and he knew, that it was make or break. The feeling was that his strength of character as a competitor would provide a positive outcome.

So it proved. He became one of the most high-profile recovering alcoholics, turned his spare energy to education and eventually founded the Sporting Chance Clinic which is a charitable foundation providing treatment, counselling and support for sports men and women who have drink, drugs or gambling addictions.

I have the utmost admiration for Tony Adams, having been party to all the honours won by Arsenal under his captaincy and watching him turn a flawed lifestyle into a truly worthwhile cause. Top of my list of plaudits for him though centres on a media campaign led by the *Daily Mirror* in 1989 that became too personal, too vindictive. An entire back page of the paper showed Tony with a pair of donkey's ears drawn on to his head. It was similar to the Graham Taylor turnip abuse. It followed a 1–1 draw with Manchester United in which Adams scored for both sides. Now you wouldn't imagine that such a big, brave man could be affected as much as he was, but Tony was hurt and increasingly so as in the weeks that followed masses of carrots were thrown at him at grounds around England. For once I saw the really sensitive edge to his personality, one that was genuinely emotionally upset. Of course very quickly he addressed the problem and – at least publicly – used it as a motivation.

Long-term it made him even more of a winner and it will not surprise me if he is eventually as successful in management as he was a player. Wycombe Wanderers, his first post, was not for Tony Adams. Portsmouth and Harry Redknapp have provided a better grounding for his management ambitions. Who knows, he might just return to the club which remember him fondly as 'Mr Arsenal'.

☺ ☺ ☺

Tony Alexander Adams

Born:
10 October 1966, Romford

Position:
Defender

Clubs as player:
1984–2002 Arsenal, 667 games (49 goals)

Internationals:
1987–2000 England, 66 caps (5 goals)

Clubs as manager:
2003–2004 Wycombe Wanderers

Honours as player with Arsenal:
1987 League Cup
1989 First Division
1991 First Division and FA Charity Shield (shared)
1993 FA Cup and League Cup
1994 UEFA Cup Winners' Cup
1998 Premier League, FA Cup and FA Charity Shield
1999 FA Charity Shield
2002 Premier League and FA Cup

Honours as coach with Portsmouth:
2008 FA Cup

Awards:
1987 PFA Young Player of the Year
1999 MBE

– *Gunners* –

In late 1886, a group of workers at the Royal Arsenal Armament Factory in Woolwich decided to form a football team. They called it Dial Square after a section of the workshops in the middle of the factory, and played their first match on 11 December of the same year, beating Eastern Wanderers 6–0. A few weeks later, they renamed themselves Royal Arsenal, and in 1888 adopted their first crest. The design was based predominantly on the coat of arms for the Borough of Woolwich and comprised three columns, which, although looking like chimneys, were in fact cannons.

After a few years of playing friendlies and entering local cup competitions, 1891 saw them become the first London club to turn professional – at the same time, changing their name to Woolwich Arsenal. In 1893, they also became the first London club to be admitted to the Football League. Starting off in the Second Division, they won promotion to the First in 1904. Despite this, their location meant lower attendances than other clubs, and so before long the club was in financial difficulty. In 1910, Fulham chairman Henry Norris took over Woolwich Arsenal with the intention of merging the two clubs. The Football League vetoed the idea, however, so Norris looked to relocate Woolwich Arsenal elsewhere. Initially sites in Battersea and Harringay were considered, before he finally chose the playing fields of St John's College of Divinity in Highbury. With the move, the Woolwich prefix was dropped and so the club became simply Arsenal FC.

In 1922, in the first match-day programme of the season, the club revealed a new crest; an east-pointing single cannon accompanied by the inscription, The Gunners. The design was amended again in 1925 to a slimmer and westward-facing cannon, but the inscription remained. Although the cannon then went largely unchanged until 2002, when it was pointed back east, the inscription had disappeared by 1949 – it was no longer required. Gunners had become the nickname for what is, without question, the greatest football club in the world!

Patrick Vieira

I'm amazed how big Patrick's elbows are. They can reach players ten yards away. Let's just give him a fifteen game ban and get it over and done with.

Arsene Wenger, 2002

What has Patrick done? He has been suspended for two games and fined £20,000 for not walking off the pitch quickly enough. What speed do you have to walk at when you've been sent off? In which rule is that written?

Arsene Wenger, 2003, following Vieira sending off at
Manchester United

⚽ ⚽ ⚽

Perhaps the greatest secret for any club in sustaining success is the ability to replace greatness with greatness in the key area of captaincy. It is easier said than done. The most seamless transition I have witnessed was when Patrick Vieira took over the captain's armband on Tony Adams' departure from Arsenal in 2002.

Patrick is a highly interesting man, much respected but largely misunderstood with a hotly disputed reputation. In the words of one of his teammates, Martin Keown, 'There is a natural warmth that surrounds him, not just a presence from his height and languid movement, a real genuine warmth.' To many, that description belies a commonly-held view of an undisciplined footballer booked or sent off far too many times.

Patrick Vieira was born in Senegal but his family moved to Dreux in France when he was just eight. AS Cannes spotted his potential early as a long leggy player with a big heart and an inexhaustible engine. He made his debut at seventeen and was captain before his twentieth birthday. Such leadership qualities in one so young attracted AC Milan but the Italian giants failed to ignite the fuse that fired the Vieira that the game came to appreciate later in his career. He made just four starts for the Milan first team. Then in September 1996 the incoming Arsenal boss Arsene Wenger asked his directors to sign Vieira for £3.5 million, a fee now looked on as one of the great football transfer bargains, but the first of many forays into the world of potential rather than proven players. Almost nine seasons later, Vieira was to depart Arsenal for a fee of £13.7 million which another giant, Juventus, paid to take him back to Italy. In the intervening years Patrick had played a massive part in re-establishing Arsenal as a top-flight club by winning three Premiership titles and four FA Cups.

In securing the seven trophies, the name Vieira was rarely absent when it came to crucial victories and controversial moments. Martin Keown was party to the Vieira contribution and is best-placed to describe the secret of the Frenchman's success:

Unlike so many players from different countries and cultures, Patrick adapted brilliantly to English ways. He even has an English/Irish Christian name and retains an English home. On days off he would try an English breakfast, was always learning from our traits – the fact that even though we might lack a degree of technique as players, the English never throw the towel in. He merged what we perceive as French arrogance with an

English determination and passion. Then he was able to pass on his views to other French players like Robert Pires, Gael Clichy, his roommate Thierry Henry and Emmanuel Petit, with whom he formed an amazing midfield partnership. Our qualities came out in them. His leadership was inspirational but different from Tony Adams when he succeeded him as captain. They had a mutual respect for each other but were different.

I'll never forget one of his earliest appearances when we were all unsure of what he could do. He came on as sub for Ray Parlour, was instantly demanding the ball and on his first touch, suddenly hit a 40-yard cross-field pass. Just one pass and we knew here was someone very special with great vision and technique.

Patrick was never the greatest of trainers but always came alive when battle was about to commence. Suddenly the loose-limbed, dreamy appearance would take on a fierce intensity and he always needed to be at the centre of events. Why then was Patrick Vieira's disciplinary record so poor? Martin Keown's view is interesting and revealing:

Because almost everything went through him, he was simply targeted by all opponents on the basis that if Vieira could be stopped you'd stop Arsenal playing. They would all try anything and everything to provoke him and although no one could intimidate him, they could make him angry. Referees have never understood these sorts of tactics and consequently he failed to get proper protection. It's the same with all big players. Initially he had a short fuse but learned as he went along. He was very frustrated in that as he saw it, there was no justice from the refs. Honestly, he rarely started a problem but if incited would usually finish it.

Apart from his Arsenal triumphs, Patrick Vieira became a World Cup-winner in 1998 and a European Championship-winner in 2000. Although his performances since leaving England have never truly reflected what we saw consistently in the Premiership, he remains what he has always been: a winner.

Juventus retained a Serie A Championship in his first season, although the club was subsequently stripped of the title, and then he helped Inter Milan become Italian Champions as well as winning the Italian Super Cup.

At his very best he was the driving force for all the teams he represented and although often a slow starter in a game, generally imposed himself and made things happen. Off the field he was the nicest of guys, but on match days would take on anyone who he felt was in need of reproach. The names of Ruud Van Nistelrooy, the Neville brothers and United captain Roy Keane spring to mind, confrontations with all borne out of the intense rivalry between Manchester United and Arsenal.

The most volatile coming together of the Arsenal and United captains came not on the pitch, but in a pre-match incident within the cramped and confined area that was the old Highbury tunnel. Vieira initially challenged Gary Neville about a previous incident during a match at Old Trafford and delivered his intent in a threatening tone. Roy Keane immediately rushed to his teammate's defence and an unseemly argument developed. Fierce competitiveness, unbelievable passion ... and all before a ball had even been kicked.

⚽ ⚽ ⚽

Patrick Donale Vieira

Born:
23 June 1976, Dakar, Senegal

Position:
Midfield

Clubs as player:
1993–95 AS Cannes, 53 games (3 goals)
1995–96 AC Milan, 4 games
1996–2005 Arsenal, 426 games (35 goals)
2005–06 Juventus, 53 games (7 goals)
2006 to date Inter Milan, 41 games (4 goals)

Internationals:
1997–2008, 105 caps (6 goals)

Honours as player with Arsenal:
1998 Premier League, FA Cup and FA Charity Shield
1999 FA Charity Shield
2002 Premier League, FA Cup and FA Charity Shield
2003 FA Cup
2004 Premier League
2005 FA Cup

Honours as player with Juventus:
2006 Serie A (cancelled and relegated due to irregularities)

Honours as player with Inter Milan:
2007 Serie A and Italian Super Cup
2008 Serie A

Honours as player with France:
1998 World Cup
2000 European Championship

– *The Battle of Berne* –

On 27 June 1954, Hungary met Brazil for the World Cup quarter-final at the Wankdorf Stadium in the Swiss capital, Berne. Pitting the beautiful flamboyance of Brazil against the free-flowing football of the Magical Magyars should have produced a classic. Instead it produced 42 free kicks, two penalties, several mass brawls and enough cards to ultimately see three players sent off, two of whom had to be escorted from the pitch by police.

In spite of the chaos, it's widely regarded that only the magisterial refereeing of the charming Englishman Arthur Ellis prevented the game from having to be abandoned. This view wasn't shared by the Brazilian FA however, who later lodged a formal complaint to FIFA that Ellis was part of a Communist plot devised to ensure Hungary won.

At the end of the game, which Hungary eventually won 4–2, the incensed Brazilians turned off the lights in the players' tunnel and waited for the victorious Hungarians to return from the pitch. Upon their arrival, another brawl got under way in which fists, bottles and boots flew in the darkness. As the dust settled, among a list of other injuries, it became apparent that Hungarian coach Gustáv Sebes needed stitches after being struck by a broken bottle in his face. 'This was a battle; a brutal, savage match,' Sebes later said. He was right, the World Cup had never seen anything like it and the British press immediately dubbed it the Battle of Berne.

Michael Owen

He showed the sureness of a surgeon in every movement, the high-speed precision of a computer in every turn and the ambition of a thief in the final shot.

> Jorge Valdano, former Argentina striker after Owen's
> goal for England vs. Argentina in the
> 1998 World Cup finals

Geordio Galactio

> Freddie Shepherd – Newcastle Chairman on signing
> Michael Owen from Real Madrid, 2005

❀ ❀ ❀

Michael Owen's story is in many ways a 'Roy of the Rovers' tale, except that Roy never suffered as many injuries in his career as the Liverpool, Real Madrid and Newcastle United striker. People have pointed to Michael's physique and height as a problem. He's just 5' 8" tall, but that never stopped other small players like Billy Bremner, Jimmy Johnstone, Kevin Keegan and co. from achieving greatness at a lesser cost of injury. Blistering pace over five to ten yards certainly drew late and desperate tackles that led to long-term lay-offs for Owen, but simple bad luck is as much the culprit as anything else.

From his earliest days at primary school in Wales, Michael broke all local scoring records. Manchester United and Arsenal chased him along with Liverpool, but after talks at all three, Liverpool won the race to sign him. A student at the FA School of Excellence at Lilleshall, the youngster soon moved to Anfield full-time and immediately started collecting medals and silverware. The FA Youth Cup was won by Liverpool in 1996. In his first season as a regular in the senior team he finished as joint top-scorer in the Premier League and was voted the PFA Young Player of the Year. The 1998–99 season brought 23 goals in 40 games. Then came the first of the injury crises and he missed most of the 1999–2000 campaign.

By then he was a full England international, having become the youngest player to represent England in the twentieth century at just eighteen years and 59 days. During the 1998 World Cup in France I watched in awe as Michael scored a wonderful goal against Argentina in the quarter-finals, a game lost only as a result of a penalty shootout. One reward came his way that year as he was voted BBC Sports Personality of the Year, the youngest ever recipient in the award's history. 2001 saw Liverpool win the League Cup, UEFA Cup and notably FA Cup, Michael scoring twice in the last five minutes against Arsenal to turn a 1–0 defeat into a 2–1 victory. His star was at its highest point when this precocious goalscorer hit a hat-trick in England's 5–1 win against Germany in Munich. Capping his year was the European Footballer of the Year award.

Twenty-eight more goals in the 2001–02 season was repeated the next season as well, but the departure of Liverpool manager Gerard Houllier and the arrival of Rafa Benitez at Anfield led to Michael's £11 million move to Real Madrid. Most Liverpool fans were in despair. In 297 games for Liverpool Michael scored 158 times. Real fans never saw the best of the lad in the white number 11 shirt but he still scored sixteen goals in 42 games, while accumulating untold wealth.

A further move back to England and a club-record £16 million paid by Newcastle increased the bank balance. All too quickly Michael was sidelined by a string of serious injuries ranging from a broken foot to a damaged anterior cruciate ligament in his right knee. It was during this period that I got to know Michael better, hosting a couple of events at which he was the guest. In the first, held at St James' Park, he was joined by his wife Louise, whom he met at primary school. The couple entertained the invited folk with real style. But it was at the end of the second evening in London that I began to truly comprehend what success in football these days can provide for rare talent.

After answering all questions and charming his audience I asked Michael where he was staying overnight in London. 'Oh no,' came the reply, 'I've got my helicopter standing by.' Personal helicopter and pilot had transported the England star back to his Lower Soughton Manor in Flintshire by the time I travelled through the congested London roads to my home in Hertfordshire, 24 miles away.

I learned that apart from the chopper, Michael also owned several cars and had looked after his family by buying an entire street very close to his original home. With horse racing and gambling one of his hobbies, you begin to fully understand the life that is possible for a very successful professional footballer of the modern era.

⚽ ⚽ ⚽

Michael James Owen

Born:
14 December 1979, Chester

Position:
Striker

Clubs as player:
1996–2004 Liverpool, 297 games (158 goals)
2004–05 Real Madrid, 42 games (16 goals)
2005 to date: Newcastle United, 45 games (20 goals)

Internationals:
1998 to date England, 89 caps (40 goals)

Honours as player with Liverpool:
1996 FA Youth Cup
2001 UEFA Cup, FA Cup and League Cup
2002 European Super Cup and FA Charity Shield
2003 League Cup

Awards:
1998 PFA Young Player of Year and BBC Sports Personality of Year
2001 European Footballer of Year

– *The White Horse Final* –

Wembley hosted its first final in 1923 having just been completed in under a year at a cost of £750,000. It saw Bolton take on West Ham in what turned out to be perhaps the most famous domestic final of all time. Although capacity for the new stadium was 127,000, the stadium entrances were not finished and so a far higher number of people made it into the ground. No one knows the final number but it's thought it could well have reached a quarter of a million with another 60,000 eventually locked outside.

With thousands having to spill onto the pitch, the game was about to be abandoned (despite the presence of King George V in the Royal Box) when mounted police were called in to push the crowds back to the sides of the playing surface. Among them was PC George Scorey and his famous thirteen-year-old white horse, Billie, who both actually had the day off but had reported for duty as word reached Scorey that the situation in the stadium had got out of hand.

Billie the horse was actually a grey but later appeared bright white in the high-contrast black-and-white newsreel footage and photography of the time. Although a number of other horses were also involved, Billie was the most distinguishable and much of the subsequent imagery gave the impression that he had controlled the vast throngs single-handedly. Billie consequently became a legend and the match became known as the White Horse Final.

During the match itself, the vast crowds had caused some fairly unusual moments for an FA Cup Final. When a player stepped up to take a corner or a throw-in, he had to wait while police negotiated him a run-up through the crowd that had formed a human wall around the perimeter of the entire pitch. Early in the first half Bolton's David Jack crashed in a shot hard enough to not only beat West Ham keeper Ted Hutton, but also to knock a spectator unconscious who was pressed against the net behind the goal. Although the goal was good, it was made somewhat controversial by the fact that West Ham defender Jack Tresadern was still trapped in the crowd after taking the throw-in. In the second half, when Bolton scored their second to secure the Cup, the ball rebounded off the spectators behind the goal and back into play so quickly, that few people realised a goal had been scored. Never again would Wembley see such a vast crowd.

Dennis Bergkamp

If he were in Star Trek *he'd be the best player in whatever solar system he was in.*

Ian Wright, 1997

Dennis has intelligence and class. Class is most of the time linked to what you can do with the ball, but the intelligence makes you use the technique in an efficient way. It's like somebody who has a big vocabulary but he doesn't say intelligent words, and somebody who has a big vocabulary but he can talk intelligently and that's what Dennis is all about.

Arsene Wenger

⚽ ⚽ ⚽

Until I began to research and write about 'The Iceman', I never realised that we shared a common secret: both of us are bearers of a christian name normally associated with the female gender. Primrose was my mum's maiden name before marriage. Dennis received Maria from his parents. More appropriately his mum and dad named him Dennis after Scotland's Denis Law, adding an extra 'n' to avoid confusion with the girl's name Denise!

The one thing you would never attempt with Dennis Bergkamp would be to embarrass him or take the mickey. Thierry Henry described it better than most:

He was given the nickname, 'The Iceman' because of his face and because he was so cool. But there are two

Dennises. The one you all saw and the one we saw as teammates. He could kill with a smile. He would look at you and you'd think he's cute. Then *the* look and you are dead.

Dennis is a very private man, rather than a shy person. He hated his time in Italy where the paparazzi tried in vain to invade his family life. When he left his first club Ajax he should have come straight to England, where he and his parents had always holidayed and followed the English game. As a boy he always hero-worshipped Glenn Hoddle's style of play. Recalling his own vision and touch for a football, it's understandable.

In his eleven years at Arsenal he changed the face of the club, both in the way in which the game should be played and ultimately in terms of the expectations of the fans. His impact on the game in general cannot be overstated either. Certainly it bears comparison at least with the way Eric Cantona turned heads at Manchester United. Dennis provided a new yardstick for all professionals. His presence at Arsenal helped Arsene Wenger attract other players of potential and ambition, including Patrick Vieira, Robert Pires and Thierry Henry.

As Arsenal's goalkeeping coach throughout his time at Highbury, I witnessed the number of hours he would put in on the training ground to ensure that all his skills remained polished ready for display. Sometimes he was left alone on the pitch after training, practising shots, free kicks, manipulation of the ball – anything and everything. Ajax and Holland had been the perfect schooling ground for the young Bergkamp. Repetition has been instrumental in the Dutch thinking on training since the late 60s and early 70s.

Most fans, in recalling Dennis Bergkamp, will visualise an extraordinary goal at Leicester City where he took on four or five players with stunning ball juggling skills, or a dummy, spin and run around Newcastle's Nikos Dabizas at St James' Park. Those goals didn't just materialise out of nothing. They were the result of practice, repetition and supreme confidence in one's ability.

Many Arsenal teammates of Dennis benefited from being alongside him at the London Colney Training Centre. Good solid players like Ray Parlour and former Arsenal, now England and Tottenham player, David Bentley. Pros at the top level can replicate skills very quickly after they see them on a regular basis during training. Dennis was a 'Dutch schoolmaster' to so many former colleagues. He understood the precise geometry of a football pitch, a skill that had been first nurtured and developed by his early Ajax boss, Johan Cruyff, who told Dennis: 'When you're young, you only see part of the pitch. You are too blinkered.'

A greater creator of goals than scorer, Dennis always retained modesty when asked how he saw the pass. 'Simple, all it takes is eye contact, knowing your teammates well and practising together.'

The Bergkamp way became something of an art form. It helped that he had in Arsene Wenger a manager who understood fully his personality and character along with his technique. Dennis' summing up of Arsene was something of a mirror image of himself as a player: 'The manager is so calm with everything, at training, before a match and after the final whistle, when even in defeat he will say little or nothing. Arsene makes players think about it themselves unlike so many other managers.'

The near-perfect professional, Dennis' only problem lay in his mistrust of flying. He is reluctant to talk about it very much. When he does you'll find it revolves around an incident during the 1994 World Cup finals in America. Delayed for a flight, the rumour spread that it was because there was a bomb on the plane. Dennis took the story seriously and it reminded him of a previous plane crash which had killed many Surinamese-Dutch footballers. The Flying Dutchman became the non-Flying Dutchman and throughout the majority of his Arsenal career, you would see Dennis getting into a train or a car as his fellow teammates boarded the team bus en route to Luton airport.

There have of course been other low points for Dennis Bergkamp in his career. One came in 1999 when he had the chance to end Manchester United's Treble dreams at Villa Park. A late penalty, if converted by Dennis, would put an end to United's FA Cup run. Peter Schmeichel saved the Bergkamp shot. Ryan Giggs went on to score a wonder goal and United made history. On such slender moments are fortunes created or ended. Back at Arsenal's training ground a couple of days later I found Dennis alone, deep in thought as I went out to coach the goalies. Our sessions began an hour before the team practice but he was already ready to train. He was naturally upset, disappointed in himself. In trying to remind him of his contribution to all that had been achieved he just sat quietly without probably listening properly, a perfectionist and artist prepared to take responsibility on his own shoulders and impatient to restore normal service.

Many great moments were left for Dennis during seven more years of entertaining all true fans across the UK. On 22 July 2006 the Arsenal directors bestowed a massive honour on Bergkamp. His testimonial game was to be the first match to be played at the new Emirates Stadium. Following the first half between the current Arsenal and Ajax teams there was a meeting of ex-players from both clubs with greats like Ian Wright, Emmanuel Petit, David Seaman, Marco Van Basten and John Cruyff taking part.

Asked by Dennis and his wife Henrita to announce the players' names at half-time and conduct the post-match interview with him, I was conscious of the overwhelming affection and awe in which the fans held him. Banners with 'The Iceman' and 'God' were everywhere and there was a standing ovation as Dennis made his farewell circuit of Arsenal's new home. My regret was that he would not be part of the first historic season in the Emirates, other than to provide support from the family box.

Dennis thanked his personal family for their love and his extended Arsenal family for their support. Monies from the day went to several charities, both in Holland and the UK.

I am unhappy that in retirement he is not yet back in football. He wouldn't need to spend every minute of every day taking on the pressures of management. But in watching, teaching and with one of those looks of his, he could further a team's togetherness and fire an individual's enthusiasm.

I am happy, very happy that I watched him play: the most entertaining footballer that I have ever seen.

☻ ☻ ☻

Dennis Nicolaas Maria Bergkamp

Born:
10 May 1969, Amsterdam, Netherlands

Position:
Striker

Clubs as player:
1983–93 Ajax, 208 games (116 goals)
1993–95 Inter Milan, 68 games (21 goals)
1995–2006 Arsenal, 424 games (120 goals)

Internationals:
1990–2000 Netherlands, 79 caps (37 goals)

Honours as player with Ajax:
1987 UEFA Cup Winners' Cup and KNVB Cup
1990 Eredivisie
1992 UEFA Cup
1993 KNVB Cup

Honours as player with Inter Milan:
1994 UEFA Cup

Honours as player with Arsenal:
1998 Premier League, FA Cup and FA Charity Shield
1999 FA Charity Shield
2002 Premier League, FA Cup and FA Charity Shield
2003 FA Cup
2004 Premier League and FA Community Shield
2005 FA Cup

Awards:
1992 Dutch Player of the Year
1993 Dutch Player of the Year
1998 PFA Player of the Year and FWA Player of the Year

– *Nutmeg* –

The name of this cheeky yet skilful move is thought to have been inspired by deceitful practice in the nutmeg trade during the Victorian era, whereby American exporters would cut their batches of nutmeg with similar looking bits of wood. The recipients who were deceived, or nutmegged as it came to be known, were left looking foolish, as is the victim of a nutmeg on a football field. In the current game, players affectionately use the term nuts when a teammate or an opponent is on the receiving end of this skill.

Thierry Henry

I remember the very first day and people laughing when Arsene Wenger said he wanted me to lead the attack. I was pretty dubious myself. I looked at him with my eyes wide open in surprise.

Thierry Henry, 2003

The only way to stop Henry is with an AK-47.

Graeme Souness, 2003, Blackburn manager

Thierry Henry could take a ball in the middle of the park and score a goal that no one else in the world could score.

Arsene Wenger

⚽ ⚽ ⚽

The 1998 World Cup finals held in France provided both my most challenging and most fulfilling experiences as a TV sports presenter. Our ITV team travelled on a daily basis to a new venue, choosing to present live from the grounds rather than sit in a soulless studio somewhere in Paris. I loved every minute of the tournament except perhaps the cheating, diving and simulation that marred the event and continues to scar the beautiful game.

I had particular interest in the host nation as two Arsenal players were in their squad, Patrick Vieira and Emmanuel Petit. Early in the tournament though, it was one of their young teammates who caught my eye. Then used by French manager Aime Jacquet as a winger, he was skilful, had an eye for a goal and possessed devastating pace, the like of which

427

I had never seen on a football field previously. He was listed in the programme as Thierry Daniel Henry, age twenty. Goals from the youngster early in the tournament set France on their way and although injury curtailed his progress and denied him an appearance in the final against Brazil, the host nation triumphed. Little did I know then that I was watching someone who would go on to mesmerise the football fraternity worldwide and do so while playing in the colours of Arsenal.

His arrival at Highbury in August 1999 received muted applause. Signed by Arsene Wenger, who had been his manager initially at Monaco where the French league and French Super Cup had been won, there were raised eyebrows at the £10.5 million transfer fee which took him to Arsenal from his second club, Juventus. Arsene Wenger, though, knew exactly what the possibilities might be if Thierry could fulfil his potential.

Thierry's time in Italy provided the least spectacular return from this extraordinary talented boy from the backstreets of Paris. The densely populated neighbourhood of Les Ulis provided a tough upbringing but despite all the hardships, it contained excellent basic sporting facilities. How the UK should learn from the French approach and other European countries when it comes to maximising youthful sporting prowess, regardless of class.

Henry arrived at Highbury as a replacement for Nicolas Anelka, another talented French striker, but moody and difficult to manage. With the £23 million Arsenal received from Real Madrid for Anelka, Wenger built a state-of-the-art training facility for £12 million and spent the surplus on Thierry Henry.

After a slow start, failing to score in his first eight games, Wenger converted his fellow countryman from winger to striker. In doing so he had simply lit the Henry fuse and now waited for the amazing footballer to fully ignite and rocket to stardom and start playing on a different planet to the vast majority of footballers anywhere in the world. It was a privilege to witness Henry at work and at play on match days, during training and away from the pressures that mounted over his eight-year reign as an Arsenal legend.

Of course it helped that alongside him was another of the game's greatest players, Dennis Bergkamp, plus the likes of Vieira, Petit, Marc Overmars, Ian Wright and the famous Arsenal back five. His impact at Arsenal was huge and in his time at Highbury two Premiership titles, three FA Cups and two European finals – including one in the Champions League – were the reward. Away from the team success he won two European Golden Boot awards, was the Premier League's top scorer for four seasons, became Footballer of the Year three times, PFA Player of the Year twice, was World Player of the Year Runner-up on two occasions, and French Player of the Year five times.

'Great' is a word misused too often in sport. For Thierry Henry it is not enough; you need to add a prefix of 'truly'. He deserves his place alongside Pele, Cruyff, Maradona and George Best as footballers who had the rarest of abilities to pick a ball up deep in defence and travel from there through the middle of a pitch, into the attacking third and score. An abiding memory is the goal he scored against Spurs at Highbury in this manner, taking on seven opponents and planting the ball in their net – amazing, brilliant, unforgettable … a privilege to watch firsthand. So too the flick up and volley from the edge of the Manchester United penalty area which flew past his international colleague Fabien Barthez in the United goal. Throughout virtually the whole of his Arsenal career, Thierry would be the first player approached by opponents at the final whistle. A number 14 Henry shirt, preferably signed, was a precious keepsake.

Although he has a reputation for moodiness, considering the pressure that celebrity burdens people with, Thierry is always respectful, thoughtful and often very amusing. He loved Arsenal, and Arsenal loved him. Leaving for Barcelona was one last challenge too attractive to turn down. The Spanish giants have yet to see the best of him. It might not happen if they continue to play him as a winger and ask him to defend rather than display his attacking talents. However well he plays, it will not be with the consistency or flair that we saw in England. Arsenal enjoyed the best of Thierry.

It is interesting to listen to Arsene Wenger's take on the decision to allow Henry to join Barcelona. Rarely if ever does the Arsenal manager stand in the way of a player who wants to move on and Arsene expressed his admiration for the young man who he developed into one of the greatest ever footballers. Wenger genuinely believes that once any player moves into his thirties he is beginning to lose a degree of fitness and is more vulnerable to injury and fatigue. However, in talking about Thierry Henry within this category, Arsene added a rider. 'Of course, in Thierry's case what is slightly below *his* very best is still way above the ability of the vast majority of other footballers currently in the game.'

This then is an Arsenal legend, one who on 17 October 2005 became the club's top goalscorer of all time when his two goals against Sparta Prague took him past Ian Wright's record of 185 goals. Then on 1 February 2006 he scored his 151st league goal for the Gunners so displacing the record of another Arsenal legend, Cliff Bastin.

When in June 2007 Thierry chose to leave Arsenal for Barcelona the fee was over £16 million, around £5 million more than he had cost, but considerably less than the £50 million offers from two Spanish clubs a year or two earlier. It's unlikely that Thierry would have gone to Spain at that time as it followed Spanish national team manager Luis Aragones' despicable reference to Henry as 'black s**t'. Henry simply turned the incident to his advantage and began the Nike 'Stand Up, Speak Up' campaign against racism in football.

Not only Nike appreciated the commercial value of the French star: Reebok, Renault, Pepsi and Gillette have used his fame and celebrity to further their sales and profits. Charities too have benefited, among them the Willow Foundation. During his time at Arsenal, Thierry signed numerous items including boots, shirts and limited edition prints, together with a £27,000 cheque he received and then gave the charity for being the Premier League's top scorer in 2005–6.

❀ ❀ ❀

Thierry Daniel Henry

Born:
17 August 1977, Essonne, France

Position:
Striker

Clubs as player:
1994–98 AS Monaco, 141 games (28 goals)
1999 Juventus, 16 games (3 goals)
1999–2007 Arsenal, 369 games (237 goals)
2007 to date FC Barcelona, 39 games (19 goals)

Internationals:
1997 to date France, 102 caps (44 goals)

Honours as player with AS Monaco:
1997 Ligue 1 and French Super Cup

Honours as player with Arsenal:
2002 Premier League, FA Cup and FA Charity Shield
2003 FA Cup
2004 Premier League and FA Community Shield
2005 FA Cup

Honours as player with France:
1998 World Cup
2000 European Championship
2003 Confederation Cup

Awards:
2000 French Player of the Year
2003 PFA Players' Player of the Year, FWA Footballer of the Year and
French Player of the Year
2004 PFA Players' Player of the Year, FWA Footballer of the Year,
French Player of the Year and European Golden Boot
2005 French Player of the Year and European Golden Boot
2006 FWA Footballer of the Year and French Player of the Year

– PFA Players' Player of the Year –

Year	Player	Club
1974	Norman Hunter	Leeds United
1975	Colin Todd	Derby County
1976	Pat Jennings	Tottenham Hotspur
1977	Andy Gray	Aston Villa
1978	Peter Shilton	Nottingham Forest
1979	Liam Brady	Arsenal
1980	Terry McDermott	Liverpool

Year	Player	Club
1981	John Wark	Ipswich Town
1982	Kevin Keegan	Southampton
1983	Kenny Dalglish	Liverpool
1984	Ian Rush	Liverpool
1985	Peter Reid	Everton
1986	Gary Lineker	Everton
1987	Clive Allen	Tottenham Hotspur
1988	John Barnes	Liverpool
1989	Mark Hughes	Manchester United
1990	David Platt	Aston Villa
1991	Mark Hughes	Manchester United
1992	Gary Pallister	Manchester United
1993	Paul McGrath	Aston Villa
1994	Eric Cantona	Manchester United
1995	Alan Shearer	Blackburn Rovers
1996	Les Ferdinand	Newcastle United
1997	Alan Shearer	Newcastle United
1998	Dennis Bergkamp	Arsenal
1999	David Ginola	Tottenham Hotspur
2000	Roy Keane	Manchester United
2001	Teddy Sheringham	Manchester United
2002	Ruud Van Nistelrooy	Manchester United
2003	Thierry Henry	Arsenal
2004	Thierry Henry	Arsenal
2005	John Terry	Chelsea
2006	Steven Gerrard	Liverpool
2007	Cristiano Ronaldo	Manchester United
2008	Cristiano Ronaldo	Manchester United

Harry Redknapp

Even when they had Moore, Hurst and Peters, West Ham's average finish was about seventeenth. It just shows how crap the other eight of us were.

With the foreign players it's more difficult. Most of them don't even bother with golf; they don't want to go racing. They don't even drink.

Samassi Abou don't speak the English too good.

Harry Redknapp

⚽ ⚽ ⚽

The 2008 FA Cup Final was very different to any from the previous decade. That's because there was none of the big four involved. No Manchester United, Arsenal, Liverpool or Chelsea. Instead it pitched a Championship side, Cardiff City, who had last won the Cup in 1927, against Portsmouth, a Premiership team but a club whose last FA Cup triumph came in 1939. Instead of devaluing the great competition the appearance of these two sides breathed life into it. They recreated a romance that had been lost to the predictable fact that money dictated where major trophies would end up. There was another reason that all neutrals and lovers of football rejoiced at the eventual Portsmouth victory: it surrounded the popularity of the club's manager, Harry Redknapp.

'H' or ''Arry', as he is known to the majority of his friends, is much-loved. When the FA was looking to appoint a new England manager to succeed Steve McLaren, the people's choice was Harry Redknapp. The governing body went for an Italian, Fabio Capello, over the boy from Poplar. This is where Harry was born on 2 March 1947 and from where he set out on a footballing journey that led him, through extraordinary ups and downs, to the new Wembley on 17 May 2008. Sixty-one years in all, and 44 of those spent as a professional player, coach and manager dedicated to a game he loves.

The secret of his popularity lies in his ability to give his time to everyone who is prepared to listen. Life's journey for Harry has been one massive learning curve ever since his schooldays in a very poor area of London. He would have loved a good education, something that was missing from the secondary school he attended that had no playground. Sport saved him, football in particular and his dad, Harry Snr, was a useful player as well as being a massive Arsenal fan. Harry would have loved to sign for the Gunners but it was Spurs and West Ham who first spotted the young Redknapp potential.

After playing for East London Boys, Harry eventually signed professional terms as a seventeen-year-old in 1964 for West Ham. The manager, Ron Greenwood, impressed him because he was a father figure and showed such great interest in the youngsters, even encouraging them to set out early in developing their coaching skills. Three World Cup-winners, Bobby Moore, Martin Peters and Geoff Hurst plus the likes of Billy Bonds, Trevor Brooking and Frank Lampard Snr, were all great players, although they failed to ignite any challenge for a league title.

Playing alongside them, watching and listening all the time, Harry began to build his beliefs about how the game operated in general and what was needed to achieve success. When he left Upton Park for Bournemouth in 1972, he mixed playing with coaching simply because the apprentices at Dean Court had no one to take them. Harry volunteered for the role of youth team coach, travelling vast distances in a tiny minibus to fulfil fixtures. Very soon he was producing players like Steve Gritt, who went on to play for Charlton and two future England players Kevin Reeves and Graham Roberts.

The die was cast for Harry's future career in management. On leaving Bournemouth, he spent time alongside Bobby Moore again, this time in the USA with Seattle Sounders and also in Phoenix, Arizona, returning to England with the 1966 World Cup captain at Oxford City where the hours were long and the pay short – £70 per week for fourteen hours a day, seven days a week. Interestingly, his view of Bobby Moore as a manager disputes the generally-held thought that he was 'just too nice'. 'Not so,' says Harry 'he simply was never given a proper chance anywhere.'

Slowly but surely Harry's coaching career was taking shape and when David Webb took him back to Bournemouth he was soon to make his mark. In late 1983 after being made manager, he created national headlines as his team knocked out the FA Cup holders, Manchester United, in the third round of the competition. In the 1986–87 season, Bournemouth amassed 97 points to win the Third Division title.

It was three years later, as Bournemouth were struggling, that the name Redknapp again made news as a result of a devastating automobile crash which claimed the lives of three young Italians and that of his mate and Bournemouth managing director, Brian Tiler. How Harry Redknapp survived remains a miracle and illustrates how tenuous a hold we all have on life. The two pals were taking in the World Cup,

Italia '90 and loving every minute of it. They had just seen Ireland play Italy in Rome and were setting off to take in the England vs. Cameroon match the following day. Brian had berated Harry for taking too long to board their minibus, driven by an Italian chauffeur. To hurry Harry up and save a few seconds in time, Brian changed seats, taking the one always occupied during the tournament by Redknapp. Some time into the journey, Harry fell asleep and didn't wake up for more than two days.

On the journey, the mini bus was involved in a 90 mph crash. Brian Tiler, sitting in Harry's normal seat, was killed instantly. On regaining consciousness and with several fractures to his skull, Harry was told the truth of an event about which he remembers absolutely nothing. In time his scars healed but never his sense of smell and his sense of taste also remains weak. Harry quietly acknowledges how lucky he is, how close it was and that, 'Yes, I guess I was given a second chance.'

After resigning at Bournemouth in 1992 he returned as coach to his first home, Upton Park and after Billy Bonds left the club, took his place as manager of West Ham United. Apart from stabilising the club, he shrewdly took a man called Jimmy Hampson from Charlton where the youth policy was reaping rewards. Together the two brought through and developed the likes of Joe Cole, Rio Ferdinand, Michael Carrick and Redknapp's own nephew, Frank Lampard. The best league position acquired was fifth in 1997 which put the Hammers in Europe where they promptly won the UEFA Intertoto Cup. In turn this earned a UEFA Cup place for the next season which never fulfilled its promise and ended with Harry in conflict with the chairman, Terry Brown and ultimately led to the exit door.

Harry Redknapp has never been down for long though and by the summer of 2001 he was back in what would be his first spell at Portsmouth. In the 2002–03 season Pompey won the Division One title against all odds, having finished fifth from bottom the previous term. It took them into the Premiership, ironically replacing the club he had recently left, West Ham. However, loyalty to his friends is a strong point in the Redknapp management philosophy and when Portsmouth owner Milan Mandaric informed Harry that he was getting rid of his pal and assistant manager Jim Smith, the boss decided to leave as well.

It was then that Harry admits making a mistake in underestimating the strength of feeling between the two south coast clubs, Portsmouth and Southampton, his next port of call. His task was to keep the Saints up, but they didn't survive and in early December 2005 he resigned and returned almost immediately to Fratton Park:

> It was not easy initially. The fans who loved me first time around were not happy. On the way to the training ground for a while, there were these roadworks and each day I had to drive past Pompey fans who were repairing the tarmac surface, holding up signs like 'Judas Bastard'. It was a real challenge.

Along the way, Harry could have become Newcastle United manager but found that he 'could not walk away again, however tempted. The fans and loyalty were always the guiding factor for me.'

As for the England manager's role made vacant by Steve McLaren's demise, Harry believes that he was 'never really going to get the job. They seemed to indicate any new manager had to have experience in the Champions League at club level. I didn't. Mind you at the time, after watching a Rangers' European game, their manager Walter Smith and assistant manager Ally McCoist told me I should do it and give it a go, and yes, it was flattering to be the people's choice.'

Had Harry gone to St James' Park or even Soho Square he would have missed out on his greatest moment at the top level, guiding a famous old club like Portsmouth, to a trophy that seemed unlikely in the modern game. On the way to Wembley, Portsmouth knocked out Manchester United at Old Trafford, a tie which, when Harry was first made aware of it on a golf course, led to him hurling his 8-iron halfway up the fairway. That was one memorable moment en route to the great prize. Another related to the Portsmouth owner, Alexandre Gaydamak, who had sent a text message to Harry after watching Spurs beat Chelsea to win the League Cup. The atmosphere of the Wembley final had evidently caught the Frenchman's imagination. His text read: 'Dear Mr Redknapp. My dream is to go to Wembley to watch Portsmouth. Please can you make this possible?'

Harry laughs when recalling this respectful text from the shy owner of the club, but clearly is bursting with pride that he was able to fulfil the request.

Harry Redknapp loves nothing more than to please people – the fans, his friends and above all his family. There is no self-proclamation by him when he talks of the moment that the FA Cup was won. 'I wanted it for my wife Sandra, for all the love and help she has given me over the years and because she had just lost her sister Pat (Frank Lampard's wife and Frank Jnr's mum) so tragically. They spoke with each other every day and have never had a cross word since they worked together in the same hairdressing business as fifteen-year-olds. It puts everything into perspective.'

More than 200,000 fans turned out to welcome the FA Cup back to Portsmouth, to applaud their team and thank their manager.

So what now Harry? 'I still enjoy it. I love football. I love talking to people,' is the reply from one of the greatest characters the game has been lucky enough to embrace.

❀ ❀ ❀

Henry James 'Harry' Redknapp

Born:
2 March 1947, Poplar

Position:
Winger

Clubs as player:
1964–72 West Ham United, 175* (8 goals)
1972–76 Bournemouth, 101* (5 goals)
1976 Brentford, 1
1976–79 Seattle Sounders, 24
1982 Bournemouth, 1

Clubs as manager:
1983–92 Bournemouth
1994–2001 West Ham United
2002–04 Portsmouth
2004–05 Southampton
2005 to date Portsmouth

Honours as manager at Bournemouth:
1984 Football League Trophy
1987 Promotion to Second Division

Honours as manager at West Ham United:
1999 UEFA Intertoto Cup

Honours as manager at Portsmouth:
2003 Football League Division 1
2008 FA Cup

– *Pompey* –

Portsmouth FC was founded in 1898 and shares its nickname with the city. Although the exact origin of the moniker is unclear, it is almost certainly of naval extraction and a number of theories abound. The simple thought is that all the pomp and ceremony synonymous with the Royal Navy and therefore on display in Portsmouth over the centuries became known as pompey, before being adopted by the city.

Some think that it lies in the fact that ships entering Portsmouth harbour enter 'Pom. P.' in the ship's log as a reference to Portsmouth Point. Navigational charts also use this abbreviation.

Others believe that it derives from the 80-gun French warship *La Pompée* which was captured in 1793 before going on to fight with distinction as HMS *Pompee* in the Battle of Algeciras Bay in 1801. It subsequently became the guardship of Portsmouth harbour in the early nineteenth century, before being broken up in 1817.

Perhaps apocryphal, but it is also said that one day when the naval temperance activist Dame Agnes Weston was delivering a lecture about the murder of the Roman general Pompey, a drunk sailor in the audience woke from a beery slumber and shouted 'Poor old Pompey!' before falling back to sleep.

In 1781, some sailors from Portsmouth also climbed Pompey's Pillar, the tallest ancient monument in Alexandria. One hundred feet above Egypt they toasted their achievement with punch and subsequently became known as the Pompey Boys.

So although I can't be sure how Portsmouth got their nickname, I do know that I always enjoyed the chant behind my goal whenever I played at Fratton Park: 'Play Up Pompey, Pompey Play Up!'

Jens Lehmann

I have to accept that there are people who don't have a clue about football.

Jens Lehmann, 2004, following criticism of him as the team's weak link during their unbeaten season

In football you can be close to being in hell then rise to heaven just like that.

Jens Lehmann, 2006, after his penalty save at Villareal put Arsenal in the Champions League Final

During his time at Arsenal he was the best goalkeeper in the Premier League. He reads the game well, he is brave and had all the assets to come into this league because he is not frightened of anybody. In all his time here I have not known Jens not to be fully committed for a single minute. That deserves a lot of respect.

Arsene Wenger

⚽ ⚽ ⚽

Few footballers represent such a contradiction in terms as Jens Lehmann. Off the field of play the German international is quiet, gentlemanly, caring and sensitive. On match day he becomes a different animal – focussed, unapproachable, tetchy and totally 'in the zone'. Whatever way you wish to view him in, there are certain footballing facts that are cast in stone: five winner's medals with four different clubs; World Cup runner-up with Germany; twice voted best European goalkeeper; and mainstay of an Arsenal team that became the

'Invincibles' during a 38-match unbeaten league campaign in 2003–04, and who went on to extend that run to a record-breaking 49 matches.

He arrived at Arsenal as David Seaman left and vacated the goalkeeping position. I retired from coaching the club's keepers at the same time. I wish I had experienced a season or two in charge of Jens. His style of goalkeeping, in terms of technique, is very close to the one I found had suited me best during my career – trusting your instinct, adventurous, brave and prepared to attack crosses where others fear to tread.

To follow an Arsenal legend such as Seaman in such an historic manner speaks volumes for the professionalism of the man from Essen in Germany. Almost always the first to arrive at Arsenal's London Colney training centre, Jens would head for the gym before his colleagues arrived, embark on his stretch routine and then turn to the multi-gym equipment. This was followed by his one-to-one work on the field with keepers' coach Gerry Peyton and then team play under the direction of Arsene Wenger. Only two things enter Jens' mind as a professional footballer and that is to win and to be the best. Why then has his career been littered with confrontation and reactions of anger befitting a bull taunted by a red rag?

A major part of the problem is his belief that referees throughout the UK and Europe fail to protect goalkeepers when they are clearly intimidated during set piece situations. Robbie Keane, then at Spurs, was well aware of Jens' fragile temperament and simply stood on the keeper's toes or blocked him off with his body. Of course it was foul play, even ungentlemanly conduct, but expecting officials to react to it or even spot the offence is unlikely. When Jens Lehmann explained how annoyed he became with such blatant gamesmanship, I was tempted to tell him that he was lucky that he didn't play in my era. In the old days, keepers were fair game in any situation.

His anger, when challenged illegally, is not restricted to life in the English game. Jens was sent off five times during his time at Borussia Dortmund. The highest profile red card that he received came in the 2006 Champions League Final between Arsenal and Barcelona when he brought down Samuel Eto'o. The referee should have awarded a penalty and left Lehmann on, admitting as such after the game. Even then Jens was named Champions League Goalkeeper of the Year for the 2005–06 season after playing for more than 500 minutes without conceding a goal.

The well-publicised rivalry between Jens and Oliver Kahn for the German number one spot was extended at competition between goalkeepers at club level and clearly Jens did not see eye-to-eye with Spaniard Manuel Almunia, who took over from him in the Arsenal goal in the 2007–08 season.

Lehmann simply believed in his own ability and didn't take kindly to being second best to anyone. After Arsene Wenger had dropped him once previously, somewhat unfairly after a last-minute Liverpool goal at Anfield, Jens sought my help and advice. It was a difficult situation for me because I was no longer the club's goalkeeping coach, but the German came to my home and we talked over the problem. His love of his craft and determination are without question and it was no surprise that he went off to the 2006 World Cup finals, ousted Oliver Kahn from the number one position and played a huge part in the host nation's advance to the semi-finals. Jens Lehman remains a driven man professionally and an appreciative guy privately.

On the day that I went to say goodbye prior to his departure from Arsenal, he gave a little grin and said 'Well Bob, I think that in my time here in England I entertained the fans, one way or another!' Much maligned and often misunderstood, I have great admiration for Jens Lehmann. He reminds me in so many ways of an original German goalkeeping hero of mine, Bert Trautmann: single-minded, abrasive, courageous.

⚽ ⚽ ⚽

Jens Lehmann

Born:
10 November 1969, Essen, Germany

Position:
Goalkeeper

Clubs as player:
1988–98 Schalke 04, 274 games (2 goals)
1998–99 AC Milan, 5 games
1999–03 Borussia Dortmund, 157 games
2003 to date Arsenal, 199 games

Internationals:
1998 to date Germany, 60 caps

Honours as player with Schalke 04:
1997 UEFA Cup

Honours as player with AC Milan:
1999 Serie A

Honours as player with Borussia Dortmund:
2002 Bundesliga

Honours as player with Arsenal:
2004 Premier League and FA Community Shield
2005 FA Cup

Awards:
1997 Best European Goalkeeper
2006 UEFA Club Football Awards Best Goalkeeper and UEFA
Champions League Goalkeeper of the Year

– *Injury* –

The greatest fear for any professional athlete is injury – it is bad enough to sustain relatively minor injuries like pulled muscles or torn ligaments. The healing time in such cases can vary between three to six weeks and, apart from a new routine of care and treatment, there is also the worry that a place in the team may be lost while rehabilitation is in progress.

Before the late 70s it was common practice for a player to be encouraged to try and 'play on', often by receiving cortisone injections in the offending area of the body. Just prior to establishing myself as Arsenal's first choice in 1968, I received a serious shoulder injury while on an end of season tour in Japan. As it was the last game of the season, I was told I was lucky that the six weeks' close season period would be enough time for a complete recovery. Yet on the first day back in training at the start of a new campaign, when I dived on the suspect shoulder it left me in pain and desperately worried that once again injury would block my route to a regular first-team place. When examined by the club doctor he told me that the injury could take a further six to eight weeks to recover. It was the worst diagnosis I could receive. However, realising my obvious distress, he told me that he could try cortisone injections directly into the point of real pain. Today, I doubt such treatment would be seriously considered. But I was desperate to make my newly acquired role as number-one choice permanent, so for more than four months, the doc would administer a painkilling injection half an hour before kick-off, after which a mixture of exercising the joint and an adrenalin rush of excitement and anticipation would get me through 90 minutes action.

The gamble worked and was worthwhile for my immediate career in the game, but long-term it has rebounded with a restriction on the left arm and hand. As with so many footballers and sportsmen in general, I suffer from arthritis, partly as a result of the abuse of the body that professional athletes accept as par for the course, partly from broken bones of one sort or another and in my case minor breaks of fingers, ribs, arm, wrist and ankle. Only the ankle break was a mild threat to my career. Top of the list as a career-threatening injury for a footballer remains a broken leg with a compound fracture, with incidents where the tibia or fibula penetrate the skin the most serious of all.

Within this book I tell the story of Derek Dooley, the Sheffield Wednesday striker, whose career was ended by such a break and the complications of gangrene which ensued and necessitated the amputation of a leg. That remains an extreme case, but others have been unable to play again following similar breaks. The career of my teammate Don Howe came to an abrupt end after a collision with Blackpool keeper Tony Waiters. A plate remains in place in his leg to this day.

The most recent example of a footballing career halted prematurely was that of David Busst. The Coventry defender suffered a compound fracture of the tibia and fibula following a collision with Manchester United defender

Dennis Irwin during a game in April 1996 at Old Trafford. Busst never played again and several players, notably United keeper Peter Schmeichel, required counselling as a result of witnessing the injury at close quarters. Play was halted for twelve to fifteen minutes in order for Busst's blood to be removed from the goalmouth. In all the Coventry player underwent 26 operations before accepting his playing days were over and taking up a clinical sports science course. The reason that Busst's injury was so serious was because it was a spiral fracture with the bone breaking in a jagged fashion and not a clean break. The MRSA bug then destroyed muscle tissue beyond repair.

As a general rule every footballer knows instantly and instinctively when he is in big trouble with an injury. In the 1972 FA Cup semi-final against Stoke City at Villa Park, I was still in mid-air, attempting to catch a high ball when, in twisting several feet off the ground, I felt something snap in my left knee. Even before I hit the ground I feared the worst. I had torn a cartilage in my left knee and sustained tendon and ligament damage as well. Operated on the following day, it took more than six months for me to play at the top level again and although my career still had a season and a half to run, I knew it was the beginning of the end for me and that I would face a decision to end my playing career prematurely at the age of 33, which is quite young for a goalkeeper. The same knee has since undergone several minor operations and remains permanently bent and likely to undergo a replacement in the future.

Knee injuries have always been as much of a threat to sportsmen's careers as legs themselves, although medical science has produced extraordinary advances in both areas with cruciate ligaments now being repaired far more successfully, and compound fractures of the leg also benefiting from new forms of repair including wiring rather than plates and screws.

Serious injury though, remains the greatest threat to talented professional athletes in any sport, depriving the watching audiences of some rare talents and the injured individual of a career and longer term income, although insurance policies provide a short-term safety net.

⚽ ⚽ ⚽

Other serious football injuries

Henrik Larsson
The Celtic striker suffered a double fracture of the left leg in a game against Lyon in October 1999. Larsson did recover and continued his great career.

Stan Collymore
Broke his leg while playing for Leicester against Derby County in April 2000. The striker required six minutes of on-field treatment, including oxygen.

Luc Nilis
The Belgian international striker was playing for Aston Villa in September 2000 when he sustained a double fracture of his right leg after colliding with Ipswich keeper Richard Wright. Nilis retired four months later.

Alf Inge Haaland
His career was effectively ended by a challenge from Roy Keane in April 2001. The tackle earned the Manchester

United player a five-game suspension and a £150,000 fine. It didn't help Keane's cause when he later revealed in an autobiography that the challenge was pre-meditated.

Djibril Cisse

A double fracture of the tibia and fibula came not as a result of a tackle or collision but from an awkward fall after the 'blade' studs in his boots stuck in the Ewood Park turf at Blackburn. The Liverpool player made a return to the game six months after incurring the injury in October 2004.

Alan Smith

He broke his left leg and dislocated his ankle while playing for Manchester United in February 2006 against Liverpool. The injury took seven months to heal and Smith now plays for Newcastle United.

Eduardo da Silva

He suffered a horrific injury while playing for Arsenal against Birmingham City in February 2008. A poor challenge by Martin Taylor left Eduardo with a double compound fracture of his left leg. Taylor was sent off for his tackle.

⚽ ⚽ ⚽

There are two tests facing any seriously injured player. One is the clinical need for the healing process to be excellent. The other is psychological and requires the player to overcome mental fear of any repeat injury from further challenges. That mental strength was never better illustrated than by the great Spurs and Derby player, Dave Mackay, who twice came back from a broken leg.

Other notable players who have overcome any psychological damage are Patrick Battiston of France and Petr Cech of Chelsea. I was covering the France vs. West Germany World Cup international for BBC TV in July 1982. Battiston was clean through on goal with only Harald Schumaker to beat when the German keeper charged into the Frenchman with such violence that Battiston suffered damaged vertebrae, a broken jaw, the loss of four front teeth and was in a coma. His jaw had to be wired back into place and, what is more remarkable, he did play again. Harald Schumaker received no admonishment of any sort except from his fellow goalkeepers, all of whom knew he had severely let down the great art of goalkeeping.

Whenever there is a one-on-one situation between attacker and keeper, it is highly possible that injury to one or the other will occur. Petr Cech of Chelsea suffered a depressed fracture of the skull following a collision with Reading's Stephen Hunt. Many observers, including Chelsea staff, blamed Hunt. In my view on this occasion, they were wrong. It was a 50-50 ball that the players were challenging for, and Hunt could easily have come off worse. Cech now plays in goal wearing a protective rugby-style scrum cap.

During my own career, in a similar situation, I was knocked out after diving at the feet of Aston Villa's Sammy Morgan. His challenge was perfectly fair and my headlong dive at his feet invited injury. I was lucky to escape serious damage. A season later in a game at the Dell, Southampton's Hughie Fisher sustained a broken leg after I dived at his feet to win the ball. Many of the Southampton fans still believe I deliberately caused the injury to Hughie without appreciating that I could easily have been the injured party.

Thankfully the Scot didn't blame me and returned to play a few months later.

The game of football is highly competitive. Players go in to win the ball and serious injury is a risk that has to be taken. My hero Bert Trautmann broke his neck in the 1956 FA Cup Final against Birmingham City, played on for the last twenty minutes and had a winner's medal to display for his courage. Bert knows only too well that he could have suffered the same fate as John Thomson. On 5 September 1931 the Celtic keeper dived at the feet of Rangers' Irish forward Sam English. In making the save and preventing a goal, Thomson's head caught the knee of the Rangers player. John Thomson never regained consciousness and died that night, aged 22. He is remembered in verse:

> *The squirrel's swift leap, the falcon's flight,*
> *The clear quick-thinking brain;*
> *All these were yours, for our delight*
> *Never, alas! again.*
>
> *We did not need your death to tell*
> *You were the sportsman true*
> *We bow to Fate, Hail and Farewell!*
> *We shall remember you.*

Extract From 'John Thomson' by T. Smith of Darvel

Theo Walcott

I didn't watch the England vs. Argentina match in 1998. I can't remember why not. It may have been past my bedtime.

Theo Walcott, seventeen years old, following his
selection for England's World Cup squad 2006

⚽ ⚽ ⚽

Almost unbelievably, the 2008 European Championship in Austria and Switzerland contained no country from the British Isles. Excuses could be found for Scotland, Wales and Northern Ireland not being there, but there was no good reason for England's absence. The finger of blame points directly at the players, at a collection of young men who can light up Champions League fixtures and finals with their talent, but who fail collectively and individually when the shirt they wear bears a badge with three lions upon it.

Consider some of the names: Beckham, Rooney, Gerrard, Lampard, Ferdinand, Terry, the Coles – Ashley and Joe. If such talented club footballers can fail, where should England look next? One hope for the future is Theo Walcott, a small bundle of exhilarating pace and ability who has re-written record books ever since he starred in a Southampton youth team which reached the final of the 2005 FA Youth Cup.

The burden of expectation placed upon him could be overpowering but it doesn't appear to disturb him in any way, shape or form. Theo is one of the most grounded young men you could wish to meet, brought up impeccably, confident of his innate talent and totally aware of responsibilities to family, friends and a public who have become critical of the celebrity status thrust upon the footballers of today.

He plays for one of the so-called 'big four' clubs. Arsenal signed him for an initial fee of £5 million which finally rose to what was believed to be £9.1 million – another record set by Theo, as the most expensive sixteen-year-old in the history of British football. Other records he holds include being the youngest player to play for the Saints' reserves at fifteen years and 175 days, and then the youngest to make Southampton's first team when he was sixteen years and 143 days old.

What caught Arsene Wenger's eye were the direct dribbling skills that accompanied blistering pace. In Year 9 at school Theo covered 100 metres in 11.5 seconds, which became 10.5 seconds by 2008. Pace is one of the greatest attributes of the modern day striker. As a schoolboy Theo had the choice of joining Southampton or Chelsea. He met both but felt overawed when visiting the Chelsea set-up and more comfortable when viewing the Saints' academy and their staff. 'It felt like family and without them I wouldn't be where I am now.'

All the big Premiership clubs were interested when Southampton made him available but, guided by his dad Don, agent Warwick Horton of Key Sports and his own instincts, he plumped for Arsenal:

> One of the main influences was the manager Arsene Wenger and how he believed football should be played, but a bigger reason was Thierry Henry. He was my idol and like me arrived needing to fulfil his true potential. He did that under Arsene and so it was Arsenal straight away. I have to admit, I was like a little fan when I first arrived at the training ground and the club photographer struggled to keep up as I asked

for pictures taken standing alongside Thierry, Dennis Bergkamp, Sol Campbell, Robert Pires and Freddie Ljungberg. I was quite scared really but Ashley Cole especially was good to me.

Since joining Arsenal in January 2006 and then signing a professional contract on his seventeenth birthday on 16 March 2006, the name of Theo Walcott was rarely out of the news, simply because of the media interest in an emerging new home-grown player. Then the England manager, Sven Goran Eriksson, selected Theo for the 2006 World Cup squad, a decision based on potential that was applauded by very few of the press and criticised by the majority.

I was as stunned as anyone, excited but stunned. At first I didn't believe it, but that evening kept watching the reports on TV alongside my dad as we played a game of 'World Cup Monopoly'. But you know it was not my fault I got picked. It was a huge experience, a brilliant learning time. Yes, I was star-struck, working alongside David Beckham and Steven Gerrard, and I was very quiet, but I took everything in and stuck close to another youngster, Aaron Lennon. In the initial squad selected Nigel Reo Coker looked after me. I was seventeen years old. Sven was brilliant, so easy to get along with. The Rooney and Owen injuries didn't help my cause although I thought I was coming on as sub versus Sweden after being told to warm up. It was brilliant training with the squad, a big, big experience.

On returning home from the World Cup, expectations increased even though Arsene Wenger made it clear that

Theo needed time and his previous record with young talent suggested that the youngster would need patience.

> Everyone seems to forget that I'm still only just nineteen. Yes, I'm 5' 9" but I'm growing. All the time I'm getting stronger. It's also easily forgotten that I was out for nearly the whole of one of the two seasons since coming to Arsenal with a serious shoulder injury. That's healed and with extra gym work I'm raring to go. It's true I asked Arsene what I have to do to become more of a regular in the first team and he told me to be more aggressive, run at players with confidence.

In almost all the games Theo was selected for or came on as substitute he influenced the course of the match. Had his breathtaking length-of-the-field run which led to Emmanuel Adebayor's goal at Liverpool resulted in Arsenal reaching the Champions League semi-final in 2008 his progress would have accelerated even more, but Liverpool ultimately triumphed. As it is, Liverpool fans recall, in awe, how Theo made the most of a Steven Gerrard mistake and took on and beat four Liverpool players – Alonso, Aurelio, Mascherano and Hyypia, the latter of whom asked for his shirt after the game.

> There was nothing particularly going through my mind. I just trusted my instinct, decided to run it and found Adebayor although three other Arsenal lads were also queuing up. Shame we went out.

One irony of that spectacular run was that Theo's dad had always been a Liverpool fan. So the young Walcott had followed suit and admits to 'going mad and shouting out loud' on the evening that Liverpool came from three down to lift the European Cup against AC Milan. Hopefully, the best is yet to come for this extraordinary talent. He is just nineteen years old and all the record-breaking and premature international experience is bound to have had a positive effect on him. He knows what he wants from football and is determined to fulfil his potential.

Remaining grounded and in touch with the real world could be the secret to Theo Walcott's ultimate success. As I write, he faces another little dilemma. The Arsenal number 14 shirt is available and that number represents the great Thierry Henry. Obvious comparisons will be drawn if it was to sit on Theo's back. 'I might ignore it and stick to my current number 32. I'm happy enough with it, but then again ...'

Following in your idol's footsteps can be the final spur and incentive for any talented young footballer.

❀ ❀ ❀

Theo James Walcott

Born:
16 March 1989, Stanmore

Position:
Winger/striker

Clubs as player:
2004–06 Southampton, 21 (4 goals)
2006 to date Arsenal, 71 (8 goals)

Internationals:
2006 to date England, 2 caps

Awards:
2006 BBC Young Sports Personality of the Year

– *Football: the ever-changing game* –

On Saturday 26 October 1963 I made a little bit of history; the last amateur player ever to appear for the Arsenal first XI. Just two months after joining the club and while having to fulfil a one-year probationary period in order to be a fully qualified schoolteacher, Billy Wright picked me to face Nottingham Forest at Highbury. There was a big media interest for the time, including photos of me teaching the boys at Rutherford School, Paddington on the day prior to my league debut. As an amateur I received no pay, just expenses, which almost equalled the salary I received as a PE and history teacher at £12 per week. Can you imagine Thierry Henry or Cristiano Ronaldo playing in a team at the top level with an amateur schoolteacher keeping goal behind them?

'Arsenal Call Up Amateur Schoolmaster' was the main headline. The copy made a play of the fact that I was the first amateur keeper to appear for Arsenal since Dutchman Gerry Keizer in the 1930s and the first amateur since Albert Gudmundsson, an Icelandic inside forward who made a few appearances just after the Second World War.

So unexpected and late was my call up that I still had to fulfil my teaching commitments on the morning of the match – officiating in a school game on Wormwood Scrubs – prior to appearing at Highbury in the afternoon. I managed to get away with refereeing the first 45 minutes. Then it was a rush by tube to Highbury and entrance via the front door into the Marble Halls. As a professional you made your way into the ground from a car park behind the Clock End, out of view to the public. Even the commissionaire on the steps had to be convinced that I was Arsenal's goalkeeper that afternoon.

Food and drink

The usual routine then would be for the players to meet at the South Herts Golf Club on the day of a home game, where we had our pre-match meal around midday. The choice of food would be tea and toast, eggs, even a steak. It was a similar menu for away games when we travelled by bus or train.

Since Arsene Wenger's arrival at Arsenal, the teams always stay in hotels overnight pre-match and travel to most away games of distance by private jet. Any food intake has to be during a set period, well before kick-off. For a 3 pm start, the pre match meal would be eaten no later than 10.30 am, ensuring digestion is completed in time. Red meat takes a long time to be fully digested and no current Arsenal players would be allowed such food even the night prior to a game. Whereas lots of cups of tea were drunk in my time, the players now are encouraged to drink lots of water – two litres on any normal day and four litres are recommended on the day of a game to avoid the dehydration, which is often the result of running up to and beyond 10,000 metres in 90 minutes.

Shirts, gloves and boots

The kit has also changed. Lightweight materials designed to aid sweating have replaced heavy shirts and jerseys, once made from wool and then cotton, and which only bore a number and a club badge. Today they also display the player's name as well as league and sponsorship logos and are made from manmade materials for the players' comfort. The look of club shirts, which for years stayed the same, now changes from year to year as there is so much revenue to be made through the worldwide sale of replica shirts bought by fans of the club.

The one piece of equipment I used to detest wearing was shinpads. Today they are much lighter but just as effective and very different to those that were first introduced in 1874. Sam Widdowson, county cricketer for Nottinghamshire, cut down a pair of cricket pads and strapped them outside his stockings when playing centre forward for Nottingham Forest to protect his ankles against steel toe-caps of boots worn by opponents. At first this idea was ridiculed but variations soon became popular with other players, including stuffing newspaper inside the front stockings.

In 1990 the FA revised the laws, stating that 'shin guards must be covered entirely by stockings and made of suitable material that gives a reasonable degree of protection. Any infringement of this law by a player and the referee must order him/her to leave the field of play until he is satisfied that protection has been added.'

In the nineteenth century players wore hard leather work boots, long-laced and steel-capped and in 1891 the FA laws were revised to allow round studs to be fitted to the soles and heels of boots if made of leather and not to project more than half an inch. Eventually work boots were abandoned and boots were specially manufactured from thick hard leather with increased protection for the ankle and with an ability to stand up to the demands of muddy winter pitches. The leather studs were originally hammered into the boots on a semi-permanent basis and players would have several pairs of boots with different length studs, but in the mid-1950s Adidas introduced boots with interchangeable screw-in studs made of rubber or plastic for varying weather conditions. After 1960 boots began to be made much lighter and from a mixture of synthetic materials and leather while in 1979 the first boots were made from kangaroo leather. Nowadays studs have been replaced, in many cases, by blades to give a more stable base in certain pitch conditions.

However, today debate rages with regards to the lack of protection given by modern football boots and the repercussions in terms of player injuries. Thicker, weightier and with much more ankle and toe protection, our boots in the 60s and 70s at least led to fewer broken metatarsals than today. And although boot companies are happy to pay today's players over £100,000 per season to be seen using their footwear – compared to the occasional fees we used to receive for wearing them in internationals or cup finals – there seems little to suggest that the major manufacturers are going to give up their quest for the lightest football boot for a more protective one.

And then there are the goalie's gloves! Mine were thin, green and made of cotton, costing five shillings and six pence; the only gloves on the market and bearing Gordon Banks' and Peter Bonetti's names in recommendation. Now there is a huge variety of big, wicket keeping-type designs with thick rubber facings and backs that cost £100 or more.

The 1970 World Cup finals in Mexico saw the first major changes in keepers' gloves and very swiftly the German national keeper, Sepp Maier, wore the larger rubber-fronted versions that we accept today. Before then goalkeepers only wore gloves in very wet conditions but usually rubbed a bit of earth into their palms mixed with some spit or even less hygienic, a mixture of spit and chewing gum which made the fingers tacky.

Since the 1970s there have been revolutionary developments in design and construction for goalkeepers' gloves in order to aid their grip when trying to catch or hold the ever-lighter balls which move so dramatically in the air. The new gloves give protection for the fingers, palms and wrists. Since the late 1990s protection from hyperextension of the fingers has become available.

Substitutes and referees

Extra spaces are now needed in dressing rooms, the one substitute allowed in the 70s now replaced by seven players ready for action. The work of physios and doctors remains vital for administering ankle strappings and the like. When serious injury occurs it is now rare, if ever, for a player to be asked to get through a match thanks to a cortisone injection, whereas it used to be normal practice in order for a player to be able to complete a game.

In 1963 when I made my debut, and for many years afterwards, a warm-up took place within the dressing room walls, not out on the pitch in full view of the paying public. Even emerging from the dressing rooms onto the playing surface has changed, both teams now lining up in the tunnel before walking out onto the pitch together and shaking hands.

At the top level there are now four match officials, as opposed to three. In practice the fourth official becomes a key member of the officiating team, one who can watch the game and advise the referee on situations that are going on out of his sight. He keeps time and separate records and also serves as a replacement official in the event that one of the other officials can no longer continue. This would have helped in earlier days when a plea would go out to the crowd for anyone qualified to step forward to assist, as was the case when Jimmy Hill ran the line at a game where he'd gone as a spectator!

Stadiums

All-seated stadiums came in after the Taylor Report following the Hillsborough disaster reducing the total attendances in many grounds. In 1963 Highbury, which had just the East and West stands with seating and the North and Clock End as all-standing, could accommodate a crowd of 60,000. Once the conversion had taken place, the maximum attendance was 38,500.

Footballs

The balls have changed out of all recognition from a hard and heavy, bladder-inflated, leather-stitched sphere to today's light, moulded ball that can be made to swerve in all directions. Earliest games of football were played with an inflated pig's bladder and eventually leather coverings were introduced to help the ball keep its shape while the rubber inflatable bladder was invented in 1850 and the first specifications for footballs were introduced by the FA in 1863. Footballs were stitched from eighteen oblong non-waterproof leather panels and laced to allow access to an interior air bladder for pumping up to the required level. Many players from my generation still bear the scars of heading a laced ball that had become heavier through the game as it gathered water from the pitch.

In the 1950s the first 32-panel football was marketed in Denmark and became popular throughout Europe. Adidas started to make footballs in 1963 and made the first official FIFA World Cup ball in 1970, which had black and white panels and they have continued to be the favoured manufacturer for all World Cups since.

For the 1982 World Cup Adidas introduced a new ball which had rubber inlaid over the seams to prevent water from seeping through, the first ball with water-resistant qualities. General wear from kicking however meant the rubber began to disintegrate after a short time and needed to be replaced during the game. This was the last genuine leather World Cup ball.

At the 2006 World Cup Adidas introduced the +Teamgeist fourteen-panel ball. Each match at the World Cup finals had its own individual ball, printed with the date of the match, the stadium and the team names. Adidas felt that the traditional 32 panel hand-stitched balls had a wider target zone meaning accuracy was hard to consistently achieve. The new fourteen-panel design resulted in a ball with the most consistent performance characteristics ever. There were fewer seams, so the ball was rounder and performed more uniformly, regardless of where it was hit. The theory was that the more perfect the sphere, the more balanced it would be, offering greater accuracy due to the predictability of its flight. They believed that the biggest difference the players would find with the new balls would be when they played in the wet: new thermal-bonding technology made the ball virtually waterproof providing identical performance characteristics wet or dry.

Players' wages

Players in 1963 were lucky boys in that their salaries were generally slightly above the national average. Today, at the top level especially, teams are made up of millionaires and multi-millionaires able to afford luxuries that are beyond the dreams of the majority of fans. After the maximum wage restriction was abolished in 1961, players' wages have risen in leaps and bounds as more money has flooded into the game from sponsorship and the sale of exclusive television rights to broadcasters. Total wages for players in the Premiership rose from €200 million in 1995 to €750 million within four years and reached €1 billion in 2001. The most recent figures available are for the 2006–07 season when wages reached €1.5 billion.

In 2005–06 Premiership League wages rose by 9 per cent and the top club wage bills were as follows: Chelsea £114 million; Manchester United £85.4 million; Arsenal £82.9 million; Liverpool £68.9 million. The average Premier League club wage bill is £48.5 million.

The ten best-paid footballers in the world as of June 2008 and based on their weekly club salary, but not including their commercial activities are as follows:

#	Player	Club	Wage
1.	Kaka	AC Milan	£150,000 pw
2.	John Terry	Chelsea	£135,000
3.	Ronaldinho	FC Barcelona	£130,000
4.	Rio Ferdinand	Manchester United	
5.	Fabio Cannavaro	Real Madrid	£125,000
6.	Thierry Henry	FC Barcelona	
7.	Andriy Shevchenko	Chelsea	£121,000
8.	Michael Ballack	Chelsea	
9.	Frank Lampard	Chelsea	£120,000
10.	Cristiano Ronaldo	Manchester United	

In yesteryear a player's loyalty was rewarded with a testimonial game. Today, with the rewards coming through the receipt of a percentage of a high transfer fee, loyalty is less obvious and testimonials a rarity.

The cost to the fan has soared over the years not only at the turnstiles and in the season tickets but also with the outlay for food, drink and programmes. Programmes that cost 5p–10p when I started are now £2–£3. An FA Cup Final programme for the Arsenal vs. Liverpool match in 1971 cost 10p. In 2008 a programme for the Cardiff vs. Portsmouth final cost £10.

⚽ ⚽ ⚽

Only one thing remains truly similar and that is a player's ability to master his nerves, focus on the job at hand and play to his maximum potential as an individual, and as a result become a well-respected part of the team. On 26 October 1963, I was a player riddled with nerves, a regular pre-match visitor to the toilets. My team's obvious concern at my selection as an amateur heightened the tension for them and for me. Only Joe Baker, a brilliant Scottish international striker, recognised my anguish and went out of his way to help. My manager Billy Wright tried to inspire me but found the wrong words: 'Bob, we want you to play like no one has ever seen you play ever before. We want you to play well.' When nerves get the better of a footballer he then turns to a last resort, Lady Luck. Without luck you can't complete 90 minutes without blatant error, whether individually or collectively.

When I faced Nottingham Forest in 1963 I was lucky. We won 4–2. The two goals I conceded were not my fault and just before half-time I enjoyed a spectacular flying catch. 'To have reached it was an achievement. To have caught it was Yashin class,' said the *Daily Mail*. Getting cramp with fifteen minutes to go and needing the attention of physio Bertie Mee surprised and annoyed Billy Wright. I never did let on that I had refereed a game that morning prior to playing in the English First Division.

What surprises me most about my league debut was that despite nerves, I relished every minute. It was like nothing I had ever experienced in my footballing life before. The atmosphere was amazing, the challenge awesome.

That game against Forest was the beginning of 309 first-team appearances, but they, in the main, came years later. Between that memorable day and March 1968, some four and a quarter years later, my total number of First Division games for Arsenal totalled just nine. In all, between 1963 and 1974 I wore an Arsenal jersey 525 times, of which 216 appearances were in the reserves. Three things sustained me: my love of playing for Arsenal, a belief in my own ability, and a passion for the beautiful game.

Bibliography

Adams, Tony with Ian Ridley. *Addicted.* Collins Willow, 1998.

Arsenal Opus: The History of Arsenal Football Club. Kraken, 2007.

Ball, Alan. *It's All About A Ball.* W.H. Allen & Co., 1978.

Ball, Alan with James Mossop. *Playing Extra Time.* Sidgwick and Jackson, 2004.

Banks, Gordon. *Banksy.* Michael Joseph, 2002.

Banks, Gordon. *Banks of England.* Arthur Barker, 1980.

Barrett, Norman. *The Daily Telegraph Football Chronicle.* Carlton Books, 1994.

Beckham, David with Tom Watt. *My Side.* Collins Willow, 2003.

Best, George, with Roy Collins. *Blessed.* Abury Press, 2001.

Brady, Liam. *So Far So Good.* Stanley Paul and Co., 1980.

Busby, Matt with David R. Jack. *Matt Busby: My Story.* Souvenir Press, 1957.

Charlton, Bobby with James Lawton. *Sir Bobby Charlton: The Autobiography.* Headline, 2007.

Charlton, Jack with Peter Byrne. *The Autobiography.* Partridge Press, 1996.

Clough, Brian with John Sadler. *The Autobiography.* Partridge Press, 1994.

Clough, Brian with John Sadler. *Walking on Water.* Headline, 2002.

Cooper, Henry. *Henry Cooper: An Autobiography.* Cassell and Company, 1972.

Dalglish, Kenny with Henry Winter. *Dalglish: My Autobiography.* Hodder and Stoughton, 1996.

Docherty, Tommy, with Derek Henderson. *Call The Doc.* Hamlyn, 1981.

Ferguson, Alex with Hugh McIlvanney. *Managing My Life: My Autobiography.* Hodder and Stoughton, 1999.

Galsworthy, Maurice. *The Encyclopaedia of Association Football.* Robert Hale, 1976.

Gascoigne, Paul with Hunter Davies. *Gazza: My Story.* Headline, 2004.

George, Charlie with Alex Montgomery. *Charlie George: My Story.* Century, 2005.

Giller, Norman. *Billy Wright: A Hero For All Seasons.* Robson Books, 2002.

Glanville, Brian. *The History of the World Cup.* Faber and Faber, 1980.

Goldberg, Mel and Alan Thatcher. *Hans Segers: The Final Score.* Robson Books, 1998.

Graham, George with Norman Giller. *George Graham: The Glory and the Grief.* Andre Deutsch, 1995.

Grobbelaar, Bruce with Bob Harris. *More Than Somewhat.* Willow Books, 1986.

Harris, Harry. *Pele: His Life and Times.* Robson Books, 2000.

Hoddle, Glenn with David Davies. *Glenn Hoddle: My 1998 World Cup Story.* Andre Deutsch, 1998.

Jennings Pat with Reg Drury. *An Autobiography.* Willow Books, 1983.

Jones, David. *Jack Taylor World Cup Referee.* Pelham Books, 1976.

Keegan, Kevin. *Kevin Keegan.* Arthur Barker Ltd, 1977.

King, Jeff and Tony Willis. *George Graham: The Wonder Years.* Virgin Books, 1995.

Law, Denis with Ron Gubba. *Denis Law: An Autobiography.* Macdonald and Jane's Publishers, 1979.

Matthews, Stanley. *The Way It Was.* Headline, 2000.

McLintock, Frank with Bagchi Rob. *Frank McLintock: True Grit.* Headline, 2005.

Motson, John and Rowlinson, John. *The European Cup 1955–1980.* Queen Anne Press, 1980.

Paisley, Bob. *Bob Paisley: An Autobiography.* Arthur Barker, 1983.

Parkinson, Michael. *Best.* Hutchinson and Co., 1975.

Pele with Robert L. Fish. *My Life and the Beautiful Game.* New English Library, 1977.

Powell, Jeff. *Bobby Moore.* Everest Books, 1976.

Redknapp, Harry with Derek McGovern. *My Autobiography.* Collins Willow, 1998.

Rees, Jasper. *Wenger: The Making of a Legend.* Short Books, 2003.

Robson, Bobby with Bob Harris. *World Cup Diary 1982–86.* Willow Books, 1986.

Rowlands, Alan: *Trautmann: The Biography.* The Breedon Books Co., 1990.

Seaman, David. *Safe Hands.* Orion Media, 2000.

Shankly, Bill. *Shankly.* Arthur Barker, 1976.

Shaw, Phil. *The Book of Football Quotations.* Ebury Press, 2008.

Smith, Martyn. *The Premiership in Focus.* BBC Books, 2007.

Stiles, Nobby with James Lawton. *After the Ball: My Autobiography.* Hodder and Stoughton, 2003.

Swift, Frank. *Football from the Goalmouth.* Sporting Handbooks, 1948.

Thibert, Jaques and Max Urbini. *Johan Cruyff: Superstar.* Calmann-Levy, 1974.

Tossell, David. *Bertie Mee: Arsenal's Officer and Gentleman.* Mainstream Publishing, 2005.

Tossell, David. *Seventy One Guns*. Mainstream Publishing, 2002.

Trautmann, Bert, with Eric Todd. *Steppes to Wembley*. Robert Hale, 1956.

Tyler, Martin. *Boys of '66*. Hamlyn, 1981.

Wilson, Bob. *Behind The Network: My Autobiography*. Hodder and Stoughton, 2003.

Wilson, Bob. *Googlies, Nutmegs and Bogies*. Icon Books, 2006.

Wilson, Bob. *Rucks Pucks and Sliders*. Icon Books, 2007.

Wilson, Bob. *You've Got to be Crazy*. Weidenfeld and Nicholson, 1989.

Winner, David. *Brilliant Orange*. Bloomsbury, 2000.

Wright, Ian. *Ian Wright: The Autobiography*. Collins Willow, 1996.